Abortion II

DEDICATION

For my wife, Joan Summers Lader,
and my agent, Roberta Pryor,
in appreciation of their unbounded help

BOOKS BY LAWRENCE LADER

1955
Margaret Sanger and the Fight for Birth Control

1961
The Bold Brahmins: New England's War Against Slavery (1831–1863)

1966
Abortion

1969
Margaret Sanger: Pioneer of Birth Control (Juvenile) (With Milton Meltzer)

1971
Breeding Ourselves to Death

1972
Foolproof Birth Control: Male and Female Sterilization

1973
Abortion II: Making the Revolution

Lawrence Lader has had a unique career as both author and crusader in the fields of birth control, abortion, and population control for almost twenty years.

His biography of Margaret Sanger was called by *Harper's Magazine*, "an absorbing and impressive book." About *The Bold Brahmins: New England's War Against Slavery*, Orville Prescott wrote in the *New York Times*: "The wonder is that in a book as brisk and readable so much authoritative information can be conveyed with so much sound historical perspective." In 1966 the publication of *Abortion* broke through the secrecy which had hidden that subject for over a hundred years, and helped launch the campaign for legalized abortion that has liberalized laws in over twenty states.

Mr. Lader became chairman of the National Association for Repeal of Abortion Laws, a militant nationwide coalition, and served on the executive committee of the Association for Voluntary Sterilization and as a board member of Zero Population Growth, Inc.

A former president of the Society of Magazine Writers, he has contributed hundreds of articles to national publications, including *American Heritage*, *Look*, the *New York Times Magazine*, and *Reader's Digest*, and was Adjunct Associate Professor of Journalism at New York University from 1967–1972.

COURT DECISION OF JANUARY 22, 1973

Still, the struggle was far from over. The night after the decision, "Right-to-Life" groups invaded a meeting in New York City of Catholic women who supported abortion and turned it into an orgy of frenzied invective. The next battleground would be in state legislatures where "Right-to-Life" would seek to push through legislative restrictions on the Court's decision. Even in the U.S. Congress, the opposition sought a constitutional amendment aimed at negating the Court's decision – a threat based on the recent Connecticut law giving the fetus the status of a person from the moment of conception.

At the same time, the National Association faces the massive challenge of promoting model clinics in nearly every state, of organizing training seminars to ensure high-standard services in areas where medical personnel have had almost no experience in abortion. It had taken over a year to make the New York law work. Now we must transfer the skills of a few states like New York and California to the rest of the country.

Above all, we must achieve complete repeal of all existing abortion statutes, eliminating abortion from every criminal code, ending forever the feudal degradation of women that lumps them with criminals on the statute books. We should not rest until the freedom of women is secured, in the words of NARAL's basic platform: "Dedicated to the repeal of all laws that could compel a woman to bear a child against her will."

(See back cover lining for summation)

ABORTION II:

MAKING THE REVOLUTION

LAWRENCE LADER

BEACON PRESS BOSTON

Beacon Press books are published under the auspices
of the Unitarian Universalist Association.
Simultaneous publication in Canada by Saunders of Toronto, Ltd.

Printed in the United States of America

9 8 7 6 5 4 3 2 1

Library of Congress Cataloging in Publication Data

Lader, Lawrence.
Abortion II: making the revolution.

Bibliography: pp. 227–236.
1. Abortion—United States. I. Title. [DNLM: 1. Abortion, Criminal. 2. Abortion, Induced. 3. Abortion, Induced—Legislation. 4. Abortion, Legal. HQ 767 L154ab 1973]
KF3771.L3 344'.73'04 72–6228
ISBN 0–8070–2180–6

CONTENTS

Preface ix

Acknowledgments xv

One Dr. Vuitch Goes to the Supreme Court: The Judicial Challenge to Abortion Laws 1

Two Roots of the Abortion Movement 18

Three Women in Revolt 30

Four Referral Services: The Gentle (And Not So Gentle) Lawbreakers 42

Five The Campaign for New Laws (1967) 56

Six The Opposition Closes In: Arrests and the Growth of Radicalism (1967–1969) 72

Seven The Big Leap: Founding the National Association for Repeal of Abortion Laws 88

Eight The Bronx Arrests (1969): The Climactic Assault on Referral Services 98

Nine Breakthrough in the Courts and Legislatures (1969–1970) 109

Ten New York: The Impossible Victory (1970) 122

Eleven The Second Crisis: Making the New York Law Work (1970–1972) 149

Twelve Winning the West, Testing the Midwest (1970–1972) 170

Thirteen Overturning the Old Abortion Laws in Federal and State Supreme Courts 186

Fourteen Ordeal and Survival: New York (1972) 196

Fifteen Climax to Revolt 209

Bibliography 227

Index 237

PREFACE TO REVOLT

It was a strange, haphazard movement at the start, only a few clusters in a few states. It was a movement of loneliness, and some would say, fanaticism, for who else but the self-contained and the driven could stand up to the abuse of those early days. It was partly a movement of chance and almost reckless determination, for there was little logical reason that all the necessary pieces should fit together in 1965 rather than twenty years later.

Yet the groundwork had long been prepared. It only needed a special mix of social and historical forces that coalesced at the right moment.

The abortion issue in 1965 was enveloped in a conspiracy of silence just as ruthless as the slavery issue in 1831. Both were too dangerous to touch. Both involved fundamental moral and religious positions that collided with the entrenched interests of their time. The abolition movement terrified the Northern merchants and manufacturers whose Southern trade was more important than their qualms about slavery. The abortion movement struck at the tenets of the Roman Catholic Church and fundamentalist faiths, but even more important, at the whole system of sexual morality to which the middle class gave lip service.

Both issues had been created by laws which were blatantly in conflict with basic rights seemingly protected by the Constitution (slavery even being written into that document). Neither slaves nor women, obviously, had any voice in the passage of these laws. If the parallel becomes slightly strained in comparing the horror of the abortion system with the ultimate cruelty of slavery, it is still true that abortion laws denied women control over their own bodies and procreation by forcing them to bear children against their will.

Both slavery and abortion divided the nation bitterly. While abortion, of course, could never unbalance the economic and political structures to the point of civil war, once abortion reached legislative debate, it split many states into irreconcilable factions. Particularly in states like New York with sizable Roman Catholic electorates, the fury of debate came close to the turbulent scenes in Congress before 1860.

Logically enough, the most striking disparity between the two is that the abortion movement never cast its movers on a heroic scale. It is hard to conceive of anyone in abortion resorting to the grandiloquent language of William Lloyd Garrison in 1831: ". . . I will not retreat a single inch—and I will be heard." Rather, the first campaigners in abortion stepped uncertainly, and often timidly, into their roles for a simple reason. To be against slavery, dangerous as it was in Boston in 1831, gave the rebel a philosophic nobility. To be against abortion laws in 1965, however, involved one in a dirty business. It not only ranged one against the Catholic Church and other religious groups which considered abortion murder, but conflicted with the deepest sex taboos of our culture. Abortion was a soiled and forbidden word. Many newspapers and broadcasting stations would not use it on their media. To advocate the right of abortion meant tearing down the key bulwark against immorality. Whether for the single girl or married woman, it meant destroying the ultimate punishment of sex, and allowing the pleasure of sex for its own sake without the concomitant obligation of childbirth. Abortion stood at the apex of all our nightmares and inhibitions about sex, and to tamper with it meant that the whole system could come tumbling down.

Not unreasonably, therefore, I hesitated to deal with the subject after writing my biography of Margaret Sanger, the birth control pioneer. In 1955, I evaded it again and turned, perhaps fortuitously if one considers the historical parallels, to a study of Garrison and other New England abolitionists. By 1962, I made the first step, soliciting dozens of editors for the chance to write a magazine article on abortion, but being rejected by all. A year later, still concerned that I could be damaged as a writer by this connection, I started work on a book that was published under the blunt title, *Abortion*, in early 1966.

Even then, at the moment of the first national press conference for my book in April, I slipped almost accidentally from the role of writer to campaigner. The reporters, fascinated by the fact that thousands of supposedly illegal abortions were actually performed in the offices of licensed physicians, insisted on knowing how women reached these doctors. I had to admit that since the publication of my first article the year before, and now my book, I had received hundreds of appeals from women to learn the names and addresses of such sources. It seemed so inconsequential, the next, obvious question. Did I send them to these doctors? Yet, as soon as I had admitted that I had, and would continue to do so until a district attorney stopped me, it was apparent that a supposedly routine dialogue between author and reporters had drawn a vivid line between a philanthropic game and dangerous reality.

Someone had tampered with the system. Someone had insisted, like an abolitionist hiding an escaped slave in 1850, that no matter how the law read, there was a higher law of moral decency that demanded no woman should be forced into an unwanted pregnancy, or the alternative horror of underworld abortion.

It was obvious, according to the laws of most states, that the abettor of an abortion broke the law as sharply as an abortionist. It was equally obvious that he could not hide under moral rights, or higher laws. There was no defense against civil disobedience except a belief in the act itself, and the faith that enough support would be roused, and enough social change effected, to make the act worthwhile.

This seemed like a slim hope in early 1966. When I finally realized, over the next few days, that I had made a public commitment, and taken on a dangerous campaign, I also recognized that I had perilously few allies. The only organized protest that could be considered the seeds of a movement were two groups: in California, the Society for Humane Abortion, little more than a loyal band of partisans drawn to an incandescent rebel named Patricia Maginnis; and in New York, the Association for the Study of Abortion, which had the advantage of a prestigious board of doctors and lawyers.

No matter what our degrees or titles, we were all considered slightly cracked, if not outright fanatics, that first year. As a result of my book on abortion, and speaking invitations to numerous broadcasts and lectures, I decided the best chance to build a movement was through public relations—to stir as much controversy and debate as possible while bringing the facts to the public. I made close to a hundred appearances that year, roughed up considerably as I crisscrossed the country. On one national television show, the commentator rose from his seat and almost struck me. On two others, Catholic spokesmen screamed obscenities. These were trivial hardships. In California later, Maginnis would be arrested; in Massachusetts, William Baird would spend 36 days in jail. The important factor was that we were rousing the public.

Since I also concluded that the referral of women for abortion to licensed physicians was the main building block of the movement, I announced my referrals at every lecture and broadcast. It was a strategy of political confrontation adopted from the abolitionists, who only began to amass national support when they confronted the law, hid escaped slaves on the "underground railroad," and rescued them from pursuing sheriffs and prison cells. Abortion referrals, it seemed to me, were the most valid symbol of resistance. On humanitarian grounds, they saved a woman from underworld abortion. But beyond that, they drew women into the movement, and provided a constant affirmation that the laws were wrong and could only be righted when enough people stepped forward to challenge them.

There were two further principles that molded the early years. Small as we were in numbers, we had to maintain a constant offensive. We had to disturb the country, whip and goad the conscience of a people, make them understand the meaning of moral wrath. If this verged on fanaticism, it was as essential in abortion as it had been in abolition. It recalled the moment when a gentle abolitionist, Reverend Samuel J. May, tried to calm Garrison at a meeting, saying, "Mr. Garrison, you are too excited—you are on fire!" And Garrison replied: "I have need to be on fire, for I have icebergs around me to melt!"

The abortion movement also needed fire—and its own style of martyrdom. It needed hundreds of clergymen who dared the law each day—a rabbi arrested in Chicago, a minister in Cleveland—and referred thousands of women for abortion. It needed resolute women to stand before television cameras and describe their own abortions to the public, proclaiming their names and suffering so that other women would be roused from their silence. It needed brawling women, shouting defiance of the law before the Governor's office in New York, marching 20,000 strong down Fifth Avenue, breaking up a meeting of the Joint Legislative Committee (where the only female witness was a nun) and crying: "Men don't get pregnant. They just pass the laws."

The abortion movement was the final step in an evolutionary process that started with the Women's Rights Congress at Seneca Falls, New York, in 1848, and developed into the birth control movement of Margaret Sanger, who insisted no woman could call herself free until she could control her own body. First, contraception, and now abortion had to be made inalienable rights if women were to escape from the bondage of unwanted pregnancy. It took only a few of us in 1966—the early fanatics—to break the silence and unleash the moral fury of women. Once the National Organization for Women and Women's Liberation groups joined the abortion movement, we were ready to shake the country.

In political terms, a second principle ruled the movement: The laws against abortion were a total evil that had to be obliterated completely, not in slow hesitant stages. Although a number of states, starting with Colorado in 1967, passed minor reform laws, the radicals insisted that the only certain and workable formula was the repeal of all abortion laws, the complete freedom of a woman to decide with her doctor that a pregnancy should be terminated. Thus, repeal became the watchword of the movement.

What we were seeking, after all, seemed so profoundly just and humane. It was simply the right of personal decision, the right of a woman to control the creative powers of her body, to bring into the world only a child she truly wanted and loved. The use of contraception gave her this right to a considerable extent. But since many contraceptives had an inherent rate of error, or could fail, or were prescribed erroneously, or simply not used in a moment of abandon, contraception without the supporting right of abortion condemned women to biological chance.

What we were seeking, further, could not infringe on the religious beliefs or political rights of any human being. The elimination of abortion laws simply meant that abortion would be treated like other medical practices. While any woman, no matter what her religion, could choose to end a pregnancy, neither a Catholic nor anyone else could be pressured into this choice.

The doctors who supported this principle represented a new type of martyrdom. No one in the movement suffered more abuse or personal danger than that handful of licensed "skilled abortionists," as the timid medical profession liked to call them, who performed abortion in their offices or clinics. None of these doctors created the movement, but they saw the necessity of challenging the law. After his arrest, Dr.

Milan Vuitch of Washington, D.C., carried his case—the first to be tried on constitutional grounds—to the U.S. Supreme Court. His trial, which brought into focus many constitutional issues on which the movement made its stand, would become an early landmark.

ACKNOWLEDGMENTS

The contributions of Prof. Cyril Means, Jr. of New York Law School to this book have been extensive. I am deeply grateful for his advice on legal decisions, historical sources, and documents, and above all for his own pioneering studies and legal briefs which have been invaluable to the abortion movement.

Similarly, Dr. Bernard Nathanson of Woman's Hospital has given unreservedly of his medical advice and his astute comments on the manuscript, as well as adding his own achievements to medical progress in the abortion movement.

Dr. Christopher Teitze, and his wife, Ms. Sarah Lewit, both of the Population Council, have been a constant source of help and support in research; and Ms. Emily Moore of the Population Council kindly made available important source material.

On legal aspects, I am deeply indebted to two attorneys, Mr. Ephraim London of New York, and Mr. Joseph Nellis of Washington, D.C.

Mr. Gerald Roscoe of New York deserves special appreciation for his generous donation of the services of his advertising agency to the abortion movement.

I want to express my thanks to Dr. Alan Guttmacher and Mr. Fred Jaffe of Planned Parenthood-World Population; Dr. William Ober of Beth Israel Hospital, New York; Dr. Samuel Goldenberg of Seattle, Washington; Dr. Jack Stack of Alma, Michigan; and Dr. and Mrs. Milan Vuitch of Washington, D.C.

For their help on political research as well as their enormous contribution to abortion legislation, I am most indebted to Assemblywoman Constance Cook, Ms. Sherry Carr, Ms. Ross Graham, Assemblyman Franz Leichter, State Senator Manfred Ohrenstein of New York and to State Senator John Rader of Alaska.

CHAPTER ONE

DR. VUITCH GOES TO THE SUPREME COURT: THE JUDICIAL CHALLENGE TO ABORTION LAWS

Although the abortion movement started at least two years before the arrest of Dr. Milan Vuitch, a 53-year-old surgeon licensed in Washington, D.C., Maryland, New York, and Virginia, his arrest in 1968 provides a coherent base from which to examine the issues behind this national revolt. The essential purpose of the movement was to change the country's antiquated abortion laws, preferably to eliminate them completely. Before we could change them, they had to be challenged. This required referral services that openly announced that the laws were wrong and that women would be sent to skilled, licensed physicians. More important, it required physicians who were rugged enough to risk arrest and carry this challenge through the courts.

In addition to filling these personal requisites, Dr. Vuitch had wisely recognized the vulnerability of the District of Columbia law.

Note: In order to limit the number of footnotes and make this study more readable the numbered citations have been kept to the essential references and placed at the end of each chapter. Further, all references in a single paragraph are grouped under one citation, with, occasionally, the references for two or three preceding paragraphs grouped together for simplicity.

Almost all other state laws prohibited abortion except to save the woman's *life.* In the District, however, the law allowed abortion for the "preservation of the woman's life and *health.*" This one additional word certainly gave the physician far greater scope in interpreting the law and deciding which cases were eligible for abortion. Since nothing in the law restricted abortion to a hospital, Vuitch seemed to be justified in performing the procedure in his well-equipped office at 1801 I Street, a dignified medical building not far from the White House.

He bolstered his position further by eliminating any semblance of secrecy. Since mid-1966, when I and other referral services started referring hundreds of women to him, Vuitch had instructed us to give his name and phone number openly. In his reception room he mixed abortion cases with his surgical patients, refusing to restrict them to early morning or evening hours when the nurse was gone and there would be fewer witnesses. Such precautions—the code words on the telephone, the secret meetings with a middleman at parking lots, which had generally been used by underworld abortionists—would have been an obvious admission of guilt.

It was the boldness of this approach, the refusal to pander to the old abortion system with secrecy and police payoffs, that assured his eventual arrest. Vuitch and the referral services—and the gathering strength of the whole abortion movement—had become a challenge that the authorities could no longer ignore.

Just after midday on May 1, 1968, while an abortion patient was on the table, Lieut. Patrick Burke of the homicide squad and a covey of detectives invaded Vuitch's office. The police took the patient to D. C. General Hospital for examination and questioned and released five other women and a man in the reception room. After seizing Vuitch's examining table and medical equipment for evidence, Lieut. Burke booked him for illegal abortion at the office of the U. S. Commissioner (the judicial official in federal territory). Vuitch was then released on bail.

According to subsequent investigation by Vuitch's lawyers, the patient at arrest, Mrs. Donald R., a secretary at the Navy Munitions Building, fully qualified as a valid applicant for abortion under Washington law. She had been deserted by her husband, a garage mechanic with a lengthy record of seductions. He had proceeded to have affairs with two other women, including a 16-year-old girl, making them both pregnant; and after talking his wife into a temporary reconciliation, made her pregnant also. Mrs. R., however, had had enough of him by now and refused to live with him or bear his child. Needing money, and possibly seeking vengeance on his wife, Mr. R. went to the police and offered to cooperate in Vuitch's arrest. According to Vuitch's lawyers, the police gave him $300 in marked bills. After taking his wife to the doctor's office, he stood in the hall to signal the raiding party, which, the lawyers claimed, carried no arrest warrant and produced a search warrant only later.

All these facts, Dr. Vuitch asserted, supported his medical decision that an abortion was necessary to preserve Mrs. R.'s mental health. "This woman had described her mental suffering—her husband's frequent desertions and extramarital affairs, an unwanted pregnancy by a husband she detested—it was all down on my chart," Vuitch pointed out. "Only I, as her doctor, could decide whether her health had been threatened. Can the police, can some district attorney make this decision? Of course not. Only a doctor has the right to decide under the law when an abortion is necessary."

The Vuitch case quickly assumed significant importance in the development of the abortion movement. It went to the core of the constitutional issues. It not only involved constitutional protection for a doctor's right to exercise medical judgment under the law; it also involved the woman's rights—constitutional guarantees of privacy of her own body, her right to decide whether she should or should not bear a child without interference by state or federal law. If the Vuitch case could prove these rights warranted constitutional protection, it was possible that the District of Columbia statute, and possibly other similar statutes on abortion, might be declared invalid.

Moreover, the Vuitch case combined a number of propitious circumstances. It occurred in the nation's capital, not only a symbolic and influential news center, but one of the few areas whose law allowed abortion for *health.* (It would have been much harder for Dr. Vuitch to support his decision on abortion on the basis of saving Mrs. R.'s *life.*) It occurred at a time when the abortion movement had changed public opinion to the extent that many people supported the medical and feminist rights involved—support that often has some bearing on a court's decision. The groundwork had also been laid by cases on similar constitutional issues, particularly in California, still proceeding through the courts. But above all, it was Dr. Vuitch himself—his brash determination to turn his arrest into a battleground—that made the case so auspicious.

Dr. Vuitch, of course, was not the first licensed physician performing abortion in his office or clinic to be arrested. There had been dozens of others whose cases lacked the timing and other essential circumstances that propelled Vuitch to the fore. Two of these shed particular light on the Vuitch case—those of Dr. Robert Spenser of Ashland, Pennsylvania, and Dr. W. J. Bryan Henrie of Grove, Oklahoma—and so deserve to be examined.

Both men were archetypes of the homespun country doctor. Spenser, who died in 1969 at the age of eighty, was a frail, wispish figure with white tufts of hair fringing his head and neck. As Ashland's leading family doctor, he saw as many children with inflamed tonsils or running noses each day in his quaint, sprawling office on Main Street as abortion patients. His office walls, and almost every room of his small frame house, overflowed with books—he would rather talk political philosophy than medicine. A statue of Thomas Paine, his particular hero, stood on his desk. He never missed a meeting of the Rotary Club, and kept a supply of ball-point pens in his pocket to give new friends. They carried the quixotic inscription: "Energy is the most important thing in the universe."

For over forty years, Spenser handled more abortion cases than anyone on the East Coast, his phone number so prized that one woman writer remarked, "Really, I think of it as the telephone number of God." This sort of gratitude arose from Spenser's unique combination of humanitarianism and medical skill. At a time when licensed physicians in New York might take a few abortions a week for at least $1,000 each, Spenser charged $10 and $50 for most of his career, only raising the price to $100 in the 1960's. If a woman couldn't afford a hotel in town, he let her stay free at his clinic.

A graduate of the University of Pennsylvania Medical School, continuing postgraduate studies at New York's Rockefeller Institute (now University), he proved his skill with a record of 30,000 abortion cases and only one death—even that of dubious cause. The patient was bleeding when she arrived at Spenser's office, and the jury exonerated him.

It is this relationship to the law and the community that differentiates Spenser sharply from Vuitch. Spenser, too, was a rebel, but a folksy, idiosyncratic rebel, far ahead of his time. There was no abortion movement in his day; he probably never envisioned a test case on constitutional grounds. As an intimate friend of the mayor, the police chief, and almost every county official (Spenser's own father had been the district attorney of a neighboring county), it was probably inconceivable to him that abortion could become a local issue. "I would say that Dr. Spenser has always ranked as one of our leading citizens," a local newspaper editor remarked. Thus, Spenser's only brushes with the law involved one death of uncertain cause, and another confused blackmail case. He became a legend, not by challenging the law, but by ignoring it. The community protected him. He treated unwanted pregnancies as well as pneumonia for over forty years because the community wanted it that way.

Dr. W. J. Bryan Henrie bore a remarkable resemblance to Spenser. Seventy-six years old at his death in 1972, he peered benignly through steel-rimmed glasses, his blue eyes crinkled and smiling, a beatific fringe of white hair over his ears. Grove, Oklahoma, is even smaller than Ashland, Pennsylvania, perhaps 1,000 people. The farmers, and their wives in cotton print dresses, came to Henrie's clinic from picturesque villages like Bluejacket. In 23 years of practice, Henrie delivered 1,250 babies. "More often, he drove to the south end of the county to see the sick in the wee hours of the night," a former patient noted. "He returned money to patients that were poor and asked them to go buy some clothes instead of paying him."

"Doc Henrie never sent a bill to nobody," a neighbor added.

By contrast with Dr. Vuitch, a Yugoslav-born, urbane specialist, making a sizable income before his abortion practice, both Spenser and Henrie represented the rural, populist tradition. Henrie, in fact, was named after William Jennings Bryan; and his broadsides and pamphlets on abortion and women's rights, which he handset and printed on a creaky, out-of-whack press in his basement, were like the words of biblical prophets alone in the desert vastness. His writings quoted frequently from the Bible. He believed in human perfectibility, even in the White House, sending each pamphlet to President Nixon, as well as the local county attorney who once prosecuted him.

After performing 5,000 abortions at a top price of $100 in his white-brick clinic, Dr. Henrie went to jail in 1962, for over two years.

Sitting down to dinner with the jailer whose grandchild he had delivered two weeks before, Henrie did not even appeal his conviction. Serenely, he accepted the consequences of a bad law, and thus he represented the link in the movement from the early stages of unsophisticated revolt to the next era of Dr. Vuitch—the militant challenge of trained, constitutional lawyers.

Henrie had been a city councilman of Grove, a generous donor to the library, cited as "father of the year" by the PTA. Before he went to jail, about half the town turned out to honor him at a farewell party. According to some newspaper accounts, women in the crowd wept, and one former patient insisted, "He's done more good for this town than any other person." Another wrote in the Tulsa *Tribune*, "I am proud to say that Dr. Henrie happens to be the nicest and most understanding doctor I have ever known. If it's a sin what Dr. Henrie did, then it's more of a sin for a woman to bear a child when she isn't fit to be a mother."

After a *Tribune* editorial, which referred to the case as "The Shame of Grove," the debate raged back and forth in the columns of Tulsa and local papers. "He was wrong, and we were all wrong in letting it go on," one man said. It was the first time that a licensed doctor (Henrie graduated from the Kansas City College of Osteopathy and Surgery) had become a *cause célèbre* after conviction for abortion. It was the first time a community, in fact, a good part of the state, had to examine its feelings about abortion and decide whether to support or repudiate a doctor who put his reputation on the line.

Henrie's sentence, moreover, proved a turning point in his own career. Even in prison, he began to release a barrage of statements, attacking the abortion law. "I believe abortion is a woman's right and decision and no one else's," he told a reporter of the *Daily Oklahoman* in 1963. "I never felt abortion was wrong. I still think the law was wrong."

Rather than hide in the anonymity of a distant city after his release in 1964, Henrie returned to Grove and devoted himself to his campaign. No longer able to practice medicine and forced to sell his clinic at a loss, he claimed that debts and legal fees had wiped out his assets of $200,000, and he had to live on his Social Security and his wife's salary of $500 a month as a nurse. Now he began a unique saga

—the first physician to wander the country, traveling by bus for days at a time to save money, in his patient search to find an audience.

At Tulsa's All Souls Unitarian Church, where the minister announced, "the time has come to look into our hypocrisy," Henrie told a meeting of two hundred that "in the progress of civilization, there comes a time when someone must stand bigger than the law." He pointed out that Grove and surrounding areas had a remarkably low rate of juvenile delinquency and crime, possibly due to the birth of only wanted children. "I delivered wonderful babies when they were wanted, and prevented pregnancies with contraception and abortion when they were not wanted."

Henrie rode the bus to San Francisco to address the first conference on abortion called by Patricia Maginnis and her fledgling organization in 1965. He came to New York, where I met him for the first time, for the legislative hearings in 1966. At almost every state or local meeting on abortion after that, Henrie would inevitably appear, passing out his hand-printed leaflets to delegates, rising to speak in his slow, slightly nasal, Oklahoma drawl, punctuated with such aphorisms as, "Contraception and abortion may be considered unnatural, but what, I ask, is more unnatural than a baby bottle?"

The main weapon in his literary arsenal was a slim magazine that he called *DESTINY, Voice of the Silent Ones.* In a defense of his own imprisonment, titled, "The Shame of Grove Reversed," he insisted that "religion will eventually adjust to advancement; the law must be dragged along." In another issue, he wrote, "I am ashamed of a law that must be broken to save the honor and respect of many women." Analyzing the argument that no physician has the right to play God in terminating a pregnancy, he concluded, "If I can be accused of playing God in abortion, I must have been greater than God when I gave a shot of diphtheria and tetanus toxoid to produce an immunity that God forgot."

"At the time I pled guilty, I wanted to scream to the world but the world was deaf," he once wrote. "It could hear no logic and would believe no reason." By 1968, Henrie's lonely, rambling campaign was being heard at last.

In the evolution of any movement, a strategic breakthrough seems to demand a combination of personal talents exactly fitted to the moment. Brash, flamboyant, and highly confident of his own ability to take on the medical profession as well as the law, Dr. Vuitch once remarked, "The medical brass always says I'm five-feet-ten-inches tall, but got a six-foot mouth." Vuitch thrives on struggle and exploding society's outmoded strictures. "I'm a tough guy, an old fox," he likes to say, his words coated with a heavy, mellifluous Yugoslav accent. "I'm breaking the way. I'm getting rid of medical absurdities. If you think that abortion is a medical service, you can't ignore it."

When he saw the standard wording of the federal warrant after his arrest, "The United States of America versus Milan Vuitch," he told his lawyer excitedly, "I've done it. They're all against me."

Vuitch gives the impression of hulking size. His voice seems to roar even when he whispers. He often says, "I was mad like a tiger," and his voice and movements take on the same aggressive qualities. He has broad shoulders, heavily muscled arms, a mane of graying, swept-back hair, and scraggly eyebrows. He moves quickly, catlike. His highly tailored suits and tasteful shirts give him the appearance of grace and gentility.

Beneath his brashness, Vuitch's sensitivity stems from the poverty of his youth and his Slavic, peasant heritage. "Women cry for help, and doctors just chase them away," he says. "I saw people dying like flies in the war, and I couldn't do much. If I can help now, why shouldn't I? Just after I got here, I saw one of the nurses at my hospital, a sweet kid, four months pregnant. I asked my department head, why can't we do something for this kid? He just shrugged and turned away. I realized then the brutality of the system. I was new here, struggling for survival, and I understood what that kid was going through. We should have stuck together and done something for her."

Although Vuitch opened four offices for general surgery in the Washington area within seven years of his arrival in 1955, and was quickly reaching the financial pinnacle of medicine, his rebellious nature demanded more than routine success. "I was always the brightest guy in my class," he recalls. "I always wanted to be best."

After Vuitch expanded his abortion cases in recent years so that he was probably handling more cases than any other doctor, he concluded, "I'm the granddaddy of abortion. I like to know I'm the best. I guess I've got that competitive spirit you find in people who start poor."

Despite his considerable profits, Vuitch probably made little more from abortion than he would have in general surgery. His income, revealed in a recent court hearing, ran about $160,000 a year, certainly in line with many successful surgeons.

Vuitch charged only $100 and $200 a case around 1960, and his top price in recent years was $300—far less than the $1,000 and $1,500 charged then by Park Avenue abortionists; and the recent rate of $600 in Puerto Rico. Frequently Vuitch cut his fee for needy patients, and charged nothing for the indigent. "If I were doing abortions just for money, I'd be asking twice the price," he pointed out.

In his office, Vuitch combines gruffness with sensitivity. For a frightened girl, he becomes fatherly, calling her "honey," relaxing her with preposterous anecdotes of his boyhood. He can also be puritanically harsh, lecturing a woman for ten minutes on her inefficient use of contraception. One father of a pregnant girl recalled: "He asked my daughter what the partner in pregnancy did, and she replied, he didn't really do much of anything. 'Oh, you mean he's just a hippy dropout?' Vuitch asked. 'What did your mother say when you told her you were pregnant? Did she say, How wonderful? My little girl is going to have the illegitimate baby of a lazy, hippy dropout. If I weren't so concerned about you girls, I could be out on the golf course like other doctors.' "

Vuitch was born in northern Serbia in 1915. His father, a peasant owning a few acres, died when Vuitch was three. His mother supported him and his two sisters by growing potatoes and beans, and leasing plots to other peasants. "Somehow we survived," Vuitch recalls (the word "survival" appearing frequently in his conversation even today).

Vuitch won a full scholarship to the University of Budapest at eighteen, and continued through medical school, graduating in 1939. Returning to Yugoslavia as an army doctor, he was captured in the Nazi invasion, assigned to a Budapest hospital, and allowed to take his boards in surgery at the University in 1944. Then the Nazis put him on an army hospital-train, which was captured by the U.S. Army in 1945.

Back in Yugoslavia he became assistant professor at Skopie's School of Medicine in 1947, and was head of obstetrics and gynecology at the Senta hospital from 1948 to 1955. He performed his first abortion in 1939. Although not fully legalized in Yugoslavia until 1952, abortion had been the traditional method of birth control for centuries (contraception being rare in middle and eastern Europe). Like all Yugoslav doctors, Vuitch handled hundreds of cases both in hospitals and his private office.

On a vacation cruise down the Dalmatian coast in 1953, Vuitch met an American girl, Florence Robinson, born in Syracuse, New York, the daughter of a Colonel of U.S. Engineers. He courted her for three weeks. Then they corresponded for a year, and she returned in 1954, marrying him in September. After she became pregnant, she went back to the United States to have her child. Finally securing a visa, Vuitch followed her.

Despite his extensive record at Hungarian and Yugoslav hospitals, Vuitch had to repeat his medical training at Doctors Hospital in the District of Columbia, first as an intern, then as resident physician from 1955 to 1960, certified by the American Board of Surgery. He secured licenses to practice not only in the District, but in Maryland, Virginia, and New York.

He did his first abortion in the United States in 1957, following the arrival of many Hungarian refugees from the Soviet invasion. His wife had told him no doctor did abortions here outside the hospital. "I guess I'm pretty Victorian," she once admitted. "I knew abortions were completely accepted in Yugoslavia—after all, the police chief brought his wife to Milan. But I grew up thinking abortions were wrong except in the most dire circumstances. I never knew Milan was doing them until 1964."

Vuitch's first patient was an airline stewardess, a Hungarian refugee brought by a Hungarian doctor. He told them he couldn't do it, he didn't even have the curettes and other instruments. She pleaded and wept. She had to make money and hold her job to bring her family from Hungary. "It seemed horrible that these American laws could ruin the life of a lovely girl who had already gone through so much tragedy and was trying to make a new start here," Vuitch said. He finally bought the instruments, performed the abortion, and kept the instruments locked away for over a year.

But the pressure increased. By the time Vuitch opened his Washington office for general surgery in 1960, he was doing a few abortions a month. On August 11, 1964, driving home after performing an abortion in his Virginia office, he was suddenly surrounded by police cars, their sirens wailing. "The lieutenant asked me if I had done abortion," Vuitch recalled, "and I said, 'Oh, yes, I've done many.' I thought they meant in the hospital. They laughed, and said I was being very cooperative. They took me to the Fairfax jail, and asked if I wanted bail. I didn't even know what bail was. It was like a comic opera."

The trial resulted in a hung jury, and charges were dropped. A second arrest at his Maryland office that fall was also dismissed when the state's witnesses couldn't be located. Vuitch now realized that a doctor could only get some protection from police harassment under the District of Columbia law with its broad wording of "health." He decided to do abortions only at his District office. "Here I was making $100,000 a year from general surgery, and I should have stopped abortions completely," Vuitch said. "My wife was terribly upset, crying all the time, begging me to stop. I should have settled down and accepted the system."

Florence Vuitch avoided all outside contacts for weeks after the arrests. She had always been active in the local PTA, and finally went to a meeting. "A friend held out her hand to greet me—I couldn't remember her ever making that conscious gesture before," Florence said. "I thought people were just trying to be polite. It made me terribly sensitive."

The Vuitches decided to tell their two sons everything. There was only one incident at school when a classmate of their youngest boy, John, said, "Your father's a crook," and John slapped him. But Florence insisted on protecting her mother who was chronically ill and bedridden at the Vuitch house. Florence always checked the newspapers first and tore out any article relating to Vuitch.

It was these very qualities of abrasiveness and pugnacity, so distasteful to his own medical peers, and even to some in the abortion movement, that made Vuitch a logical candidate for challenging the abortion law.

This concept of legal challenge was drawn directly from Margaret Sanger's own experience. In the early days of birth control, she clashed sharply with most of her own movement by breaking the federal and New York State laws on contraception. First, she sent contraceptive information through the mails. Then she opened a birth control clinic in Brooklyn in violation of state law, staffing it with nurses, her sister, and herself, since she could find no doctor to take the risk.

In 1966, the abortion movement tried at first for a more conservative approach. An *ad hoc* committee, consisting mainly of Professor Cyril Means, Ephraim London, and Ms. Harriet Pilpel, all experienced civil liberties lawyers, Aryeh Neier of New York Civil Liberties Union, Dr. William Ober, and myself, met for months to develop a test case. We tried, but failed, to enlist a respected obstetrician-gynecologist who would perform abortion openly in his hospital on a patient with only minor health problems—a case that clearly contravened the New York law. We would then notify the district attorney, and the doctor's arrest and subsequent trial could hopefully be carried to the highest courts.

Our basis was the landmark *Griswold v. Connecticut* decision in 1965 in the U.S. Supreme Court, which overthrew Connecticut's birth control law and guaranteed "the right of privacy in marital relations." In a *New York Times Magazine* article in 1965, and my book, *Abortion*, the next year, I theorized that abortion as well as contraception must be included in the options of marital privacy, and deserved the protection of the Constitution. Quoting Ms. Pilpel, both works raised an inflammatory issue: "Does it not constitutionally deny a woman's life, liberty and pursuit of happiness if, despite her wishes and the opinions of concurring doctors, she is forced to bear a child she doesn't want, and objectively, shouldn't have?" [1]

Fortunately, in 1968, Vuitch and his lawyers, Joseph L. Nellis and Joseph Sitnick of Washington, D.C., agreed to make a frontal attack by testing the constitutionality of the District law itself. The pretrial brief hammered at all constitutional issues, primarily the abridgment of the rights of both doctor and patient under the First, Fourth, Fifth, and Ninth Amendments. Under the First Amendment, the lawyers argued, the right to give and receive medical treatment had been guaranteed by previous Supreme Court decisions. Why should not abortion as well as contraception be included in such treatment? The *Griswold* case encompassed contraception in the right of privacy. Why not abortion? "If an individual may prevent conception," retired Supreme Court Justice Tom C. Clark insisted, "why can he not nullify that conception when prevention has failed?" [2]

The fundamental issue was a citizen's sovereignty over her own body. Once contraception failed, or a woman was unable or unwilling to use the most effective contraceptive for a variety of medical, emotional, or personal reasons, governmental mandate under the present abortion law forces her to bear an unwanted child. It may damage her health severely, and punish her economically and socially. Without the right to eliminate contraceptive failure, other rights of privacy or family rights would be largely negated.

Further, Nellis and Sitnick argued, the government could gain no benefit or self-interest by preserving punitive abortion laws in 1969 that were passed for different reasons and under sharply disparate conditions seventy or one hundred years before. At that time, internal surgery produced high death rates from infection and pain-induced shock. Aseptic techniques gained little acceptance until the 1880's. These critical medical hazards of the last century were in large part responsible for the old laws. In 1901, the District law could probably qualify as a public health measure. Today, its purpose has been negated by medical advances and the safety of abortion techniques.

In fact, the law now produces exactly the opposite effect. Unable to obtain a safe hospital abortion, a woman may resort to the horrors of self-abortion—rubber tubes, knitting needles, soap solutions, and other chemicals which invariably lead to mutilation and often death. Or she may turn to the filthy back rooms of the untrained, nonmedical abortionist where infection, lack of anesthesia, and lethal techniques often create similar butchery. At least 350,000 patients are admitted to hospitals annually with complications from such abortions. From 500 to 1,000 die.

An equally disturbing result of these laws is that hospitals have established a system of standards and abortion-approval committees that discriminate drastically against one group—the ward patients, particularly blacks and other minorities. In New York City during 1960–62, private hospitals aborted one pregnant woman in 250; municipal hospitals only one in 10,000. Five times as many white women were accepted as nonwhite, and thirty times as many whites as Puerto Ricans. "The effect of these wide-ranging interpretations is to deny abortions to the poor, thus adding a gross factor of statutory discrimination to those hardships which the government is otherwise trying to correct," the lawyers concluded.

Moreover, the government today retains no compelling interest in increasing population, one of the original purposes of these abortion laws. United States population has already increased a third since World War II, and may add one hundred million more by the turn of the century. Demographers predict a doubling of world population in this same period, and another doubling fifteen years later. "This abortion statute intensifies the problem of population by largely excluding voluntary abortion as a means of regulating family size when contraception failed or was not used," the Vuitch brief pointed out.

Then Nellis and Sitnick attacked the unconstitutionality of the law from a different approach—the vagueness of its language, "necessary for the preservation of the mother's life or health." These few words, the only direction in the statute, hardly give suitable guidance to a physician (or a judge and jury) on what physical, mental, or social conditions should be considered in assessing "necessity."

Since abortion policies of "necessity" not only vary widely from hospital to hospital, but from service to service within the same hospital, the physician faces an impossible burden. When two Stanford University researchers submitted 11 typical cases of abortion to 26 California hospitals, not one type of case achieved anything close to unanimous approval. As another example of divergent opinion within the profession, a 1969 poll by the journal *Modern Medicine* showed that 51 percent of U.S. physicians, and 61.4 percent in the District of Columbia, wanted abortion available to any woman upon her request to a competent physician.

In no other sphere of medicine does the law impose such a burden on physicians. No other operation—even a prefrontal lobotomy possibly altering a patient's personality—legally requires the surgeon to prove necessity for life or health. "On any analysis of this vague requirement, altogether lacking acceptable standards, there will never be an instance in which a physician is able to defend his actions successfully where the evidence shows an exercise of medical judgment which the Government seeks to challenge," the Vuitch brief observed.

The statute is equally vague in defining the words "life" and "health." Does "life" mean immediate survival? Or survival for a period of days, months, or years? There is no indication that "health" means mental as well as physical. It can be defined narrowly, or as the World Health Organization and other medical groups insist, encompass the complete state of mental and physical well-being, not merely the absence of disease or infirmity. "The statute is plainly unconstitutional," concluded the lawyers, "for its failure to meet the specificity requirements of the due process clause of the Fifth Amendment."[3]

On November 10, 1969, before a hushed audience filling every seat in the U.S. District Court of the District of Columbia, Judge Arnold Gesell handed down a decision that exonerated Dr. Vuitch and declared the District law unconstitutional. It was the most impressive advance made by the abortion movement until then, the first time a Federal Court had overthrown an abortion law. Judge Gesell found that the law contained "no clear standard to guide either the doctor, the jury or the Court," and that it failed to give the clarity and certainty required by due process.

"There has been, moreover," he continued, "an increasing indication in decisions of the Supreme Court of the United States that as a secular matter a woman's liberty and right of privacy extends to family, marriage and sex matters and may well include the right to remove an unwanted child at least in early stages of pregnancy."

Turning to discrimination against the poor, Judge Gesell ruled: "It is legally proper and indeed imperative that uniform medical abortion services be provided all segments of the population, the poor as well as the rich."

Finally, the Judge urged a prompt appeal to the Supreme Court, and at the request of the U.S. Solicitor General, the High Court agreed to hear the case.[4]

The immediate impact of the Gesell decision was to allow any licensed physician in Washington, D.C., to perform abortion according to his medical judgment in a hospital, clinic, or office. Vuitch himself was suddenly lifted to national prominence, interviewed on television and by the press, lionized by the movement. With Washington then the only completely legalized area for abortion, Vuitch's appointment schedule became more crowded than ever. Even after he moved to larger quarters, patients often had to wait hours to get through on his telephone, and another three or four weeks for an appointment. He was still, however, a pariah to the medical societies, and although he enjoyed goading and bullying his associates at medical meetings, "those stuffed-shorts," as he called them, still clung to their old practices of approving abortion by committee and confining it to hospital premises.

In the rest of the country, the Vuitch case had a profound impact on the growth of legal challenges to local abortion laws, inspiring dozens of test cases in federal and state courts.

This policy of "confrontation politics" proved the decisive factor in building the movement. The first radicals who established referral services, and laid down the philosophy of complete repeal of abortion laws—Patricia Maginnis in San Francisco, William Baird of the Parents' Aid Society on Long Island, and myself—jolted and shocked the public into understanding the issues. It was a crude, inflammatory approach, but the only way to shake the country.

It was also a dangerous approach, considered by many we were trying to reach, and even by some already in the movement, nothing more than outright law-breaking. It could have failed. Yet it succeeded because it had justice and humanity on its side, and was the only strategy that could produce immediate results. Like the abolitionists long before, and Margaret Sanger in the birth control campaign, we gambled that a confluence of historical and social forces had reached the breakthrough point, and fortunately we gambled accurately.

NOTES

1. 381 U.S. 479 (1965); Lawrence Lader, *Abortion* (New York: Bobbs-Merrill, 1966; Boston: Beacon Press, 1967), pp. 154, 170, 172, 173.

2. Tom C. Clark, *Religion, Morality and Abortion: A Constitutional Appraisal*, 2 Loyola Univ. (L.A.) L. Rev. 1 (1969).

3. For all references to the Vuitch brief, see *Brief for Milan M. Vuitch, M.D.*, In The Supreme Court of the United States, October Term, 1970, No. 84; Joseph Sitnick, Joseph L. Nellis, Roy Lucas, Attorneys for Milan M. Vuitch, M.D.

4. *United States v. Vuitch*, 305 F. Supp. 1032 (D.D.C. 1969), jurisdiction postponed to argument on merits, 397 U.S. 1061 (1970).

Special References

The sources on Dr. Robert Spenser are the author's interviews with him, with editors, and with town officials in Ashland, Pennsylvania.

The sources on Dr. W. J. Bryan Henrie are the author's interviews with him and other residents of Grove, Oklahoma, and Dr. Henrie's notebooks and clipping files, particularly the Tulsa *Tribune*, July 17, 1962, and the Tulsa *Daily World*, December 7, 1964.

CHAPTER TWO

ROOTS OF THE ABORTION MOVEMENT

"What made you do it?" Ms. Betty Friedan, author of *The Feminine Mystique* and neofeminist leader, once asked me as we were exploring the roots of our interlocking campaigns many years after that moment in 1966 when I announced I would send any woman to a licensed physician for abortion. It was Margaret Sanger, I explained. "No woman can call herself free who does not own and control her own body," Ms. Sanger taught me. "No woman can call herself free until she can choose consciously whether she will or will not be a mother." [1]

Until then I had never grasped the implications of this principle. Whatever the original feminists demanded for women, or Betty Friedan and the neofeminists today, whether equality before the law, in education, business, and professions, or the equality of shared responsibility between the sexes in home management and child rearing, all of these things were meaningless unless a woman controlled her own procreation. No woman could achieve these other freedoms without the basic freedom of birth control.

I first met Margaret Sanger in 1953 when I started my biography of her, and for three years, often for months at a time, we spent whole days and nights working and talking together in Tucson, Santa Barbara, and New York. At seventy-five, she was all fragile grace and laughter. At the same time, she possessed the most powerful creative energy I had ever known. Her mouth and chin, expressing this duality were "all compassion and sweetness and yet all resolution and strength," a friend noted. Beneath the surface softness she had boundless will. She moved against walls of prejudice and ignorance, and toppled them. After a half-century of struggle, she was still roaming from country to country, organizing an international birth control movement from a suitcase in hotel bedrooms, creating a network of staffs and clinics that would circle the world.

Her beauty seemed ageless. On many nights, when we sat together over a bottle of champagne, her favorite drink, and she talked in that cool, shimmering voice with her head cocked slightly to one side and laughter always rising in her throat, she was still a child. "A lover's face, a child's face," a friend had called it. Another remembers, "At a party where I met her, she took off her shoes and danced on the grass —a delicious little girl."

At the end of an exhausting day of talk and note-taking in Tucson, she would slip into an evening dress in ten minutes, and we would drive twenty miles to a dinner party. Her entrance invariably made a room come alive. Or in the middle of the morning she would decide to show me a restaurant in Nogales, and we would take off for the Mexican border seventy miles away. Even when I was back in New York, she sent a constant stream of letters, mixed with bubbling anecdotes and incisive advice. "Nothing can really be right unless you're in love," she liked to say.

In her vision of the revolutionary impact of birth control, Margaret Sanger predicted a "new woman" who would gain "the greatest possible fulfillment of her desires upon the highest possible plane"—a precursor of the Women's Liberation movement today. She wanted fulfillment for women not just in creative energy and careers, but in love and sex. The new woman would have to cleanse the social fabric of puritanical debris and inhibitions that had perverted our thinking for centuries. Above all, long before the popularization of ecology, Margaret Sanger wanted birth control to restore the harmonious balance between nature and its human inhabitants.

She could reign as both the woman rebel and the woman in love. Many men pursued her, particularly in England, where she held court amidst rose gardens and moonlit lawns for Havelock Ellis, H. G. Wells, and Hugh De Selincourt, the poet. "What man could help falling in love with you?" asked Janet De Selincourt, Hugh's wife. "Can't I carry you off somewhere for a day or so?" asked Wells in one of his frequent, insistent notes. "I have loved you beyond my power to understand it," exclaimed Bill Williams, a Kansas City *Post* executive, working with her on a book. This was a side of her life she treated discreetly because of its potential damage to the birth control movement. Yet it was just as essential to her fulfillment as her public campaign. She had to live, as Shelley wrote long before, as if "to live and love were one." Her triumph was that she could incorporate both in perfect fusion: the radiant, social emancipator, and the woman in love.

Ironically, I would eventually split with Margaret over abortion —only in a theoretical sense since, by 1963, she was too ill to carry on our old discussions. Margaret had always opposed abortion. In her work as a nurse on Manhattan's Lower East Side around 1910, she would watch in horror the long lines of immigrant women, worn out by poverty and constant childbearing, waiting outside the offices of nonlicensed abortionists with five dollars clutched in their hands. The rate of injury, and even death, from this crude, underground surgery was frighteningly high. Margaret detested the waste and degradation of human life, and pleaded for contraception as a rational and humanitarian alternative.

Naturally, she was right in the context of her time. But the context had changed by 1962. Abortion by a licensed physician had now become a safe and simple procedure—new techniques making it far safer than childbirth itself, and even safer than such minor operations as tonsillectomy. Despite the gains of the birth control movement, most contraceptives still had a broad margin of error or misuse, or were not used at all. Since these factors resulted in a minimum of 550,000 unwanted births each year, plus an estimated 1,000,000 secret abortions, I became convinced that abortion must be completely legalized as a backup, emergency measure to contraception.[2]

In the evolution of my thinking, perhaps the biggest step was to demand legalization as an inalienable right of women, protected by the Constitution's Bill of Rights. This position, strengthened by the U.S. Supreme Court's *Griswold* decision, had never been advanced before (although Patricia Maginnis and Professor Garrett Hardin of the University of California, Santa Barbara, came to this conclusion about the same time).

It seemed to me that for the state to force any woman to bear a child against her will was a flagrant and brutal abuse of personal liberty. This belief undoubtedly stemmed from my hatred of interference with the sexual conduct of any individual, married or single, and of enforcing morality by law. I supported the right of a woman to use her body as she saw fit, and opposed any dictatorship over these rights by puritan moralists and religious dogmatists.

What seemed most outrageous about our abortion laws, when I began to examine them in 1962, was the way they punished and degraded women through the "system." The combined hypocrisy of legislators, the medical profession, and law enforcement made them virtually laws for the wealthy and influential, discriminating heavily against the poor and minority groups.

These laws had been passed during the Civil War period. Before that, under common law inherited from England, abortion was not punishable as a crime if performed before "quickening" (the movement of the fetus in the womb at about the start of the fifth month of pregnancy). They had been passed, as Dr. Vuitch's lawyers pointed out, to protect women against the medical hazards of that time, and to stimulate the growth of population, then a critical need. But as these purposes evaporated, the laws became mainly a bludgeon against women, an enforcement device to support moral and religious codes. With intensified pressure from the Roman Catholic hierarchy, moral dogmatists, district attorneys, and politicians, most hospitals barricaded themselves behind the final absurdity of the system, the Therapeutic Abortion Committee.

These committees restricted abortion so drastically—one New York hospital cutting its quota by two-thirds, a Los Angeles hospital by over 800 percent—that by the 1960's only 8,000 abortions annually were performed in hospitals. Low abortion rates became a status symbol. "The fewer abortions, the better we look," a Philadelphia hospital administrator told me. By establishing a quota system, approving a small, fixed number of abortions each month, TA committees practiced medicine by statistics, rejecting cases of critical need simply because the quota had been filled. Each committee had its own labyrinth of regulations, some rejecting all cases with psychiatric grounds, for example. "What must I do to prove how desperately ill I am?" one patient asked a prominent Baltimore physician. "Must I attempt or finally commit suicide, or finally be committed to a mental hospital to prove it to them?"

The most disgraceful result of the committee system was its discrimination against the ward patient, which in urban areas meant blacks, Puerto Ricans, and other minorities. In New York City in the 1960 period, only 7 percent of hospital abortions were granted to nonwhites. In a survey of sixty leading hospitals across the country, the rate of abortions for private patients proved to be almost four times greater than for ward patients. Many municipal hospitals, which handle the majority of poor and minority-group patients, virtually eliminated abortions, New York's Metropolitan Hospital, for example, performing only one in 13,000 live births between 1959 and 1961.

Even wealthy and influential women who had some chance of getting through TA committees, were forced to crawl and beg before godlike doctors (almost always male), who had been granted by the state supreme power over a woman's right of choice in childbearing. Women had to perjure and degrade themselves to comply with the system, paying exorbitant fees to psychiatrists for "letters of approval" that would convince the committee a patient was on the point of suicide. Even worse was the "punishment syndrome." After approving abortion, one committee reversed itself on discovering the woman was unmarried. Another committee reported, "Now that she has had her fun, she wants us to launder her dirty underwear."

But what of the majority of women who lacked the money and influence to get through a TA committee? The best statistical estimate was that 1,000,000 women had to seek nonhospital abortion. A limited number managed to get to licensed physicians like Henrie, Spenser, and Vuitch. The rest, particularly minority groups, were driven to the underworld of abortion, and suffered the worst punishment of all.

The horrors of this underworld became the final factor that drove me into the abortion campaign. An analysis of 111 New York City convictions showed that less than a third were physicians or former physicians, the others boasting such qualifications as clerks, barbers, and salesmen.

A twenty-year-old Pennsylvania fashion designer was recommended to a Brooklyn hospital attendant with no medical training, who offered a bargain price of $100. When she died on a table in his apartment, he dismembered her body and disposed of the wrapped pieces in trash cans along Broadway. A Los Angeles girl, brought by her mother to an abortionist who turned out to be a real estate salesman, died on the table from four times the correct dose of anesthesia. Two women, indicted in New York, alternately worked as prostitutes and abortionists.

Even those underworld abortionists with medical degrees often represented the worst depths of physical and mental disintegration—one diagnosed as a schizophrenic, another treating his patients at half-price if they catered to his perversions. Alcoholism was common in this group, one physician "so drunk that he . . . perforated the vagina, tearing loops of bowel with the curette."

The most disturbing aspect of underworld abortion was that these incompetent practitioners concentrated in depressed urban areas. As one barometer of bungled abortion, 10,000 "incompletes" were admitted to New York City municipal hospitals in 1964. As a second barometer, deaths from abortion in New York increased 200 percent in the last decade. Thus, minority groups were punished doubly. Not only was it hard for them to get through TA committees for hospital abortion, but they invariably ended up in the grasp of hacks and butchers of the underworld.

At the bottom level of the underworld was self-abortion. One pathologist showed me a case which had entered his emergency room with a catheter or rubber tube, easily obtainable at local drugstores and used to dislodge the fetus, still protruding from her cervix. She had pierced her uterus, and like many similar cases, died a few hours later.

Other hazardous implements and chemicals for self-abortion ranged from wire coathangers, umbrella ribs, and knitting needles to ergot, lead salts, kerosene, and castor oil. Perhaps the most lethal technique was the injection of a soap or detergent solution which could cause death within hours or minutes. A mother with three children, admitted to Boston's Massachusetts General Hospital with a temperature of 105 after douching herself by syringe with soap and bleach solution, died twenty-six hours later.

The abortion system enabled doctors and hospitals to make exaggerated profits from a few patients at the same time as they self-righteously pretended to screen out unjustifiable cases. The Catholic hierarchy and other religious dogmatists claimed they were protecting the rights of the fetus even if hundreds of thousands of unwanted children ended up in adoption services and foster homes, or became the victims of the "battered child" syndrome. Millions of women fed the coffers of abortion rings, or if they could afford it, respectable Park Avenue doctors who took a few tax-free cases a week at $1,000 and up. Even district attorneys could exploit the system with an occasional arrest and a flurry of headlines that advanced their political careers.

Only the woman—tortured, degraded, and psychologically scarred—got nothing but what she considered her inalienable right: A safe abortion if she was lucky, often injury and death.[3]

Until 1965, I had studied the system through academic research. Now I was to meet this anguish head-on. With the publication of my book and the start of radio and television appearances, the letters and phone calls increased. I was engulfed in misery. "I just don't know how long I can hang on," wrote a 44-year-old Iowa mother, supporting five children and a crippled husband on Social Security. "I am sure if I don't take an overdose of pills, I will lose my sanity."

"My husband got injured, and he can only do light work when he can get it, and I am the main support of my family of five," wrote a black mother from Florida. "Having lost my home, I had to move to a much smaller home, and if I lose this one, my family will be in the street."

A 41-year-old Minnesota mother described her third child, crippled by curvature of the spine, and her fourth, born mentally retarded and physically disabled. She had just started to work and pay off their large medical debts when she became pregnant again. "I feel like I'm drowning and no one will help me."

A 26-year-old New Jersey husband described how his wife "broke down uncontrollably during her fourth pregnancy" and "I was afraid at times to leave her alone with the children." A psychiatrist recommended abortion, but their doctor refused. During the next pregnancy, her husband heard a crash of glass from the bedroom. "My wife was kneeling down, picking up the sharpest pieces of glass. I grabbed them away from her. When I looked at her, tears were streaming down her face. She begged me to let her kill herself. I just held her tight and cried like a baby."

It seemed almost impossible to ignore these appeals. "There are two things that are more important than writing," Erik H. Erikson, the Harvard psychoanalyst, once said. "One is action, and the other is silence." I knew I could go on in no other way but action. Since almost every state law included penalties for helping a woman secure abortion, it implied considerable risk—constant surveillance, tapped telephones, possible arrest.

If my referrals were to have real meaning, they had to produce an open and massive confrontation announced constantly at every interview and broadcast so that women knew the secrecy of the abortion system had been cracked. They would have to become the rallying point of a movement, and give cohesion to women long isolated in lonely, secret compartments. Above all, they would put district attorneys and police officials on notice that the hypocrisy of the old laws was being challenged.

Strangely enough, I found, one becomes quickly immunized to personal risk, and even a phone call from the district attorney with a summons to the grand jury becomes a detail in the daily swarm of technical problems. The real challenge in the first few years was the volume of requests. Each interview or broadcast produced a wave of letters and phone calls. It would take much of the morning writing my answers, and since I refused payment, returning checks and cash that were often enclosed.

To protect my family from intrusion, I insisted on a letter of request, rather than a personal interview. But this could hardly deter women arriving unannounced at my door from Georgia or Indiana, often with no money for hotel or travel to another city, and desperate to find a New York doctor within the day. Nor could it prevent the phone calls in the middle of the night. A woman seeking abortion, understandably, loses all track of time, particularly of the time-gap between East and West Coasts. Somehow, long distance calls always arrived after midnight.

Perhaps the most complex factor was personal involvement. Women would call back to report that the doctor I had suggested was away or that they could not afford the doctor's price. I felt responsible for each case—admittedly dangerous since my own objectivity could be wrecked if each case became a personal torment. Yet I often had to spend hours on the phone, finding another doctor, pleading with a doctor to reduce his price, or simply searching out an inexpensive hotel room for a stranded applicant.

The greatest problem that first year was to find enough qualified physicians to perform in-office abortion. Dr. Spenser had virtually retired, and would only take an occasional case after insistent pleading. The few clues I had for potential doctors came from Paul Krassner, the incisive, satiric editor of *The Realist*, and through his editorial pages, probably the first proponent of open referrals. These clues got me past the first few months. Then a noted Southern physician, a man whose reputation I had known for years through his medical papers and lectures, volunteered to handle a dozen cases a week. Late in 1966, I met Dr. Vuitch, my principal outlet until his arrest.

Finally, I found an excellent medical group, organized by Louis Brown, a physiotherapist, in a New York City apartment. His staff included three or four doctors, each giving a few hours a day apart from their own practices, and thus able to accept more than fifteen cases a day. Brown and his wife developed a unique service. They met all out-of-town patients at the airfield with their car, often took them out for lunch or dinner, and if a snowstorm delayed their departure, or their cash was low, the Browns would house them without charge in their own apartment.

The top price of the Browns' doctors was $300—the same limit that Dr. Vuitch had accepted. They also agreed to take a reasonable number of indigent cases at half-price or without charge. Naturally, the Browns made money, probably $30 or $40 on each case. Still, these figures—and one must include the risks and legal fees that Vuitch and the Browns' doctors incurred after their indictments—were minimal compared to the standard $1,000 and up charged by many fashionable gynecologists at the time.

There was another factor underlying the strain of those early months—a simple matter of loneliness. I was closed off from everyone except my wife, who bore an immeasurable share of the load. The small New York group, known as the Association for the Study of Abortion, comprised lawyers, doctors, and other professionals who were uninterested in referrals or my confrontation thesis. While the New York Civil Liberties Union had taken a stand against abortion laws, it would be a year until its executive director, Aryeh Neier, telephoned me—a call I would always treasure—to offer any necessary legal defense.

Everything changed at the end of a cross-country trip of radio and television appearances in April 1966. In San Francisco I met Patricia Maginnis, President of the Society for Humane Abortion, the first woman to demand repeal of all abortion laws. It was like coming out of a dark tunnel. We talked for two days—at Fisherman's Wharf where the bay danced with the skimming, white sails of pleasure boats, at the Japanese tea garden in the public park, at her tiny disheveled downtown office where she slept on a blanket roll to save money, amidst mimeograph machines and stacks of pamphlets. We drank and talked, and I took a few hours off to appear on radio shows. There was always an aura of gaiety about her. She painted in her spare time, pastoral scenes in water color, but more often, squiggly cartoons, keyed to her slashing, bitter wit. A woman fighting off the advances of the all-powerful male, requesting: "Please don't rape me yet. I'll need your name, address and phone number for the district attorney." She had taught herself to play the flute and was remarkably accomplished at Handel sonatas. Later, when she visited us in New York, my wife, a professional musician, accompanied her on the piano while we roamed across Handel scores till late at night.

Pat Maginnis was thirty-seven when I met her, a slender, almost frail woman with soft, brown eyes, and a hesitant, high-pitched voice that seemed to disguise the flamboyant campaigner who had already made abortion an issue on the West Coast. There was a hint of toughness, however, in the thrust of her chin. When she talked about abortion, her words rasped and stung. She had gone through three herself, the first by a doctor in Mexico, the last two using risky, self-abortive techniques she had learned during her hospital service with the Women's Army Corps. She had developed an infection and high fever, and put herself into a San Francisco hospital. "That's when you learn how they make terror part of the system," she said. "The hospital staff was more interested in getting me to talk to the police than curing me. The police love to hound women in abortion cases. They kept pounding me with questions—who did it? Where? What did it cost? When I insisted I did it myself, they said I was lying. After the doctors curetted me, they kept talking about a piece of fetal tissue and wanting to have it baptized. They assumed from my name I was Catholic. Of course, I was born one, but outgrew that long ago. When they asked about my religion, I told them I was a Buddhist."

About the same time I started my referrals in New York, Pat Maginnis decided that California abortion laws had to be challenged by direct confrontation. She went to Tijuana on the Mexican border and visited a dozen doctors performing abortions in small clinics—no more legal in Mexico than California, but long tolerated there by authorities. She put the best clinics on a mimeographed sheet with their telephone numbers and addresses, and began standing on the busiest street corners of San Francisco, handing them out to women. Although she insisted she was violating three sections of the Penal Code (Sections 274, 276, and 601 of the State's Business and Professional Code), no one arrested her. She even sent her handbills to the State Attorney General and local police officials, but continued to be ignored.[4]

Finally, after reporters and broadcasters began covering her daily vigils on the street, a policeman stopped her on July 23, 1966, insisting she needed a permit. "Of course I don't need a permit," she told him.

"You're littering the streets," the policeman insisted.

She denied it. "I'm picking up every discarded leaflet, and handing them out again."

Still, she was arrested under Section 188 of the Municipal Police Code (distributing lewd and obscene literature), and released on bail. When the case came to trial on August 17, Municipal Judge Leo Friedman declared that the arrest should have been made under Section 601 of the State Code, which was not within his jurisdiction and Maginnis, therefore, was released. Further, he called Section 188 unconstitutional as a violation of free speech. Jubilantly she announced, "Now I can paper the town with leaflets."[5]

She did nothing in a small way. In a few months, she had become the abortion gadfly of California, provoking arrests, rousing a storm in the papers and broadcasting media, making women aware that the Society for Humane Abortion could become the agent for their demands. She angered many, of course. That was her style: noisy and passionate. It was exactly what was needed from the first woman: to throw off all constraints and take her chances in the furnace of confrontation politics.

NOTES

1. Margaret Sanger, *Woman and the New Race* (New York: Truth Publishing Co.; 1920), p. 94.

2. Larry Bumpass and Charles F. Westoff, "Unwanted Births and U.S. Population Growth," *Family Planning Perspectives*, Vol. 2, No. 4, October, 1970, pp. 9–11.

Mary S. Calderone (ed.): *Abortion in the United States* (New York: Paul B. Hoeber, Inc.; 1958), p. 180; Marie E. Kopp: *Birth Control in Practice* (New York: Robert M. McBride & Co.; 1934), p. 122. The estimate of 1,000,000 abortions annually, although accepted by most public health authorities, is based on limited and outdated data. As a result of legal abortion statistics for 1972, the figure probably is closer to 750,000.

3. For an analysis of the abortion "system" prior to legalization, see Lawrence Lader, *Abortion* (Boston: Beacon Press, 1967), particularly Chapters I, IV, V, VI, VII, VIII, IX, X.

4. Section 274 forbids supplying any woman with the means of procuring abortions; Section 276 forbids soliciting a woman for abortion, or use of any means to procure abortion; Section 601 forbids offering any service to produce abortion, or assisting abortion by publishing or other means.

5. *Society for Humane Abortion Newsletter*, Vol. 3, No. 1, January–February, 1967.

Special References

The sources on Margaret Sanger are interviews with her by the author, and personal letters of hers, Havelock Ellis, and others in the author's possession, mainly included in Lawrence Lader, *Margaret Sanger and the Fight for Birth Control* (New York: Doubleday & Co.; 1955).

CHAPTER THREE

WOMEN IN REVOLT

The most puzzling issue in the revolt against abortion laws is why women suffered quietly for so long. A leaden apathy suffocated all protest even after birth control had reached respectability by 1935, and other nations (notably Japan in 1948, and the Soviet Union and its Eastern bloc in 1955) had completely legalized abortion. Abortion never became a feminist plank in the United States among the suffragettes or depression radicals. It was ignored, even boycotted by Planned Parenthood women in those days, and only surfaced in California when individual desperation outweighed public taboos. The trauma of her own abortion undoubtedly converted Pat Maginnis from apathy to action.

"I was ashamed of my country," Maginnis concluded in 1957 when she was forced to go to Mexico for an abortion she considered her natural right at home. In the Women's Army Corps as a medical technician, stationed at a Panama Canal Zone hospital, her insight expanded. "I saw the brutality of the system—a soldier's wife who had attempted suicide after being refused abortion, held captive like an animal in the hospital ward, literally forced by the staff to continue a pregnancy she hated."

Ms. Lana Phelan, a pert, handsome blonde, Maginnis' closest associate, who remarked later when breaking the laws with abortion referrals, "I'm married to a cop," was pushed into her first marriage at fourteen by family pressure. The man was twice her age, but her parents insisted that motherhood was the only fitting role for a girl. "I didn't even know where babies came from," she recalled. "After a long, dangerous labor, and the birth of my first daughter, the doctor instructed me to wait a few years before another pregnancy. I asked him what to do. He snapped, 'Stay away from your husband.' Three months later I was pregnant again. We hadn't even paid for the first delivery, and the doctor treated me like a criminal."

Through friends, Phelan located a local midwife-abortionist. "The pain was awful, indescribable," she remembered, "but at the end this gentle old lady said a few words I'll never forget, 'Did you think it's so easy to be a woman?' " Lana reported the abortion to her doctor and asked why he hadn't prescribed contraception. "I figured you were a smart kid and would find a way out," he told her. At that moment, Phelan decided that the whole system was rigged against women.

The first stage of protest often seems to be rooted in class discrimination. Margaret Sanger, daughter of an impecunious, Irish-born stonecutter who raised eleven children in Corning, New York, looked up as a girl at mansions on the hill of her town, and noted bitterly that the rich possessed some secret to keep their families small while those nearest the poverty level added a new baby almost every year. Maginnis and Phelan came from the same marginal backgrounds, supporting themselves at an early age. Phelan had to quit school in the seventh grade for a drugstore job, the only income in her family in the late depression years. After both went through abortions, they quickly found that the system was made for the wealthy women who could pressure her way through hospital committees, or buy the same service at an outrageous price from a physician in his office.

Political radicals first before becoming feminists (there was not even an organized feminist movement then), both Maginnis and Phelan rebelled at this "law for the rich." When Assemblyman John Knox submitted an abortion bill to the California legislature in 1961, Maginnis organized citizens groups and collected petitions in support although complaining the bill hardly scratched the surface of the problem. By 1966, she had gathered enough converts to hold an abortion conference in San Francisco where the "repeal" position—"Any woman at any time should be able to procure a legal abortion without even giving a reason," Prof. Garrett Hardin put it—was formally adopted.

Phelan came up from Long Beach (where she had settled after a second marriage to Barney Phelan, a Department of Corrections supervisor), and saw Maginnis standing outside the conference hall in a driving rain, handing out leaflets. "If she could get soaked to the skin for this cause," Phelan recalled, "I had to join it." Within a year, they had formed an ebullient partnership.

Maginnis now took the ultimate step in confrontation politics, which would embroil her in personal abuse even from many early radicals. She announced a series of free, public classes throughout California to teach women the techniques of self-abortion that she had twice used on herself. The technique involved the use of the forefinger to stretch the opening of the cervix, and through the cervical opening digitally irritating the uterus to bring on contractions and eventual miscarriage. Like all methods of self-abortion, this was highly condemned by the medical profession. Maginnis herself admitted its risks. She knew she was dealing in sensationalism, yet insisted that the shock value was necessary to dramatize the refusal of hospitals and doctors to assume responsibility in fighting the present laws. If medicine and society coldly ignored the needs of women, the only resort was for women to act on their own.[1]

If her approach was flamboyant, Maginnis shrewdly saw that the first objective of the movement was to attack the law head-on. "Law enforcement, from Attorney General Lynch to the policeman on the street, realizes that once the law stands trial in court, it will collapse," she told reporters.

Her classes, starting on July 27, 1966, in San Francisco, covered contraception, abortion referrals overseas and at home, after-abortion care, and police tactics, as well as self-abortion. A policewoman, taking notes, covered almost every session. "The first people we invited were the police," Rowena Gurner, Maginnis' associate, noted. By December, the average attendance ran well over a hundred, and meetings were picketed regularly by a new Catholic group, "Mothers Outraged at the Murder of Innocents," or MOMIS, as the press called them. Although picket leaders demanded that the governor and law officials arrest Maginnis, no one seemed eager to increase the rash of publicity she had already roused.

Eventually, the District Attorney of San Mateo County announced he would arrest Maginnis and Gurner under Section 601 of the State Code if they held classes in his jurisdiction. They accepted the challenge with a meeting at Redwood City on February 20, 1967, where the District Attorney arrested and jailed them for eighteen hours without bail. Their defense, handled by the Civil Liberties Union, claimed that Section 601 resulted in a constitutional abridgment of free speech and press. At the trial in June, the judge upheld this position, exonerated the women, and declared the law unconstitutional. Although the District Attorney appealed the verdict to higher courts, Maginnis had achieved her purpose of making women confront the cruelty and hypocrisy of existing abortion laws.[2]

Maginnis and Phelan then decided to expand their offensive into a national tour. Their starting point was Washington, D.C., where an International Conference on Abortion had been called for early September. Financed by the Joseph P. Kennedy, Jr., Foundation, this conference, despite the trappings of objectivity, seemed to those of us who had been trying to build a movement to be primarily aimed at smothering recent progress. Only three women were represented among fifty-nine panelists (a few more were added, after considerable pressure, to the "at large" delegation). The speakers and panelists were largely Catholics or antiabortion in their views, and the "repeal" position was virtually ignored.

To disrupt the flow of opposition press releases emanating from the Washington Hilton Hotel, Maginnis and Phelan marched before its doors with signboards demanding, "End Butchery," and decorated with metal coathangers, knitting needles, and other crude, abortion instruments. The Washington *Post* consequently headlined its story, "Conference Termed 'Stacked,' " and for two nights in a row Maginnis drew further press coverage and standing-room audiences with her self-abortion lectures at the All Souls Church.[3]

They moved on to Oberlin College in Ohio, and Rocky River, a Cleveland suburb, where both lectures were picketed by the predominantly Catholic "Right to Life" movement, and counterpicketed by hundreds of students. Free speech, beyond abortion itself, was now becoming the central issue of their tour. Although they had signed a contract with the Albuquerque, New Mexico, Civic Auditorium, and paid a deposit, city officials canceled out at the last minute, claiming the talks "would be injurious to the health, welfare and morals of the community." They had to book a motel auditorium while the New Mexico Civil Liberties Union attacked officials for "attempting to stifle the propagation of an idea which is distasteful to them."

The climactic struggle over censorship came in Milwaukee when the local YWCA, two hotels, and the Jewish Community Center in turn accepted their booking, and then canceled out. "ABORTION 'CLINIC' STARTS ROW," explained the Madison *Capital Times* in a front-page, banner headline. Finally, Maginnis and Phelan secured the auditorium of a union hall. "That Milwaukeeans have tried to deny this group the right of free speech is disgraceful," concluded the Milwaukee *Courier.* "Next week we might hear that no place is available for those who wish to discuss police brutality or taxes or graft or street lights and garbage collection." [4]

No one, of course, enjoyed this controversy more than the women themselves. Both were brash and irrepressible in their attitude toward established tradition. They loved the tumult of grass roots politics (Phelan having been elected to local office in Hollywood, Florida, years before). They prodded and whipped their audiences with florid phraseology. "Abortion laws are a lie, a farce, and slavery in its cruelest sense," Phelan liked to proclaim. "At the instant of impregnation, a woman's body becomes the property of the state." They broke through the deadweight of apathy—women talking to women, angry voices demanding anger and action. They were firebells disturbing the night, and nothing was more essential in this early period.

Yet neither the Society for Humane Abortion, nor its political arm, both of which Maginnis founded and headed, ever built a broad base of support among California women. What was needed was a larger vision to link abortion to the whole fabric of suppressed feminist demands, and turn this vision into a national uprising that would radically alter the status of women in our time. This role would eventually be taken by Betty Friedan.

The early feminists, starting with the Seneca Falls convention of 1848, had blotted out sexual issues like the plague. Their demands were social and economic. They not only denigrated sex, but in their efforts to attain any form of equality, often tried to look and act like men, cutting their hair short and wearing bloomers as standard dress.

By the turn of the century, the vigorous movement of Susan B. Anthony and Elizabeth Cady Stanton had dwindled away to the solitary objective of women's suffrage. When the vote was finally secured in 1920, a step having minimal influence on the status of women, the old feminism expired. Even the radical women of the 1930's, grasping for power on the campuses, and in the unions and political parties, never dared to include birth control or abortion in their platforms.

Only Margaret Sanger fought—although briefly—against this total blackout of sexuality among radicals. As a Socialist organizer herself, she tried to sell contraception to the unions and working class, but was soon ignored and rejected by the political Left (except for such splinter groups as the International Workers of the World). By 1920, she had to turn for support to the middle and upper classes.

This blackout of sexuality among feminists originated in fear. The puritan tradition linked sex with evil and guilt. To the puritan mind, laws against contraception and abortion were intended to punish and degrade women, and above all, to deprive them of the possibility of enjoying sex for its own sake. By outlawing contraception and abortion, male-dominated society assumed that a woman would be terrified to indulge in sex when a pregnancy would expose her "sin" to the world (or punish her with the ordeal of underworld abortion).

This national obsession with the "punishment syndrome" reached its peak in the Victorian period. Even for married women, sex was considered unwholesome; they were expected to tolerate—but certainly not enjoy—their husband's advances. When Anthony Comstock, the ultimate puritan fanatic, pushed his law through Congress in 1873, contraception and abortion were lumped together with "obscene literature and articles of immoral use." Such traditional fears of sexuality and physical pleasure still persist. When Colorado passed the first slightly liberalized abortion law in 1967, a State Medical Society official found it necessary to explain, "[The law] wasn't written for the secretary in Chicago who went out one night and had a good time." [5]

The struggle of early feminists for economic and social rights, and even such a prosaic objective as the vote, was painful enough without venturing into the fearsome territory of sex. This crucial step could not be taken until the publication of Friedan's *Feminine Mystique* in 1963, and the founding of the National Organization for Women in 1966. The two events mark the dividing line between the old feminism of rights, and the new feminism of liberation—a total revolution against the subjugation of women as sex objects and suburban stereotypes as well as second-class citizens in offices, factories, and universities. "The real revolution is the emergence of women from passivity to full self-determination, a process that had to include both brains and sex, a totality," Friedan insisted.

Significantly, even Friedan, one of the most impressive militants of her time, avoided the abortion issue at first. We had known each other for years, and while she was writing *Mystique*, I occasionally suggested that all feminist demands hinged on contraception and abortion and a woman's control over her own body and procreation. Yet her book hardly touched this fundamental problem and mentioned Margaret Sanger only peripherally. Friedan, too, had not emerged from the straitjacket of guilt and sexual taboos that society had clamped on women. Even to her probing mind, sex was still ostracized from the grand pattern of feminine emancipation. "I was so obsessed with the issue of equality that I still couldn't face the meaning of sex," she explained. Another neofeminist leader, Ms. Jean Faust, concluded, "We were all blocked at first by traditional labels. We were afraid of being called 'loose women' if we included abortion in our platform."

The breakthrough came slowly. In June 1966, at a meeting of the Commissions on the Status of Women in Washington, Friedan emerged from the status of author to activist. A small caucus demanded a resolution to place the Government solidly against sexual discrimination in hiring practices, but when the Commissions' leadership tried to muzzle them, they met at lunch and planned a new national organization to implement their demands. On her napkin, Friedan scribbled three letters, "N.O.W.," the National Organization for Women. That fall, hundreds of delegates met for the founding convention in Washington, and Friedan was elected first president.

Although pounding away at the abortion issue in her lectures, she still hesitated to force it into the NOW platform for fear of splitting off Catholics and conservative professionals. But the following year, she led the younger delegates of New York State NOW in adopting a "Bill of Rights for Women" that included abortion as "a civil right of every female person." That winter, while the Constitutional Convention was meeting to revise state laws, she brought a NOW delegation to Albany, the state capital, and lonely and chilled in the freezing rain, they paraded back and forth with their abortion signs.

At the national NOW convention later in 1967, Friedan and the younger leadership, including many Catholics, decided to push for an abortion plank. The long, strident debate dominated the convention. "The professional women demanded we concentrate on economic goals—they were scared of harming the organization's dignity with abortion and sex," Faust recalled. "It was the kids, and not just the New York bloc, who led the fight. Kids from Michigan, Ohio, and Texas kept standing up and shouting, 'We've got to have an abortion plank.' We pushed it through finally, but a lot of delegates resigned."

Friedan has dominated NOW and the feminist campaign against abortion laws like a hurricane. She sweeps through meetings, telephone calls, dinners, and speeches with frantic bursts of energy as if each day might be her last. Everything is in motion, not just her words which come so fast she seems to ignore the necessity of breathing. Her hands gesticulate, wave, flail. Her eyes are deep, dark, charged, and violent as her language. Her nose is long, her hair, despite patient attention at the beauty parlor, often askew. Nothing fits the accepted model of beauty. Yet she exerts a powerful, haunting attractiveness—that special combustion which lights up a few, rare individuals interacting with their audience.

"She walks like a tipsy penguin, carrying herself belly forward like a woman in the third month of her pregnancy," a writer once described her. "With her slim arms and legs, her pregnant posture, wearing her no-bra bra under clinging jerseys, she could be the fertility icon of a pagan tribe. It is, perhaps, a reflection of a mercurial personality that she never looks the same twice. At a lectern she is sometimes earth mother, sometimes bitch, sometimes child. People who admire her find her attractive. To her enemies she is all the witches from Macbeth." [6]

She became a phenomenon through boundless ambition, and some claim, aggressiveness—her "greatest strength" and "also her greatest weakness," an associate defined it. She started late, *The Feminine Mystique* not published until she was forty-one. Before that came seventeen years as a fumbling, precocious Jewish girl in Peoria, Illinois, a lonely outcast from the dates and sororities essential to Midwest conformity. She went east to Smith College where her brains and drive came closer to acceptance, making Phi Beta Kappa as a junior, graduating *summa cum laude.* After graduate study, she came to New York City, met Carl Friedan, now an advertising executive, and married. Outwardly she accepted the suburban stereotype—a home across the Hudson near Nyack, raising two boys and a girl, an attempt at meaningful community projects like organizing the professional skills of local parents to implement the school curriculum. Eventually, she started magazine writing, four or five pieces a year squeezed between household chores, a foothold in the world she coveted.

It wasn't enough. Her marriage was volcanic almost from the start, a succession of brawls that often reached physical violence, and ended in divorce in 1969. Carl demanded a housewife, and the very word, when she had to describe her role on the census form, made her ill. She had to break out of the prison she would define in *Mystique* as "the problem that has no name," a problem that disturbed most of her classmates at their fifteenth reunion: the misery, the inner rage, the futility of capable women longing for more satisfaction than bedmaking and barbecues.

It was Friedan's vision that recognized the growth of this fierce, feminine discontent, and molded it into a perceptive tract. Still, many books as good or better have disappeared in weeks. What established her as a force was that she made the book almost singlehandedly, created a market for over 53,000 hardbound and 1,500,000 paperback copies. Through television, radio, and lectures, she established almost instant communication with an audience waiting to be stirred. Often sharp and overbearing, she grated on many nerves, disturbed and even terrified others. What really mattered, however, was not the women she displeased, but those she touched with fire. Particularly on college campuses, and among young professionals, she roused an increasing number to the realization that tidbits of equality would not satisfy the demands of women.

Her unfettered aggressiveness and star image have been attacked not only by conservatives, but by the radical Women's Liberation groups which consider NOW a bourgeois organization nibbling at the edge of the feminist problem. None of these carpings has diminished her accomplishments. The wall of opposition facing the neofeminist movement, particularly its struggle against abortion laws, demanded imperious leadership. No one but Friedan exuded the excitement to spread neofeminism across the nation. If this required a star image, she simply gave what the broadcasting and press media demand—the focus on an individual, like Ralph Nader in consumer protection, who can project the aims of a whole movement.

Whether more concerned with reforming the present system (including such symbols as her sit-ins at all-male bars and restaurants), rather than total revolution of the nuclear family as required by Women's Lib, the pertinent fact is that she produced immediate results. When the abortion movement needed picket lines outside of uncooperative hospitals, she activated NOW groups by phone in a dozen cities. Despite the surface impression of bedlam surrounding her daily schedule, she became remarkably organized in crisis. The Women's Strike for Equality March of August 26, 1970, which brought a parade of at least 20,000 to Fifth Avenue, and similar demonstrations in other cities, were a testament to this skill. The coalition behind this march started with chaotic and bickering factions. At meeting after meeting, the plan never got past the blueprint stage. Yet Friedan's grasp and persistence—begging, cajoling, screaming—held the coalition together and produced a stunning success.

Friedan and neofeminism erupted on a wave of technology. For it was the technology of contraception, the birth control pill, that made possible the radicalization of women. Only when technology—and abortion is a crucial step in this process—allowed women to free themselves from the prison of incessant childbearing could they grapple with the possibility of achieving themselves on every plane. By bringing NOW, and eventually Women's Lib into the abortion campaign, Friedan ensured that the struggle for feminine liberation was solidly rooted in the one base that could turn theory into reality—a woman's control over her own body and procreation.

Everything that denigrated women had to start from this point. Ibsen's Nora, fleeing her own prison, asserted, "I have another duty just as sacred . . . my duty to myself . . . I believe that before everything else I'm a human being—just as much as you are . . . or at any rate, I shall try to become one." Margaret Sanger insisted in 1920 that a woman's "mission is not to enhance the masculine spirit, but to express the feminine." [7]

Friedan's *Mystique* carried the vision further. It demanded not only equality, but a full partnership between the sexes. The right to the same education, the same jobs and careers at the same pay as men, the right to the same social responsibilities and political influence—yes, even the right to eat and drink at the same restaurant or bar. If this meant erasing some of the sacred boundary lines between the sexes (Norman Mailer wistfully pleaded, "Who finally would do the dishes?"), the neofeminist vision required a sharing of all parental and household responsibilities. Technology could produce the childcare centers, the publicly supported nurseries and after-school facilities which would free a woman for full-time education or employment. But it was the male who would make the revolution complete: eradicate the stereotype of centuries, share the oppression of dishes or diapers.

Thus Friedan's concept of liberation depended on men as well as women, and as she reiterated endlessly, "Man is not the enemy." It was a blueprint that appealed particularly to youth and college campuses, where the technology of the pill had already ushered in the sexual revolution, as the popular press likes to call it. Those bastions of prudery, the parietal rules, had collapsed at one campus after another, and men and women mingled freely. The next logical step was an equality beyond sex, the complete eradication of the old boundary lines between male domination and female subservience that Friedan predicted in her book. Here was a concept to stir a generation, and it was Friedan's skill as the siren of revolt that carried the battleground from the printed page to the classroom, home, and office. She gave breath and passion to what might have remained an esoteric theory. She transformed a literary tour de force into picket lines, turned passive women into militants of the barricade.

It was the surge and fervor of neofeminism that paved the way for the abortion movement. Each was essential to the other, and neither could have advanced without the other. Still, it was the voices of angry women, organizing across the country, that shook legislatures out of their complacency, and produced the first breakthrough for new abortion laws.

NOTES

1. For a description of the self-abortion technique, see Patricia Maginnis and Lana Clark Phelan: *The Abortion Handbook* (No. Hollywood, Calif.: Contact Books; 1969), pp. 139–142.

2. Sacramento *Bee*, November 6, 1966; *Berkeley Barb*, November 25, 1966; San Francisco *Examiner*, December 2, 15, 1966.

3. The Washington *Post*, September 7, 8, 9, 1967.

4. Cleveland *Plain Dealer*, October 7, 14, 1967; Madison (Wisc.) *Capital Times*, July 16, 1968; Milwaukee *Courier*, July 20, 1968.

5. *New York Times*, April 30, 1967, p. 60.

6. *McCall's*, May 1971.

7. Margaret Sanger, *Woman and the New Race* (New York: Truth Publishing Co.; 1920), pp. 8–9.

CHAPTER FOUR

REFERRAL SERVICES: THE GENTLE (AND NOT SO GENTLE) LAWBREAKERS

The Rev. Howard Moody of New York City's Judson Memorial Church, a hefty, six-foot-tall, forty-six-year-old, Baptist minister with crew-cut hair, known for having tackled such inflammatory problems as the Tammany Hall boss-system, made a startling announcement on the front page of the *New York Times* on May 27, 1967. He and twenty-one Protestant ministers and Jewish rabbis were opening the Clergy Consultation Service on Abortion. Henceforth, any woman could phone the Clergy Service's number in New York, and make an appointment with one of the clergymen on duty that week to find out how she could terminate an unwanted pregnancy.

Moody was understandably hesitant to define the legal standing of his service. The clergy would offer options, he told the press. They would help a woman adjust to keeping her baby or offering it for adoption. They would help her obtain a hospital abortion if her medical background supported the possibility. And they would refer her to a list of doctors in the United States and Puerto Rico (and eventually London) for in-office abortion—a choice that would be made in the next few years by about 95 percent of the clergy's cases.

There is "some legal risk," Moody observed, "but we are not willing to admit it is illegal." Still, he always recognized the possibility of tapped telephones and police surveillance. An insistent woman on the telephone often demanded, "Is this where I can get an abortion?" Moody would reply cautiously, "This is the Judson Memorial Church, ma'am. We do abortion *counseling* here." One irate voice retorted, "I don't need the Sermon on the Mount, Reverend. I need an abortion."

The fact that thousands of women would soon get an abortion through the clergy, after a counseling session that ran from ten minutes to an hour or so, was a turning point in the campaign. It brought the moral weight of prominent and outspoken clergymen behind the principle of referral—something that Maginnis and I with our radical orientation could never provide. The cloth had dignity, authority, and sanctity that might dissuade a district attorney from investigation. As a religious counterforce to Roman Catholic attacks, the Clergy Service gave us another decided advantage. It put into daily practice the philosophic stand that many denominations had already adopted—that abortion was not murder, as Catholic dogma claimed, but a humane solution to a critical social problem. "We affirm that there is a period during gestation when, although there may be embryo life in the fetus, there is no living child upon whom the crime of murder can be committed," the Clergy Service stated in its first position paper.

In practical terms, the Clergy Service added an equally important factor—a rapid increase in the number of cases that could be handled. Once the New York service functioned smoothly, Moody could extend it to other cities—an expansion policy that soon made it one of the most powerful forces in the abortion campaign.

Except for the Unitarian-Universalists, only a handful of ministers had spoken out on abortion, mainly Moody and Rabbi Israel Margolies of New York City, the first to support Mrs. Sherri Finkbine in 1964 when she was denied an abortion by Colorado hospitals despite the danger of fetal deformity from thalidomide. At my first press conference, Margolies joined me in defense of the "higher law" doctrine, enunciated by the Boston abolitionists when they broke federal laws supporting slavery after 1850. "When rulers have inverted their functions and enacted wickedness into law which treads down the inalienable rights of man to such a degree as this," the Reverend Theodore Parker announced in 1850, "then I know no ruler but God, no law but natural Justice."

Since I called upon this doctrine in my referral service (obviously a philosophic defense with no standing in court), it was a notable advance in building the abortion movement for the Clergy Service to take the same position. "Believing as clergymen that there are higher laws and moral obligations transcending legal codes," Moody put it, "we believe it is our pastoral responsibility and religious duty to give aid and assistance to all women with problem pregnancies."

It had taken Moody eight months of intensive planning to put the Clergy Service together. The idea developed on September 6, 1966, during a luncheon with Moody and two Episcopal priests, Lester Kinsolving of San Francisco, and John Krumm of New York (later Bishop of Southern Ohio). At some point, they asked me what they could do to help the campaign. I replied bluntly, "Start with the women. Organize the clergy to refer women to qualified doctors."

Moody was the ideal candidate for such a project, combining a commitment to social responsibility with hardheaded realism. He had come out of World War II with an Air Medal and three battle stars. As a Marine attached to the Air Corps shortly after Pearl Harbor, he fell out of the underside of a B-17 bomber with a heavy camera in one hand, clutched at a strut with the other, and managed to pull himself back into the plane, still grasping his camera.

After graduating from Yale Divinity School, Moody served as chaplain at Ohio State University before coming to Judson in 1956. He soon turned it into a dynamic community center, pioneering in narcotics treatment, avant garde music, theater, and even politics. Moody led the new Democratic reform club in 1957 against the omnipotent Tammany boss, Carmine De Sapio—a campaign which failed, but helped produce the eventual downfall of De Sapio and Tammany Hall.

To organize the Clergy Consultation Service, Moody invited about forty clergymen, mainly friends or, like Margolies, known opponents of abortion laws, to a series of meetings. The Reverend Jesse Lyons of Riverside Church, for example, had seen his niece denied abortion after German measles, which resulted in the delivery of a malformed child, institutionalized for life. Reverend Finley Schaef of the Washington Square Baptist Church had struggled with the pregnancy of a fifteen-year-old girl raped by her father. "I felt stunned and helpless when the law said I couldn't prevent this tragedy," he recalled.

At an early meeting of the group, Prof. Cyril Means of New York Law School outlined the legal risks of referrals, an issue causing the resignation of a few clergymen whose congregations opposed their stand. One rabbi was told he would lose his post if he persisted.

Ephraim London, noted legal advisor of the Civil Liberties Union, drew up a set of rules to minimize the risks. New York clergymen should only refer a woman to a doctor *outside* the state, under the assumption that a district attorney might hesitate to pursue a case into another jurisdiction. Clergymen should have no personal contact with doctors, and accept no money from doctors or women. No names or addresses, only a number, would be attached to each case record.

This fear of the law came to a head at the last meeting when the name of the service was debated. The policy draft suggested, "Problem Pregnancy Consultation Service." Lyons, Schaef, and I, among others, opposed this evasion, stressing that the impact of the service depended on open and total commitment. "Abortion's a loaded, fearsome word," Moody observed, "but we decided we didn't want to chicken out on it." After intense debate, the clergy voted to call themselves the Clergy Consultation Service on Abortion.

Now the main hurdle was to find enough qualified doctors to meet the demand quickly roused by the publicity given the clergymen. The limited list Paul Krassner and I could offer was hardly enough for a start. A women's committee, headed by Ms. Arlene Carmen, Moody's executive assistant, was delegated to open up new sources and evaluate them. A doctor's medical training and professional experience, particularly in gynecology and abortion, were obviously the first requisites. But the Carmen committee also gave considerable attention to personal and psychological qualifications, the cleanliness of offices, excellence of equipment, type of anesthesia used, postoperative care, and price scale. Five doctors from the Philadelphia area were scrutinized and rejected in one week.

A constant check was kept on doctors through the postoperative reports of patients. At a Puerto Rican clinic, a patient told Moody, the doctor had failed to show up for her appointment and his nurse performed the abortion instead. The clinic was immediately banned.

Puerto Rico became the most important early source for the Clergy Service. But after doctors started boosting their prices to $500 and $600, Moody found he could control prices at $400 or less by sending most cases to one clinic, which maintained superior medical and pricing standards.

Another expert source soon developed in Pennsylvania—an obstetrician-gynecologist who took a few cases a day at $300 top and an occasional poverty case without charge. The applications from New York ghetto areas, however, were less than expected. Red tape and travel costs to Pennsylvania and other states limited most black and Puerto Rican women to neighborhood abortionists despite low medical standards. Not until late 1969 was the Clergy Service able to open up a New York source at St. Luke's Hospital. Through the insistent courage of Dr. Bernard Nathanson, an obstetrician-gynecologist, and the social service department, St. Luke's was soon clearing most poverty cases simply by giving the broadest possible interpretation to the old abortion law.

The Clergy Service also found a remarkable source in New Orleans. The contact happened accidentally when a woman dropped into Moody's office after a New Orleans abortion which she praised highly. Arlene Carmen made an investigatory trip. She gave a top rating to the doctor's medical credentials and facilities, and agreed on a $300 price, with about a fourth of the cases free. The doctor and his staff laid special stress on supportive counseling before and after abortion, and taught each patient the fundamentals of contraception. "He made women feel they were good people—a positive experience we had rarely developed elsewhere," Carmen noted. "He quickly became our prime source."

To relieve the pressure on a clergyman, Moody rotated the list of ministers and rabbis on the official answering service so that each was on duty one week out of every four or five. Still, this meant an individual case load of at least twenty a week. The aim of the counseling process was to supply information—most women knew little about the medical or legal aspects of abortion—and to allay their fears. "I tried to put a woman at ease, to make her realize abortion was not a matter of eternal damnation," Lyons explained.

The clergy soon found that guilt rarely stemmed from religious concern over fetal destruction, but from the judgment imposed by society on a woman's harrowing search for help. "You could see the stigma disappearing as the abortion campaign changed public attitudes," Lyons noted. "At first, I used up a box of Kleenex in a few counselings. Within a year, the tears and guilt were gone."

The deep-rooted prejudice against the word "abortion" was so intense that Carmen, who handled many of the phone calls, had to struggle to get the women to define their problem. "Is it a personal matter?" she would ask. There would be hesitant agreement. "Is it a problem pregnancy?" Again, a whispered assent. "Most women were so tortured by anxiety at their first visit, they were almost physically crippled," Carmen observed. "But when they came back to report after the abortion, they were smiling and happy—literally different people. We could hardly recognize them."

Most clergymen agreed that the most painful cases were teenagers accompanied by parents. "The parents were crushed, the girl humiliated by the shock to her parents," Moody explained. "I tried to make parents understand their daughter was not a freak. They wanted a minister to tell them this. They wanted help with their guilt."

Another difficult category was the post-twelve-week pregnancy, often caused by the delaying tactics of physicians. A patient, coming for a pregnancy test, was often told: "Wait until you miss another period, and then we'll see." Consciously or unconsciously, doctors often delayed women past the period of safe, early abortion in order to force her to bear the child. "These late cases—telling a woman you couldn't do anything for her—were a frightening ordeal for us," Lyons said.

Fortunately, the new British law, which took effect on April 26, 1968, solved the problem of late abortions, at least for women who could afford the London plane fare. The law was a landmark, the most comprehensive yet passed by any Western nation (excluding the Communist bloc). It allowed abortion by a licensed physician to preserve total family health—not just the mental and physical health of the mother, but if another birth would damage "the existing children of the pregnant woman." It went even further, including damage both to the woman's present health and her "reasonably foreseeable environment."

Such indications gave wide latitude to medical judgment, and almost any case could be approved. Although abortion was free to Britons using the National Health Service, Americans and other visitors at private hospitals and clinics paid about $300 for early pregnancies, higher for post-fourteen-week cases. Even with a $400 plane fare, the cost was comparable to Puerto Rico, and the medical standards and care unequaled.

Despite problems with Catholic and conservative physicians in Birmingham and some rural areas, the British law worked well from the start. About 40,000 cases were handled in the first year with only 5 deaths—a rate of 12 per 100,000 compared with the maternal mortality rate of 24 per 100,000. Statistics from Scotland in 1968 showed that over 60 percent were performed on women with two children or more. A few British newspapers played up the invasion of overseas applicants, mainly from Germany and France, but these cases only averaged about 7 percent of the total. By 1971, Britain was performing 100,000 abortions a year.[1]

When Moody put together his New York Clergy Service statistics in June 1970, after 30,000 cases, perhaps the most remarkable result was that there had been no deaths, and the rate of medical complications, all minor, ran only 2 percent.

Equally remarkable was the fact that the New York clergy had never been blocked by arrests. Moody's only threat was an attempt at blackmail. He received a phone call one day from a man, claiming that his girl had been referred by the service, and demanding $5,000 or he would name the doctor to the police. Moody stalled and asked the man to call back. Concluding it was better to face the blackmail issue bluntly, he called a friend in the district attorney's office who instructed him how to proceed. When the man called again and demanded that Moody meet him in Washington Square Park with the cash, detectives "wired" Moody with hidden microphone and tape recorder. As Moody talked to the man, detectives made the arrest.

Not long afterwards, the father of a girl who had been counseled by the service visited Moody to express his gratitude. "If I can ever be of help to you in my line of work," he offered, "please let me know." Moody asked what work he did. "I'm a police captain," the man said.[2]

Once the New York clergy functioned smoothly, Moody embarked on a network of services across the country. For any woman outside the metropolitan area, the cost and time of a trip to New York for consultation, and a second trip to a doctor in Washington, D.C., or Puerto Rico, were serious obstacles. Moody envisioned clergy services in key cities within convenient distance of every woman. Each service would be independent, yet could draw on the blueprint, experience, and medical sources of New York.

Moody built the network at first through friends—Reverend Allen Hinand in Pennsylvania, Reverend Charles Straut in New Jersey, Reverend Clyde Dodder in Massachusetts. Other services were started by clergymen from the New York group—Reverend Farley Wheelwright who had transferred to Cleveland, Rabbi Lewis Bogage who had gone to Denver.

Despite Colorado's 1967 reform law, the first in the country, Rabbi Bogage soon found that few cases were covered by the law. "It was a shock to me personally when I moved to Colorado and discovered that this state's supposedly liberal law was actually a tight abortion law, and that the problem here was the same as in New York," he observed. "That's why we had to offer abortion counseling here." But the Colorado service, like many others, quickly assumed a second function—an aggressive campaign for new laws that would guarantee abortion as an inalienable right. "Our real objective is to become a lobbying group," Bogage announced, "that can fight for changing Colorado's abortion law so it becomes really liberal, or to have it repealed entirely." [3]

The Michigan Clergy Service, headed at first by Reverend Carl Bielby, became one of the most innovative in the country. Over 100 clergymen took referrals, including a few Catholic priests working behind the scenes. Although based in the Detroit Council of Churches' office, where Bielby directed social services, it maintained local branches and counseling in a dozen Michigan cities. Its clerical support, in fact, was so prestigious that a group of ministers and rabbis sat down to explain its purpose and methods with state officials, legislators, and ranking police officers. As a result, the Clergy Service was never touched by any Michigan police or district attorney.

The service screened its clergymen carefully for psychological maturity and counseling experience, and put every applicant through an intensive training program. It never used doctors in Puerto Rico or Mexico, but kept a steady roster of about five sources in neighboring states.

The only potential problem came when a clergyman spotted a car in his parking lot with an older man and girl, apparently his next counseling appointment. The license plate roused his suspicions, and a quick check verified that it was a police number. Nervously, the clergyman gave the couple a broad range of options. It turned out that the visitor was indeed a detective, but a legitimate applicant who had accompanied his daughter for help.

The Los Angeles service, largest in the country, soon processed almost 1,000 women a month. Headed by Reverend J. Hugh Anwyl of the Ecumenical Fellowship, who lost his parish as a result of abortion referrals, the service had over 100 affiliated clergymen and its own building.

Significantly, it made few referrals for in-office abortion once it established cooperative agreements with many hospitals and clinics under the 1967 California reform law. The expensive and time-consuming technique of pushing cases through hospital boards with letters of approval from two psychiatrists was virtually eliminated. The service cleared most cases for hospital abortion within a day or two. "Delays cause the problems to escalate—more emotional, medical, and financial costs," concluded Anwyl. "We provide service on a kind of crisis basis."

The clergy services—the "gentle lawbreakers"—were soon augmented by a variety of other referral groups. This had been my concept—the first wave, Maginnis and I, rousing an ever-widening circle of converts until local referrals were available in almost every area of the country. They came from many sources: Cindy Cisler from the National Organization for Women, Robert McCoy who had put together the first Minnesota organization against abortion laws, Bill Baird who started his own birth control clinic on Long Island and became the ultimate exponent of shock tactics.

McCoy, a freckled, boyish, forty-two-year-old salesman for a steel company, had long been frustrated by his inability to help women who came to him on abortion. "A girl I couldn't help rode a bus to Chicago to find an abortionist, and called me from a hospital where she was standing with her shoes full of blood," he recalled. "Someone had butchered her, and the hospital called the police and refused to treat her until she agreed to testify against the abortionist."

McCoy found that the only recourse for a Minneapolis woman was to walk down Hennepin Avenue with $800 or $900 in her purse, searching out one of five unqualified practitioners, all using the dangerous catheter technique. A former president of the American Humanist Association, who still retained his ministerial license, McCoy located an experienced Mexico City clinic, and another in Canada, investigating them during personal visits. Both were short trips from Minnesota by air, and charged $300 or less. He sent his cases in groups over the weekend so they would be bolstered by companionship. McCoy, according to the Minneapolis *Star*, looked like "the neighbor across the fence," and the gatherings at his suburban home on Saturday and Sunday mornings "like a secretarial placement service."

When a Catholic women's group demanded a grand jury investigation, and the County Attorney warned that referrals were "treading on very dangerous soil," McCoy simply announced he was enlarging his case load. "My family doctor treated me like I was some kind of thing with no morals," one woman told reporters, "but McCoy was thoughtful and understanding. He didn't give any moral lectures."

The only referral service with its own clinic in those early years was the Parents Aid Society of Hempstead, Long Island, which Bill Baird had enlarged from a contraceptive service to abortion referrals in 1967. Baird was the master manipulator of screaming headlines and incendiary issues. Flamboyant, aggressive, never granting the opposition a moment's peace, he sought arrest to focus public opinion on his program, and achieved this objective four times, including a 35-day stint in a Boston jail. He loved the game of charges and countercharges, badgering both the opposition and anyone in our own movement who lagged behind his goals. Once he staged a sit-down strike, accompanied by his followers, at the New York City headquarters of Planned Parenthood, which he labeled a wasteful, hidebound bureaucracy. "I teach more people in a day than they reach in a month," he proclaimed, "and I do it free."

With his strategic skill at poking the most exposed nerves of society at the opportune moment, and exploiting his forays in the press, Baird soon accumulated equal numbers of admirers and detractors. Former New York City Commissioner of Human Rights William Booth, for example, called his campaign "dynamic, inspiring and courageous." Others, particularly in Planned Parenthood, were outraged by his inflammatory tactics. Still, after each Baird hurricane, the movement made considerable progress. Each of his arrests affected the law in question. Each innovation—the mobile van, for instance, with which he brought contraceptive and abortion information directly into ghetto areas—set a pattern that was finally followed elsewhere.

Thirty-five years old in 1967, a cowlick of brown hair over his forehead, his suits and shirts always matching his blue eyes, Baird was born in Brooklyn. "A lot of hoods came out of our neighborhood in East New York," he observed. "I might have been one if it hadn't been for my mother. Once when I was six or seven, I stole some comic books. My mother whacked me across the hand, and made me take them back and apologize to the storekeeper."

Baird continually stressed the poverty of his youth. He had to hold a full-time job at high school. His sister died when she was twelve, "because we were poor—she'd be alive today if we had competent medical help." He dropped out of medical school because of lack of funds. Eventually, he went to work for a manufacturer of foam contraceptives, setting up demonstration units at drugstores. Convinced that birth control services failed to bring contraception to the poor, he bought an old mobile van, decorated the interior like a comfortable living room and consulting room, painted the sides with the message, "Free Family Planning," and drove it night after night into ghetto areas. Since he demonstrated all types of contraceptive techniques, his employer frowned on the "plan van." When he started challenging the law, the company fired him.[4]

The New York State law at the time only allowed contraceptives to be distributed by physicians, nurses, and professional personnel. At Hempstead on May 13, 1965, Baird gave out contraceptives from his van, insisted that the police arrest him, and spent the night in jail. Less than a month later, the U.S. Supreme Court overturned the Connecticut law, and shortly afterwards, the New York law was amended to allow unrestricted distribution of contraceptives—a reform possibly hastened by Baird's arrest.

With this taste of notoriety, he repeated his shock technique by bringing a picket line from the Parents Aid Society to St. Patrick's Cathedral on August 13, 1966, brandishing such signs as "Rome fiddles while the world yearns for birth control." It was the first protest march before the Cathedral itself, according to reporters. In September, he took his "plan van" to Freehold, New Jersey, to tackle another state law, which was reasonably similar to the old New York law. Again convicted of distributing contraceptives, he refused to pay the fine, and chose twenty days in jail—a sentence terminated after a day because of his illness. Later, the New Jersey Supreme Court reversed his conviction, and ruled that display of contraceptives to a woman asking to see them was not prohibited by law.

After opening his Hempstead clinic, Baird tried in 1967 to apply his arrest technique to abortion. Inviting an Inspector of the Nassau Police and the press to his clinic, he described the abortion process, using dilator and curette. "A woman planted in the audience asked Baird for the name of an abortionist," reported the *Village Voice*. Baird read off the names and phone numbers of a few Japanese and Mexican doctors; then announced he was in violation of the law. The Inspector denied it. "I am," Baird insisted. "You're not," protested the Inspector.

"It is your duty to arrest me."

"It is not."

"At this," according to the *Voice* article, "Baird began wildly to berate the Inspector . . . . He called him chicken. He beat the air with surgical instruments." The Inspector fled to the street, "leaving Baird utterly bereft."[5]

The Parents Aid Clinic in Hempstead is a two-story, red brick building open every evening from 5 p.m. to midnight. It has a consulting room, examining room, lecture hall, and laboratory. The reception room is manned by volunteers. In fact, all Baird's staff, including the medical director, served without pay, except for an administrator at $75 a week. Baird financed the clinic through contributions or a rare foundation grant, but mainly through his lecture fees. He was so broke once he had to work as a hospital guard, and his wife, Evie, as a switchboard operator while his mother took care of their four children.

Baird tried to interview every case himself in the early years. Within an hour one evening, he saw a woman of thirty-three, separated from her husband but supporting their two children; two college students, the boy black, the girl white; and a young couple with three children, the wife only twenty-two. At about 10 p.m., a phone call came in from a Brooklyn woman, begging help for her teenage daughter. "Don't cry," Baird assured her, "we'll stay open till you get here."

Toward midnight, Baird complained to a reporter, "The five-year fight has drained me physically and emotionally." He often describes his life in tones of martyrdom. ". . . Baird seems to have grown increasingly and irritatingly fond of hearing himself cry 'betrayal' and 'oh, how I've suffered,' and has occasionally gotten self-righteous about imagined snubbing by those whom he assumes owe him uncritical loyalty on demand," observed Boston's *Phoenix*.

On April 6, 1967, Baird staged his most flamboyant challenge to a state law in a lecture to 1,500 students at Boston University's Hayden Hall. He had been invited by the student newspaper and plans for a court test had been well laid. Three policemen stood in the wings; a lawyer from the Civil Liberties Union waited in the audience. After discussing the crisis of overpopulation, Baird offered to distribute packages of contraceptive foam (sold at almost every Massachusetts drugstore without prescription), and read off the names of Tokyo clinics specializing in abortion. Twelve unmarried girls accepted the contraceptives and the police stepped forward to arrest him. "History is being made in Massachusetts today," Baird concluded, "and you, the students, are part of it."

Since the Massachusetts law, primly labeled "Crimes Against Chastity," forbade distribution of contraception to unmarried persons, Baird was indicted under Section 21A. Ostensibly, he also broke Section 21 of the law, forbidding abortion information, but this was ignored.[6]

The Assistant District Attorney called Baird's speech "an invitation to promiscuity and sexual license." Baird, however, "has never advocated premarital sex—that's not his bag," the Boston University *Informer* pointed out. "He has only advocated freedom—the freedom of choice." In fact, Baird, who once taught Sunday school, admitted, "I'm sort of a square because I do not drink or smoke."

From the vehemence of the District Attorney's assault, and the curtness of the Roxbury District Court ("I am not interested in giving you any publicity here," the judge snapped), it was obvious the authorities did not consider this a token trial. The judge referred the case directly to Superior Court, and on October 17, 1967, Judge Donald Macaulay handed down a verdict of guilty. Baird's lawyer immediately appealed to the Supreme Judicial Court, and the stage was set for final confrontation.[7]

While the appeal dragged on in the courts, Baird thundered against the state's "chastity" law in lectures, rallies, and picket lines.

He was an old hand at exploiting a confrontation. Yet histrionics seemed justifiable considering the prison term he risked—and eventually served. His strategy always brought progress in the long run. His style added a wild, unorthodox zest that was essential to the campaign.

We needed the unexpected and irreverent. We needed tumult. We had to create a sense of danger and urgency. The risks were considerable, but the movement was built on risks. The hope they would produce a fruitful outcome in the courts kept us going in those early days.

NOTES

1. Abortion Law Reform Association *Newsletter*, Winter 1967, No. 20, p. 3; Health Bulletin, Vol. 27, No. 3, July 1969; New York *Post*, July 23, 1970.

2. Susan Brownmiller, "Abortion Counselling," *New York Magazine*, August 4, 1969, p. 26.

3. Olga Curtis, "Clergymen Who Offer Abortion Aid," *Empire Magazine*, January 25, 1970, p. 26.

4. Boston *Sunday Herald Traveler*, June 8, 1969.

5. *Village Voice*, February 23, 1967.

6. Boston *Herald Traveler*, April 7, 1967.

7. Boston *Herald Traveler*, October 18, 1967, p. 73.

CHAPTER FIVE

THE CAMPAIGN FOR NEW LAWS (1967)

Often I would lay awake at night after a hectic day of referrals, hearing again the anguished voices of women on the telephone, or running over in my mind the letter of despair in that day's mail, and I had to ask: Was this enough? Was it only a palliative? Could my referrals, and a few other services, even with the increasing load taken on by Clergy Consultation, ever make more than a dent in this mountain of suffering? We hoped for a test case in the courts that would eventually change the laws. We searched for an outstanding gynecologist, like Dr. Aleck Bourne in England in 1938, who would openly perform an abortion in his hospital and seek arrest to confront the law. But no doctor here wanted this role. And it might be years before an in-office abortion case—the Vuitch decision came in 1969—reached the federal courts.[1]

Meanwhile, the one alternative was to fight the laws in the legislatures, a bleak prospect at the time. Only a rare legislator—mainly State Senator Anthony Beilenson in California and Assemblyman Percy Sutton in New York—had been interested enough to introduce a bill. Legislative opposition was glacial. And a precedent for this route in the birth control campaign hardly added encouragement. Margaret Sanger had spent decades struggling with state legislation, and even a federal bill in Congress, without changing a single law—her triumph finally coming in the courts.

The legislative route could still serve as a vehicle for debate and public education. As an officer of the Yorkville Democratic Club, therefore, I induced Sutton to join me in a public forum on abortion on April 8, 1965, which was the first program at a political club in New York, perhaps the first in the nation. Significantly, most of the club's officers were Catholics, who not only favored the meeting but afterwards confided that they supported abortion reform. This gave me an inkling of our potential allies among lay Catholics, and henceforth I urged a policy that would split the violent opposition of the church hierarchy from our increasing alliance with lay members.

Both Sutton and his cosponsor of the abortion bill in the State Senate, Manfred Ohrenstein, maintained their leadership in abortion through the years. Ohrenstein represented the mid-West Side of Manhattan, a strong liberal constituency. Sutton, who represented Harlem and later became Borough President of Manhattan, gave us a special asset because of his continuous resistance to the claims of some black militants that abortion could promote race genocide. On March 7, 1966, the first hearings on the Sutton-Ohrenstein bill were held at the Capitol in Albany, and along with a few outspoken New York City doctors and representatives from the Liberal Party and New York Young Democratic Club, I went up to testify. All our grand works produced nothing, the bill dying in committee. But we made a considerable impact in the press, the first serious attention paid abortion legislation in the state. That spring and summer, I spoke at least a dozen times to Democratic clubs throughout the city, hoping to enlarge our political base and promote community resolutions that would influence Albany.[2]

The most vexing problem was the bill itself, based on a blueprint proposed by the prestigious American Law Institute, and generally called the "ALI plan." It was a reasonable improvement over the old laws, which in almost every state allowed abortion only to save a woman's *life.* It made the principal criteria for abortion the serious impairment of a woman's physical or mental *health,* which certainly gave hospitals more leeway if they interpreted "health" broadly enough. It also provided for abortion if the child might be born with a grave physical deformity or mental retardation; or for abortion in the case of rape or incest, including statutory rape of a girl under sixteen.

Still, the ALI plan fell far short of the "repeal" position held by

Pat Maginnis, Prof. Hardin, myself, and a small group of radicals like the Unitarians and New York Civil Liberties Union. We insisted that abortion be removed completely from criminal codes and become purely a medical choice between doctor and patient.

Rather than remain aloof from ALI legislation, I favored a strategy of temporary cooperation which would eventually draw supporters like Sutton and Ohrenstein into the repeal camp—a strategy that proved effective by 1968. Meanwhile, our weakness was that except for the California organization and a fledgling group in Illinois, we lacked any real repeal base, particularly in New York. Although the Association for the Study of Abortion was incorporated in New York on March 30, 1966, it chose to remain an educational body in order to increase its fund-raising chances through tax exemption. This removed it from direct political action, and as a result, ASA could never become the vehicle for the neofeminists, clerical activists, students, and other militants soon pouring into the movement.

Within its limited scope, however, ASA proved effective in the early years. Its president was Dr. Robert Hall of New York's Columbia-Presbyterian Medical Center; its chairman Dr. Louis M. Hellman, a noted obstetrician-gynecologist, soon to become Deputy Assistant Secretary for Population of the U.S. Department of Health, Education, and Welfare. With a group of equally prominent physicians, lawyers, and theologians on its board, ASA gave abortion the prestige and authority that was invaluable at the start.

The startling breakthrough made by the Clergy Consultation Service now galvanized many of the official religious bodies to take a stand on abortion. By spring of 1967, the American Lutheran Church, New York City's Protestant Council of Churches, the Episcopal Diocese, and the New York State Council of Churches, among others, had come out in support of the ALI bill. One of the greatest assets the Diocese provided was the services of a staff officer, John V. P. Lassoe, Jr., a modest, highly efficient organizer, who set out to build a coalition behind the bill. Adding to the religious nucleus a list of lay supporters like the National Federation of Temple Sisterhoods, Americans for Democratic Action, American Friends Service Committee, and State Charities Aid Society, Lassoe created the Organizations for Abortion Law Reform.

It had just begun a program of gathering thousands of petition signatures for the 1967 bill (introduced by Assemblyman Albert Blumenthal of Manhattan since Sutton had been elected Borough President) when the Roman Catholic hierarchy produced its first lesson in power politics. The state's eight bishops, with Cardinal Spellman of New York as their spokesman, issued a pastoral letter urging six and a half million Catholics to combat the bill with "all their power." On Sunday, February 12, 1,700 Catholic churches throughout the state were ordered to read the pastoral letter at their services and implement its message with a flood of letters and phone calls to legislators. It was hardly surprising, therefore, when Senate Majority Leader Earl Brydges, a Catholic, and one of the most influential Republicans in the state, announced that his mail was running 100 to 1 against the bill.[3]

We didn't have the strength yet to meet this kind of attack. All we could muster—and even our religious coalition would have been impossible a few months before—was a joint statement by the New York City Protestant Council, Association of Reform Rabbis, and other Protestant and Jewish organizations deploring "the harsh and unbending posture of our Roman Catholic brothers," and condemning the abortion laws as "unduly restrictive, tragically uncharitable, and unjust."[4]

Catholic strategists knew exactly what it took to assure a legislative vote. The abortion movement and its religious allies, on the other hand, had not learned how to convert pressure into votes. We were dealing with the most sensitive issue of our time—certainly more sensitive than divorce-law reform or parochial school aid, and even more so than birth control in its day. What the abortion movement was grappling with, perhaps for the first time in U.S. history, was how to turn an issue that overlapped religion, law, and sociology into a workable political campaign. We needed new techniques, a new type of politics. And except for a handful of reform Democrats in the Legislature, we lacked political leadership.

The opposition concentrated its wrath on Assemblyman Blumenthal, and consistently linked abortion with godlessness. Blumenthal was fired as chairman of the influential Democratic Advisory Committee, probably by Assembly Speaker Anthony J. Travia, a Brooklyn Catholic, "because of complaints from other regulars that Mr. Blumenthal's views were 'too far out'," according to the *New York Times*. At the hearings, the Albany district attorney, a Catholic with six children, demanded of Blumenthal, "Is anybody on your committee an atheist?" Although Blumenthal begged the legislators to "keep an open mind" and avoid religious prejudice, Assemblyman Dominick Di Carlo, a Queens Republican and Catholic, "traded loud and angry words" with him after an NBC television debate, reported the *Times,* and shouted, "Atheists are willing to destroy life, but I don't think most people want any part of this." [5]

However, a remarkable new ally, State Senator Basil Patterson, a black Catholic from Harlem, insisted, "We're not telling other Catholics they have to get abortions, we're only asking them not to dictate to the rest of the population what they can and cannot do." This rent in the Catholic opposition was followed by a statement of support for the bill by forty prominent Catholic laymen, who declared, "Legislating morality has always been a fruitless and wrong act . . . ." [6]

The bill was still buried in the Assembly Codes Committee by March. In an attempt to swing a few more votes, Blumenthal compromised an already weak bill by limiting the "mental health" provision to a definition that virtually required an abortion applicant qualify for institutional mental care. Even then, the bill was killed in committee by a 15 to 3 vote (with one abstention and one absentee), and never got to the Assembly floor for debate.[7]

It now seemed obvious that the old-fashioned politics of lobbying and compromise could never produce a popular groundswell for abortion. We had to generate a new kind of excitement, put the issue in vivid, personal terms, and the radicals were convinced that only total repeal of abortion laws—the right of choice between a woman and her physician—could lead to a realistic platform.

The drive to build repeal organizations throughout the country was haphazard at best. The Wisconsin Committee to Legalize Abortion—such grandiose names generally hid a membership of a few dozen people—was led by a pert, determined housewife named Ms. Edith Rein, who contacted me for legal advice in 1966 after my book, *Abortion,* was banned from circulation by the Milwaukee Public Library on the grounds that "It may be pornographic." Her Committee worked on a total budget that year of $124, its main supporter being Lloyd Barbee, a black State Assemblyman, sponsor of one of the nation's first repeal bills. The Governor's Commission on Human Rights even refused to let Rein testify, denying that abortion fit into any category of rights.

In October 1966, I flew to Chicago to make an abortion speech, and decided to use this chance to have a breakfast conference with one of the stormy petrels of the movement, Dr. Lonny Myers. Annoyed with the approach of the Association for the Study of Abortion, Dr. Myers had constantly peppered ASA with pungent notes to pierce its sleepy dignity. Although I had been a founding, board member of ASA, and chaired two of its committees, I was delighted to find after two hours of talk that Myers' platform was a rational and constructive force for repeal.

A graduate of Vassar and the University of Michigan Medical School, Myers was married to Dr. Shu-Yung Wang, a plastic surgeon, and raised five children while serving as an anesthetist at Chicago hospitals. Startled that Illinois public health agencies were forbidden to offer contraceptive information, she plunged into a campaign which overturned this ban and was awarded Planned Parenthood's Volunteer of the Year Award.

Recognizing the irony of her own sizable family, she once commented, "Until six years ago, I was one of the ignorant, a member of the American Fertility Cult. Had I known what I know today, I could not in good conscience have planned to bear five children."

In 1966, with Reverend Spenser Parsons, Chaplain of the University of Chicago, and Norval Morris, a noted law professor at the University, among others, Myers founded the Illinois Committee for Medical Control of Abortion (ICMCA). Its repeal platform insisted on a decision between doctor and patient, completely rejecting the ALI blueprint. "To ask me to rejoice at a modified abortion law on the ALI model," Myers explained, "is like asking a person opposed to witch-burning to rejoice because a law had been passed permitting burning of witches under sixteen or over forty years old. Moderate reformers don't want babies of rape victims to suffer, but those of unwed mothers should."

With an aggressive campaign of newspaper ads and radio and television programs, ICMCA soon built a membership of 10,000, and Illinois joined Maginnis' California group as the two most potent repeal bases in the country. Now a firm supporter of Myers' work, I urged ASA's cooperation with the Illinois unit with no success. Ms. Ruth P.

Smith, ASA's executive director, had already split with the board. ASA's constitution gave only twenty board members the right to vote. In 1968, ASA adopted a "rotation" policy which conveniently rotated a number of militants, including myself, off the board. This produced a turning point in the movement. When the militants eventually organized a nationwide coalition of repeal groups, Myers, Smith, and I were instrumental in putting the coalition together.

Still, the ALI blueprint would dominate abortion legislation throughout 1967 and 1968. The first two laws passed in Colorado and North Carolina resulted from a new strategy: the "inside" campaign, involving only a small core of political leaders, working inside the legislature. Both states had special characteristics—small populations and few Catholics. Colorado's two million population was about 17 percent Catholic, and its electorate had recently approved a sensitive law, giving free, public contraceptive service to the medically indigent.

The crucial factor, however, was the Colorado campaign's leadership—especially Ms. Ruth Steel and State Representative Richard Lamm. A former president of Planned Parenthood of Colorado, then on the national board, Ms. Steel was a gentle, persuasive woman in her forties, with sparkling blue eyes and a consummate political instinct. Mother of two daughters, she had battled fifteen years to extend birth control services, making it a rule to preserve an impeccable, ladylike image at the State Legislature. Day after day, buttonholing legislators in their offices, she dressed immaculately, even wearing white gloves. One crusty Senator called her the "Carrie Nation of the Bedroom."

Lamm, a handsome, dark-haired, first-term Representative of thirty-one, grew up on an Illinois farm, and strongly supported conservation and population control. With a law degree from the University of California, Berkeley, he migrated to Colorado in 1961. Within three years, although knowing no one on arrival, he became vice president of the Colorado Young Democrats, and was elected to the House of Representatives in 1966.

Logically, abortion should have been the last measure for a political novice to tackle. Lamm not only came from a district with a heavy Catholic vote, but, as a Democrat, his close political ally and friend was Lieutenant Governor Mark Hogan, a devout Catholic. Still, Lamm grew increasingly convinced of the necessity of an abortion campaign and set two provisions before Steel's committee. He wanted a realistic bill with reasonable chance of passage and would introduce it only after securing at least twenty cosponsors.

The bill, modeled on the ALI blueprint, provided that abortions could only be performed in state-licensed hospitals after unanimous approval by a special board of three physicians.

Lamm's first target was to enlist an influential Republican legislator as primary cosponsor. He chose Representative Carl Gustafson, a successful Denver businessman. With Steel, they analyzed the legislature, and concentrating on Protestant and Jewish members, particularly those inclined toward humanitarian and social causes, canvassed the House and Senate in the next few weeks.

The drive for sponsors was a startling success—37 Representatives and 16 Senators, a total of 53 out of 100 legislators in both houses. Four of the five women members became sponsors, the fifth pulling out after pressure from her district, the heaviest Catholic concentration in Denver.

The next step was to get the bill assigned to a sympathetic committee. They chose Health and Welfare since Gustafson was a member, and the chairman known for his impartiality. In the Senate, they enlisted Senator John Bermingham, a Republican from Denver who headed the Health and Welfare committee and had managed the 1965 birth control bill.

Now Lamm and Steel set out to win the support of the news media. Accompanied by carefully selected doctors and clergymen from Steel's committee, they visited editors and executives of metropolitan papers and broadcasting stations and many of the rural media. Eventually, the Denver *Post*, the leading newspaper in the state, ran three editorials supporting the bill, and most other major papers backed it.

An important part of the strategy was to avoid public furor, and draw support from medical, religious, and legal leaders, using their testimony in daily packets of material placed on the desk of every legislator. "It was our opinion that one letter from a doctor or minister supporting the bill, particularly if the legislators knew the person writing, was worth twenty adverse letters," Lamm said.[8]

Lamm made a special effort not to polarize religious opposition. "We tried desperately not to provoke the Catholic Church, and I said numerous times that I did not want to view the issue over the smoke of a fifteenth-century battlefield."

Once Lamm introduced his bill on February 22, however, the Catholic opposition reacted bitterly. A telegram from the Colorado Catholic Conference to all parish priests demanded, "Will you allow Colorado to become the abortion center of the U.S.?"

When the House committee hearing opened on March 9, women brought their children to parade outside the Legislature with signs on their backs proclaiming, "I'm glad I was born." The president of the Catholic Lawyers' Guild of Denver warned that Colorado "would become the abortion mecca of the world," and a Catholic Representative called the bill "a form of euthanasia." [9]

Lieutenant Governor Hogan, presiding officer of the Senate, had entered the hospital for minor surgery, and the sponsors wanted to reach Senate debate while Hogan was absent, and a non-Catholic in the chair. After a series of crippling amendments were beaten down, the bill passed the House on March 29 by an impressive 40 to 21 vote.[10]

At 2 p.m. the day following House passage, a friendly Senator was presiding over the upper house when the bill reached it. Within an hour, the bill had been introduced, read for the first time, and assigned to Senator Bermingham's favorable committee.[11]

"A pugnacious, quarrelsome and sometimes shouting crowd dominated by members of the Roman Catholic Church jammed a State Senate hearing room Tuesday morning," reported the Denver *Post* on April 4. "At one point, Senator Bermingham lost his poise entirely and shouted at the unruly, spillover crowd: 'Be quiet!' Bermingham was explaining that limited time would require a five-minute restriction on each speaker when out of the audience came the bellow: 'The public be damned; just run it through.' The man repeated the same phrase as he stalked out of the hearing later, just after Bermingham had ordered an anti-abortion bill physician (a past president of the Catholic Physicians Guild) to remove from the committee table two bottles containing alcohol-preserved fetuses. So unruly was the crowd that two members of the Catholic Lawyers' Guild, which had requested the hearing, left the meeting to draft a quick, formal apology to Bermingham." [12]

"The Catholic forces participated in their own destruction," one study noted. With only a minor amendment, immediately accepted by the House, the Senate passed the bill 23 to 12 on April 6, and sent it to Governor John A. Love, a Republican.[13]

Although he had previously indicated that the bill "sounds like something I can support," the Governor now came under intense pressure. Pickets surrounded his house with signs demanding a veto. More than 5,000 letters and telegrams piled on his desk, running about 2 to 1 against the bill. Two Senators gave him a petition with 10,000 signatures opposed to the bill. Realizing they could not match this deluge numerically, Lamm and Steel concentrated on sending the Governor letters from supporting medical and clerical committees. The Governor delayed his decision, periodically announcing he was studying all facets of the problem, giving the public impression of a dignified statesman calmly working his way through a crisis.

On April 25, in almost a "circus atmosphere" of bright lights, flashing bulbs, and whirring cameras, Governor Love signed into law the first new abortion statute in the country. Noting that the bill is "completely permissive," not requiring any hospital or staff member to perform abortion against their will, and that the fear of Colorado's becoming an abortion center "does not seem to me well-founded," he declared that the bill was "designed to do something about areas of suffering which have been of concern to a great many people for a great period of time." [14]

"It offers dignity and decency in place of present pitiless restrictions throughout the nation which have resulted in more than a million illegal abortions and the needless death of four thousand mothers each year," the *New York Times* concluded.[15]

The "inside" campaign, limited to the ALI blueprint, was now adopted in North Carolina by another freshman legislator, Arthur Jones of Mecklenburg County (which included Charlotte, the state's largest city). North Carolina had the advantage of an even smaller Catholic population than Colorado—56,000, or 1 percent. As in Colorado, Jones was able to remove the abortion issue from partisan politics. To complete the similarities, Jones, like Colorado's Lamm, was an outsider to the state—born in Philadelphia, raised in New Jersey, one of the few Northerners in the General Assembly, and a recently retired executive of the North Carolina National Bank.

Forced to drop out of high school in the eleventh grade to earn a living, Jones was accepted at Oberlin College in Ohio ten years later in 1925. Majoring in sociology, he wrote term papers on birth control, Margaret Sanger, and abortion, and formed on campus probably Ohio's first planned parenthood unit. "For forty years I have been aware of the ineffective, antisocial laws in this area, imposing upon a whole people legal restrictions which have their roots in the theological doctrine of a religious minority," Jones remarked. "Like many another college student who feels impelled to rebel, I decided then that if I ever had a chance to bring about a change, I would do so."

After drafting the bill with state medical society officials, Jones secured the agreement of the president-elect and other prominent physicians to testify at the hearing. The only opposition came from Catholics—one Senator on the committee, doctors and lawyers who organized letter-writing campaigns to legislators, a few priests attacking the bill in their sermons. Church officials played only a marginal role. With the bill maneuvered to the floor while the Senate was embroiled in other debate, it passed the Senate easily.

Jones now asked the House Health Committee chairman to sit on the bill for two weeks while he personally canvassed 75 of 120 House members and enlisted 68 committed votes. He also contacted all county medical society chairmen and other influential physicians, who informed their legislators of their support. Although the bill came under heavy fire after its second reading on May 4, all amendments were beaten down. On May 8, both House and Senate concurred on technical changes, and the bill passed the House by more than a 2 to 1 majority, becoming law since the North Carolina governor has no veto.[16]

After the Colorado and North Carolina "inside" strategy, the struggle now moved to California, repeating the fiery confrontation seen in New York. In fact, the California debate reached an emotional pitch surpassing that of New York and unequaled in recent California legislative history.

This resulted not only from the state's large Catholic population (about one-fourth), and its bitter division between liberal and right-wing blocs, but from further explosive factors. An abrasive first-term governor, Ronald Reagan, intervened both in legislative debate and final structuring of the bill to an extent unique in abortion politics. In addition, the abortion movement was split over the bill. Finally, the bill followed hard on an existent *cause célèbre*—the punishment of nine prominent San Francisco obstetricians for performing "rubella abortions" in their hospitals.

After the first hesitant attempt in 1961, the drive for an abortion bill was taken over in the 1963 and 1965 sessions by Assemblyman Anthony Beilenson with the support of the California Medical Association, the State Board of Public Health, the Northern and Southern California Council of Churches, and the Northern California Board of Rabbis, among other groups—a coalition stronger than previously developed in any state. Beilenson, a graduate of Harvard College and Law School, had learned his politics in Adlai Stevenson's and President John F. Kennedy's campaigns. Elected twice as an Assemblyman, and in 1966 as a State Senator from the wealthy, liberal Beverly Hills area, he had the advantage of heavy pluralities in a district committed to a new abortion law.

The political climate had been prepared by the repealers and the notoriety of Maginnis' arrests. In 1966, the California Committee on Therapeutic Abortion, a middle-road organization, began to enlist a broad spectrum of doctors, lawyers, and other professionals. Headed by Dr. Keith Russell, professor of obstetrics at the University of Southern California and officer of many medical groups, CCTA was strictly educational. Like ASA in New York, it distributed pamphlets and newsletters to a mailing list of 20,000, ran a speakers' bureau, organized conferences and recruited an expanding list of women's clubs, bar associations, and clerical groups.

One proof of the changing political climate was the contrasting opinion polls of 1966 and 1967. The first showed 65 percent of Californians (51 in the case of Catholics) for liberalization of the law. Ten months later, 73 percent favored liberalization with the most dramatic increase among Catholics, now 67 percent.[17]

Although CCTA unofficially supported a political action unit, the Ad Hoc Committee for the Therapeutic Abortion Act, Beilenson complained that CCTA would have been more valuable if it "had only got me a few votes up here." [18]

CCTA's first act was to coordinate the defense of the "San Francisco nine"—Dr. J. Paul Shively, chief of obstetrics and gynecology at St. Luke's Hospital, and other noted obstetricians charged with "unprofessional conduct" and the threatened loss of their licenses before the state Board of Medical Examiners. Since 1941, and particularly since the British and Australian studies of 1960, virologists had described the drastic fetal damage—heart disease, blindness, deafness, mental retardation—resulting from a woman's exposure to rubella, or German measles, in early pregnancy. The risks of deformity ran as high as 50 percent, and some 30,000 defective infants, according to the National Institute of Health, were born as a result of the 1964–1966 epidemic. Consequently, while most state laws allowed abortion only to save a woman's life, the majority of U.S. hospitals decided that a defective birth increased the risk of suicide, and approved rubella cases for legal hospital abortion.

In New York, over half of all hospital abortions were performed for rubella in 1964. In California, 77 percent of nearly 750 diplomates of the American Board of Obstetrics and Gynecology considered "the material risk of significant fetal abnormality" a valid indication for abortion.[19]

After a national magazine described rubella abortions in San Francisco hospitals, Dr. James V. McNulty, a fashionable Los Angeles obstetrician, member of the state Board of Medical Examiners and a Catholic, stated at a medical meeting that he intended to stop such "criminal acts." Investigators arrived at a number of San Francisco hospitals late one Saturday in May 1966, when administrators were absent, and secured abortion files from clerks unaware the state had no right to them without a court order. From the doctors, they secured frank admissions—secretly taped—of the rubella abortions. Then the Board charged the nine doctors with unprofessional conduct.

To quash these accusations, 200 of the nation's leading physicians, including 127 deans of medical schools, joined the legal defense and CCTA in an *amici curiae* brief, and petitioned the state Supreme Court to know the evidence against the accused. A Citizens Defense Fund raised money for court action; leading newspapers, including the San Francisco *Chronicle* and the *Examiner,* supported the doctors in editorials.

While the case served to focus public attention on one aspect of the law, it dwindled into obscurity as the Beilenson bill took over the stage in 1967. Dr. McNulty, who had brought the original charges, found increasing coolness among his associates, and resigned from the

Board. The Board finally slapped a few wrists, one doctor being reprimanded, the other eight having their licenses suspended for ninety days—but the sentences postponed for a year. Meanwhile, the doctors went to the courts, and even these reprimands were nullified.[20]

Dr. McNulty's offensive, however, galvanized Catholic opposition against the Beilenson bill. The Los Angeles Catholic Diocese hired Spencer-Roberts Associates, the political strategists whose clients had included Ronald Reagan, to organize Right to Life Leagues across the state in defense of "the rights of the fetus." With the pressure intense on Catholic legislators supporting the bill, one state Senator heard his priest tell the congregation: "Let us pray for the Senator's soul." Chartered airplanes flew opposition groups to the state capital. The mail on both sides reached record proportions—an average of 22,500 a day compared with 10,000 the previous year. Still, this frontal attack on the Legislature seems to have backfired. A number of Senators, opposing the bill, concluded that the Church had overplayed its hand. "You just don't go around threatening legislators," one Senator remarked.[21]

Beilenson moved astutely to enlist as the bill's cosponsor Assemblyman Craig Biddle, not only an influential Republican with access to Governor Reagan, but chairman of the committee to which the bill would be assigned. In the Senate, with the Judiciary Committee split down the middle, hearings began on April 27. When an overflow audience of hundreds had to watch from another room by closed-circuit television, one veteran Senator remarked he could not remember an issue that had drawn "such a mob." The hearing lasted until 2 a.m., when the committee sent the bill to the floor and recommended passage by a slim 7 to 6 majority.

Beilenson now got a substantial boost when Lieutenant Governor Robert H. Finch, presiding officer of the Senate, endorsed the bill. The Governor, however, announced he still had strong reservations and, after a telephone talk with Cardinal McIntyre, ordered his liaison man to inform Senate Republicans to oppose it. Reagan finally admitted to a press conference that he wanted the fetal deformity clause deleted, and statutory rape allowed only at fourteen years of age or less. After making these changes to suit the Governor, Beilenson forced the bill to the Senate floor on June 6, where it passed 21 to 17.[22]

Meanwhile, the Biddle bill in the Assembly had been amended to conform with Reagan's demands. Despite this, the Governor held another press conference on June 13, and continued to raise questions about the bill, including a residency requirement which Beilenson had already rejected. The Governor's tactics, intended to cast doubt on whether he would sign the bill, "seriously breached legislative courtesy," according to Dr. Sagar C. Jain in his legislative study. "The legislature was obviously annoyed by this eleventh-hour move and Reagan's prestige suffered because of it." [23]

That afternoon, the vote was called in the Assembly, and the bill passed 48 to 30. Two days later, the Governor signed it.

With three bills passed in 1967, the abortion movement seemed to have made impressive political strides. Amid general jubilation, however, there were grave doubts. For the first time repealers had openly opposed an ALI bill. There was a serious question as to whether the passage of ALI bills would not lull the public into a sense of exaggerated accomplishment and deflate the drive for repeal for years to come.

Further, the real issue was whether these laws could prove of any practical value. Maginnis claimed that the bill would simply legalize those cases already being approved at hospitals under the psychiatric umbrella of the old law. "Far from ameliorating the situation for women," she insisted, "the 'liberal' law was simply designed to protect the physician from prosecution in disputable cases."

Despite its seeming success, the movement had actually reached a crisis. We had only partially converted a social revolt—the deep abhorrence of millions of people against the old abortion laws—into a political structure. The abortion repealers, still only a segment of the movement, now had to translate their momentum into legislative votes—a process that had already started in New York. We had to take an immovable position—repeal or nothing. It would be at least a year before the hard-line approach proved its validity. By 1968, "repeal" would become the only word that could galvanize the country.

NOTES

1. For an analysis of the Bourne case, see Lawrence Lader, *Abortion* (Boston: Beacon Press, 1967), pp. 103–107.

2. New York *Herald Tribune,* March 3, 1966, p. 17; Cyril C. Means, Jr., "The Law of New York Concerning Abortion and the Status of the Foetus: A Case Study of

Cessation of Constitutionality," *New York Law Forum*, Fall, 1968, pp. 493–498.

3. *New York Times*, February 13, 1967, p. 1; Buffalo *Courier-Express*, February 17, 1967.

4. *New York Times*, February 25, 1967, p. 1.

5. *New York Times*, February 13, 1967, p. 1; New York *Daily News*, February 14, 1967, p. 3.

6. *New York Times*, January 30, 1967, pp. 1, 7; February 12, News in Review, p. 5; February 18, p. 1; February 20, p. 1; February 23, p. 41; March 6, p. 28.

7. *New York Times*, March 8, 1967, p. 1.

8. Richard Lamm, Sam Downing, Jr., M.D., Abraham Heller, M.D., "Legislative Process in Changing Therapeutic Abortion Laws," *American Journal of Orthopsychiatry*, Vol. 39, No. 4, July, 1969, p. 688.

9. Fort Morgan (Colo.) *Times*, April 3, 1967; Denver *Post*, March 10, 1967, p. 3.

10. Denver *Post*, March 29, 1967.

11. Douglas G. McConnell, "The Coming of an Idea: Abortion Reform in Colorado," a study for the Eagleton Institute Seminar in Practical Politics (N.J.), May 6, 1968, pp. 56–57. The author is indebted to this study for other background material.

12. Denver *Post*, April 4, 1967, p. 1.

13. Douglas G. McConnell, "The Coming of an Idea," p. 48.

14. Denver *Post*, April 26, 1967, p. 1; Pueblo (Colo.) *Chieftain*, April 26, 1967.

15. *New York Times*, April 29, 1967, p. 34.

16. The North Carolina section is based partly on letters, memoranda, and speeches of Art Jones and Wallace Kuralt, director of Mecklenburg's department of social services, but mainly on the monograph by Sagar C. Jain and Stephen Sinding, "North Carolina Abortion Law 1967: A Study in Legislative Process," Monograph No. 2, Carolina Population Center, University of North Carolina, Chapel Hill, 1968; *New York Times*, May 14, 1967, Sec. 2, p. 71.

17. Sagar C. Jain and Steven Hughes, "California Abortion Act 1967: A Study in Legislative Process," Carolina Population Center, University of North Carolina, Chapel Hill, 1968, pp. 18–33, offers important background for the California campaign; *New York Times*, June 14, 1967, p. 19; Bernard Burton, "The Story of California's Abortion Law," 1967 (unpublished), pp. 1–15; San Francisco *Chronicle*, May 9, 1967.

18. Jain and Hughes, "California Abortion Act 1967," *op. cit.*, p. 38.

19. Lader, *Abortion*, *op. cit.*, pp. 36–39 and *n.*, pp. 181–182; *Wall Street Journal*, February 15, 1966, p. 1; K. Niswander, "Therapeutic Abortion: Indications and Techniques," 28 *American Journal of Obstetrics and Gynecology*, 124 (1966); E. Overstreet, "Therapeutic Abortion: Attitudes and Practices of California Physicians," 105 *California Medicine* 337 (1966).

20. Keith Monroe, "How California's Abortion Law Isn't Working," *New York Times Sunday Magazine*, December 29, 1968; San Francisco *Chronicle*, June 21, 1967; *New York Times*, February 15, 1968, p. 14.

21. Jain and Hughes, "California Abortion Act 1967," *op. cit.*, pp. 48, 49, 64; Monroe, *New York Times*, *op. cit.;* Los Angeles *Times*, May 10, 1967, Part 1, p. 20.

22. Los Angeles *Times*, May 10, 1967, Part 1, p. 3.

23. Jain and Hughes, "California's Abortion Act 1967," *op. cit.*, p. 82.

CHAPTER SIX

THE OPPOSITION CLOSES IN: ARRESTS AND THE GROWTH OF RADICALISM (1967–1969)

The passage of three abortion laws in 1967 had caught the opposition, particularly the Catholic Church, off balance, but not for long. By May, Catholic bishops across the country had appointed the Family Life Bureau to coordinate their counteroffensive. The *National Catholic Reporter* noted that "diocesan lawyers and state Catholic welfare officers were urged to mount intensive campaigns against abortion law liberalization in their home states at their annual conference." It was the start of a nationwide pattern of harassment.

It was a dangerous time for the early radicals. The indictments—against the "San Francisco Nine," against Dr. Leon Belous and Pat Maginnis in California, against three clergymen for abortion referrals in Ohio, Illinois, and Pennsylvania—all showed that the opposition recognized referrals as the core of the abortion movement and intended to crush them. After publication of my *Redbook* article (February, 1968), describing my own referral system, detectives asked me to come in for interrogation—an inquiry postponed for a year until two agents finally arrived at my door with a subpoena to the grand jury.

In Los Angeles, Dr. Belous had long attacked the old abortion law on radio and television, and openly announced referring emergency cases to qualified abortionists. Unlike Dr. Vuitch or Dr. Henrie, always on the fringe of the professional hierarchy, Belous personified medical status. A distinguished, ruddy-faced obstetrician-gynecologist of sixty-five, he had been chief of his service at Cedars of Lebanon Hospital and a Naval Commander in the Medical Corps in World War II. In a prestigious practice of almost forty years, he had delivered the babies of many of Hollywood's business and acting elite. The California Supreme Court would later note that he was "considered by his associates to be an eminent physician in his field."

"A prominent judge I know warned me privately that the district attorney wanted my referrals stopped," Belous recalled. "They made it clear they were out to get me."

Still, Belous kept hammering at the cruelty of the old abortion law and the hypocrisy of hospital abortion committees. "Doctors like to sit around pontificating on a woman's fate," he would say on television. "They've made it their religion."

Early in 1967, before California's moderate reform law was passed, a young couple, Cheryl and Clifford, contacted Belous by telephone. They explained that they were at their "wit's end." Belous said there was nothing he could do, but after Cheryl pleaded tearfully, threatening to go to Mexico for an underground abortion, the doctor made an appointment at his office.

An examination confirmed her pregnancy. When Belous again said he could not help her, Cheryl begged him to give her an address in Tijuana, Mexico. Belous had visited the underworld clinics there and studied them carefully. He lectured the couple on the risks, stressing that "women who went to Tijuana were taking their lives in their hands," as the California Supreme Court opinion noted. Sobbing, Cheryl insisted she would take any chance rather than have an unwanted child. Belous finally gave her a California phone number and a prescription for antibiotics, and told her to return for examination after the abortion. "The doctor believed that if the young couple carried out their threats, Cheryl's very life was in danger," the Court opinion concluded.[1]

The phone number belonged to Dr. Karl Lairtus, a physician licensed in Mexico, who had recently moved to California to apply for a license. Belous, from personal observation, considered him a qualified physician, skilled at abortion, and had sent him other emergency cases.

After her abortion, Cheryl was resting in the recovery room when the police, apparently tipped off by another woman patient, broke in and arrested Lairtus. They found two notebooks containing a list of women's names and physicians' names. One of these was Belous, whom the police considered a referring doctor. On this information alone, the police arrested Belous, seizing his office files without a proper warrant, as his lawyers later claimed.

Now Belous began three years of tortuous and expensive legal struggle—"my own personal hell," as he described it. His associates at the medical society, and even friends and patients at his country club, cut him completely, or at best considered him demented. Although supported by the California Civil Liberties Union and other groups, he insisted on retaining A. L. Wirin, a prominent lawyer, on a fee basis.

In Municipal Court, the judge, a woman, dismissed the case on the basis of illegal search and seizure of Belous' office. The district attorney immediately called a grand jury and had Belous reindicted on Cheryl's admission he had given her Lairtus' phone number. This time, Belous was convicted in Superior Court by a Catholic judge, and the conviction sustained in the Appellate Court, where two of three judges were Catholic.

Although some legal advisers favored a guilty plea with the possibility of suspended sentence, Belous insisted his defense should be made on constitutional grounds. Wirin considered it a gamble, with only a 20 percent chance the California Supreme Court would accept an appeal. Belous, at the same time as the Vuitch case, was determined to test the old law and overthrow it. An *amicus* brief, signed by 178 deans and other professors of medical schools across the country pinpointed a "hard—almost brutal—reality": that the abortion law "designed in 1850 to protect women from serious risks to life and health had in modern times become a scourge." "I decided to make a stand on constitutional grounds because I knew I was right," Belous concluded. "I had always insisted on a doctor's prerogative to prescribe abortion in emergency cases. I never made a penny. There was an exhilaration in doing what you believe in. Even if I lost and went to jail, I still knew the laws were wrong."

While Belous' case was pending, the Rev. Robert W. Hare, a 35-year-old Presbyterian minister and founding member of Cleveland's Clergy Consultation Service, was indicted on June 12, 1969, by the grand jury of Middlesex County, Massachusetts, on a charge of aiding and abetting a criminal abortion. The police claimed that a

Cleveland woman had been driving to the airfield from the office of Dr. Pierre Brunelle at Chelmsford, Massachusetts, when she became ill, and stopped at a police station for help. The police arrested Brunelle, finding in his office notebooks with the names of Cleveland clergymen, including Hare. At least a dozen Cleveland women were questioned; two testified before the grand jury in Massachusetts. After his indictment for referrals Hare noted, "the ironic fact is that I've never met Dr. Brunelle, and had never been in the state of Massachusetts in my life, but we were charged with committing a crime together." [2]

The prosecutor of Middlesex County, a Catholic in an area at least 50 percent Catholic, sought to extradite Hare to Massachusetts on a charge of "aiding and abetting" which could bring a jail sentence of one to seven years and a $2,000 fine. "A first and very threatening infringement of ministerial rights," Hare called it.[3]

"We are satisfied we are operating completely within the law," the Rev. Farley Wheelright, director of the Clergy Service which had already counseled over 1,000 women, announced. Each clergyman offered a range of options. "We do not tell a woman what to do," Hare pointed out. "Rather we urge a woman to make her own decisions." Hare and his lawyers agreed he should not fight extradition to Massachusetts. Rather, he should stand trial as a symbol of the clergy's rights.

"If it is a crime for a Protestant minister to practice his ministry," Dr. Richard A. Schwartz, chairman of the Association for Reform of Ohio Abortion Law, wrote in a letter to the Cleveland *Plain Dealer*, "then we might as well be living in Rome instead of the United States where the Constitution supposedly guarantees freedom of religion."

The *Plain Dealer* in an editorial went even further. ". . . The main point of the episode is that he [Hare] should not have been in jeopardy of breaking the law by discussing an abortion with a woman," it argued. "Nor should an Ohio woman have to leave the state and sneak around like a common criminal to obtain an abortion. Ohio's present abortion law is inadequate, unfair and inhumane." [4]

A wide range of religious organizations quickly came to Hare's defense. The Presbytery of Cleveland voted to go on record as affirming that "it corporately as well as Mr. Hare individually should be held responsible for the alleged violation of the criminal law of the Commonwealth of Massachusetts, and that any further prosecution in the case at hand should be carried out against the Presbytery also. We further affirm that Mr. Hare was acting on the basis of his ordination vows and the confessional position of this church."

On March 23, 1970, the Rev. Hare appeared in Massachusetts' Middlesex Superior Court. His attorney argued that Hare's counseling did not constitute aiding and abetting abortion, and that the Massachusetts abortion statute was unconstitutional for denying the rights of women, freedom of speech, and the ministerial function of counseling. On March 27, the judge dismissed all charges, exonerating Hare.

This victory was shortlived. The State proceeded to take the case to the Supreme Judicial Court, and possibly harry the Clergy Consultation Service all the way to the U.S. Supreme Court. ". . . The Presbytery saw the potential consequences for the church if I should be convicted," Hare concluded in 1971, with the case still pending. "It would virtually open the door for any clergyman to be put in jeopardy if he had prior to the fact counseled with a person whose actions then became the subject of prosecution."

The Chicago Clergy Consultation Service now came under an even cruder form of attack—the planting of a detective decoy as a woman seeking abortion help from Rabbi Max Ticktin. The Chicago Service, which had already counseled about 500 applicants, announced its program publicly with a full-page ad in the Chicago *Sun-Times* on December 14, 1969. Nine days later, Rabbi Ticktin, one of twenty-four Protestant ministers and six rabbis in the Service, and director of the Hillel Foundation at the University of Chicago, received a phone call from a woman, later identified as a detective, calling herself "Kay Grabel."

Ms. Grabel asked for an appointment for December 30, and arrived with a man, also a detective. Ticktin discussed several alternatives. Grabel rejected them. "I stressed that I do not advocate abortions," the rabbi noted. When he offered London or Puerto Rico as an abortion alternative, Grabel insisted on a local doctor. The rabbi finally suggested the name of Dr. Jesse Ketchum, a Michigan obstetrician-gynecologist, explaining that the clergy took no fees and that arrangements should be made directly with the doctor.

On January 6, 1970, the District Court of Oakland, Michigan, issued a warrant for the arrest of Rabbi Ticktin; the Circuit Court of

Cook County, Illinois, issued a warrant authorizing the police to search and seize the rabbi's files at his home and at the Hillel Foundation. That evening, Chicago police rushed up two flights of creaky stairs at the Foundation to Ticktin's booklined office. "They broke through a door panel, and then they took some folders from Max's office, and they took a telephone," reported the Rev. E. Spencer Parsons, director of the Clergy Service. They did not, however, find Ticktin himself. He was on a tour of Israel with a group of rabbis under the sponsorship of the United Jewish Appeal.[5]

With lurid headlines in Detroit and Chicago papers, Thomas F. Plunkett, prosecutor of Oakland County, Michigan, announced he had unveiled an "abortion ring"—an "international system of abortion referrals involving many clergymen and many doctors around the nation." The Rev. Parsons added wryly, "We regard our ministry as one of counseling women with problems. Apparently, the State of Michigan regards it as a conspiracy." [6]

Dr. Ketchum and his wife were arrested at the same time. Grabel had arranged to meet the doctor at a Southfield, Michigan, hotel, and after she passed over $500, the police broke into the room. Both Ketchum and his wife pleaded innocent in court, and were released on $20,000 bond each.[7]

By the time Rabbi Ticktin returned home from Israel, the case had become "a *cause célèbre,* and the unprepossessing campus clergyman a celebrity of sorts," the Detroit *Free Press* reported. The American Civil Liberties Union protested: "Historically, the professional files of clergymen, attorneys, and physicians have been regarded as sacrosanct—not primarily to protect the professional man but his clients." Students passed petitions from door to door, demanding Ticktin's exoneration. A dean announced the University's backing, calling him "an absolutely unique bridge to the generation gap." The executive director of the Chicago Board of Rabbis described Ticktin as "a moral leader of great integrity." [8]

This attempt to crush the Clergy Service now produced a rebound phenomenon. Within a week of Ticktin's arrest, the Rev. Robert F. Marshall, minister of the Unitarian-Universalist Church at Birmingham, Michigan, warned Plunkett, "You will have to jail every rabbi in Oakland County, every Unitarian cleric, at least half of the Protestant clergy and even a few Catholic priests." The Michigan

Clergy Service, which had just come out for repeal, joined with dozens of other groups to form the Michigan Organization for Repeal of Abortion Laws. State Senator Coleman Young, a Detroit Democrat, announced he would introduce a bill to repeal the Michigan law.[9]

A few days later Plunkett agreed to address an audience of 250 women at the Birmingham Unitarian Church. "Kept at the podium for two hours while angry women demanded to know his exact position on the repeal of what they called an 'archaic and inhuman statute,'" reported the Detroit *Sunday News*, Plunkett refused to be pinned down. "I still think it needs a lot more thought . . . ." A Michigan legislator on the program announced that 80 percent of his constituents were for repeal. Another called "total repeal one of the most important issues to face the current legislature."

At an overflow meeting of the Women's Guild at Sinai Hospital in Detroit, three-fourths of the audience signed "repeal" cards. On January 20, the Detroit *Free Press* stated in an editorial: "After 124 years, repeal of Michigan's abortion law is an idea whose time has come." As the revolt spread, the Oakland County prosecutor capitulated. On January 24, Plunkett announced he would not seek to extradite Rabbi Ticktin to Michigan. As far as the Clergy Service was concerned, the case was closed—although technically Rabbi Ticktin remained open to prosecution until Dr. Ketchum's case had been settled.[10] *

In Boston, Bill Baird's ordeal moved slowly through the courts. On May 1, 1969, the Supreme Judicial Court supported Baird's right of free speech at his lecture—the right to discuss and exhibit contraceptives, and presumably to name Japanese abortionists. At the same time, it declared that the state had a legitimate interest in preventing the *distribution* of contraceptives which might have undesirable or dangerous consequences. With Baird guilty on this count, the judge—

* The Rev. Robert Wallace of the University Baptist Church, State College, Pennsylvania, was arrested in September 1970 for two referrals in a case that has never come to trial. Although not then affiliated, he and other local clergymen subsequently joined the Clergy Consultation Service.

noting that he had "never received as much mail as I have on this case"—sentenced him to three months in jail.[11]

Intractable as ever, Baird was arrested again in Wisconsin. Displaying contraceptive and abortion devices in a speech at Northland College, he was indicted for breaking the Wisconsin law, which ranked as high on the scale of antiquity as that of Massachusetts.[12]

He delighted in poking fun at these targets. If a Massachusetts court had convicted him for distributing contraceptives, how could drugstores throughout the state openly display and sell contraceptive foams without prescription? Did profit make the difference? Accompanied by a reporter, Baird walked into a Boston drugstore with a single girl who purchased vaginal foam. The Sunday *Herald Traveler* concluded that "a crime was consummated," but the district attorney seemed to have had enough of Baird's goading and refused to press charges.[13]

If he had to go to jail, Baird was determined to turn the state into an arena of protest. At his sentencing, demonstrators filled the courtroom, overflowed into the corridors, and marched outside with signs like "Don't Let the Poor Down." He led another group of college students into the Boston State House with a petition of 3,000 signatures opposing abortion and birth control laws. Despite freezing winds on the day he entered jail, a hundred pickets marched for hours on the sidewalks outside.[14]

To rouse the public further, Baird announced on August 7, 1969, that he would run for the U.S. Senate against Ted Kennedy. As an independent candidate, he needed about 62,000 petition signatures to get on the ballot, but soon complained that Framingham and Natick police wouldn't let him pass petitions in public places. When he filed suit against the Secretary of State, the Federal Court in Boston decided he lacked enough signatures. Baird protested, "A qualified poor man just can't run for office in this state. I love this state. It's the most fouled-up state I've ever been in. I've never seen so many politicians so cowardly and so gutless." [15]

Another furor started when Baird entered Suffolk County Jail on February 20, 1970. Dean Robert Drinan of Boston College Law School (later elected U.S. Representative) and three other Catholic priests signed a statement asking Baird's release. One priest came to jail to visit Baird, but the Catholic chaplain refused admission. A few days later, over fifty women, carrying signs like "It's the Massachusetts Legislature that Raped Me" and "Doctors Profit, Women Suffer," invaded the Boston hearings of the Legislative Committee on Social Welfare. Guards forcibly evicted them from the room.[16]

"Going to jail," Baird wrote in his Prison Diary, "I worry about Evie [his wife]. She has been getting sick phone calls and crank letters. Last night the phone rang and I answered it and somebody said, 'Baird, while you're in the can, I'm gonna rape your old lady,' and hung up." [17]

Thousands of letters, telegrams, and phone calls poured into the office of Governor Francis Sargent, demanding Baird's release, and even newspapers rallied behind the cause. "Let's give each woman, married or single, freedom over her own body. And let's stop the hypocrisy that this law breeds," the Somerville *Journal* stated editorially. "We owe a lot to Bill Baird," observed State Representative Martin Linsky. "He had focused attention on this issue." [18] Governor Sargent, a Republican whose supporters generally favored birth control and abortion, finally granted Baird parole, and he was released from jail on $1,000 bail on March 27, 1970.[19]

Baird had already appealed his conviction, and on July 6, the U.S. First Circuit Court of Appeals issued a stunning decision, overturning the old "Crimes against Chastity" law. "We consider that it conflicts with fundamental human rights," stated Chief Justice Bailey Aldrich in the majority opinion. "In the absence of demonstrated harm, we hold it beyond the competency of the state." Baird's lawyer called the decision "a landmark for the country." [20]

Baird's troubles were still not over—the State would appeal the decision to the U.S. Supreme Court. Yet, he had reached his objective, won temporarily in the courts, and proved the effectiveness of public shock tactics.

It was these tactics, I believed, that would produce a wave of anger across the country, particularly among women, and usher in the next phase of the abortion movement. We could not move the country from moderate reform to complete repeal without such anger. We had to have the support of the mass feminist movement, literally bring women "into the streets" for repeal.

The rapid growth of referral services and the arrest of clergymen and doctors helped to produce a new brand of militant feminism—a boisterous upheaval on campuses and among hundreds of cadres of the Women's Liberation movement. For the first time, the feminists were speaking for themselves—facing the fact of their own abortions, no longer afraid to express their demands in strident tones.

"The hardest step was to make your own abortion into public property, to stand up at a public meeting or before a television camera and let your personal degradation become a symbol of anger for others," explained Ms. Constance Billé, a pert, dark-haired University of Pennsylvania student in 1968, later a full-time Women's Liberation organizer, who had an abortion at sixteen. "When I decided to tell about my abortion openly, it became the most mature decision of my life."

The turning point in mass anger took place at the Washington Square Methodist Church in New York City in March 1969 at a meeting of hundreds of women organized by "Red Stockings," a Women's Liberation affiliate. Women stood up to describe their abortions: the anguished search for doctors, the groveling before anyone that could help them in their search, the dingy rooms of backstreet abortionists, the surgical cruelty, often without anesthesia, the degradation which affected them for years. For the first time a group of women had made the public confront their personal horror—names, faces, their most intimate secrets exposed to television cameras and the world.

"ABORTION IS A RIGHT! We refuse to be considered 'criminals,'" announced the Seattle (Washington) Radical Women.

"For us abortion can be a matter of life or death, physical and psychological suffering, and slavery to laws we had no voice in making," stated Female Liberation in Boston.

"The compulsory breeding of women by church and state is nothing more than ecclesiastical and legislative pimpery in which the bodies of all women are utilized for state profit and pleasure," Lana Phelan told the California Conference on Abortion in Santa Barbara in February 1968.

The feminists now gained support from an unexpected quarter. President Lyndon Johnson had recently appointed a Presidential Advisory Council on the Status of Women, probably expecting standard platitudes on accepted issues. Instead, its chairwoman, former U.S. Senator Maurine Neuberger of Oregon, produced a report in 1968 that recommended the repeal of all abortion laws—the first time anyone in a government circle had taken this position.

In 1968, Women's Liberation groups in Washington, D.C., published a fiery booklet, "It's All Right, Ma. (I'm only bleeding.)" Action, violent action if necessary, was urged as national policy: "We have to be in the streets. By this we mean we have to create enough visible energy, noise and pressure to put our issues into the mind of all America."

Demonstrations and disruptions now ushered in the second phase of the abortion movement. In New York, about fifty pickets from the "October 17 Movement," "New Women," and "New York Radical Women" marched outside the Criminal Court building on Center Street during the trial of a prominent abortionist, while a similar number invaded the hearing room, interrupting the proceedings with their questions and cries.

At the American Medical Association convention in New York in 1969, women pickets surrounded the Coliseum with signs and leaflets demanding that doctors sign a petition for repeal. Dr. Lonny Myers of Illinois invaded the hall to confront her colleagues, dressed in a white lab coat, her hands tied with red tape as a symbol of medical restrictions under present laws.

In Los Angeles, NOW women picketed the Hall of Justice and marched into the district attorney's office to announce their "refusal to capitulate to laws which deny women sovereignty over their bodies and minds." They submitted stacks of signed statements from women who had undergone illegal abortion. "Do all 100,000 of us [the estimated, annual number of California abortions] have to come forward and say we insist on being prosecuted before you'll change the law?" they demanded.[21]

The first violent confrontation—"WOMEN BREAK UP ABORTION HEARING," the *New York Times* described it—took place in New York City at the hearings of the Joint Legislative Committee on the Problems of Public Health on February 13, 1969. The hearing panel consisted of eight members, all male. Of fifteen witnesses, all were men except a Catholic nun. A former judge of the state Court of Appeals had just finished his testimony when Ms. Kathy Amatniek stood up and shouted, "All right, now let's hear from some real experts—the women!" State Senator Norman Lent, the chairman, pounded for order, but she demanded, "Repeal the abortion law instead of wasting more time talking about these stupid reforms."

Lent banged his gavel while another woman cried, "Men don't get pregnant. Men don't rear children. They just make the laws."

"But wait a minute, dear," Lent protested.

"Don't call me 'dear.' Would you call a black person 'boy'?"

Another member of the panel, State Senator Seymour Thaler, broke in, "There are people here who want to do something for you."

"We're tired of being done for," snapped the woman. "We want to *do* for a change."

Everyone seemed to be shouting at once. "Why are fourteen men and only one woman on your list of speakers—and she a nun?" demanded another woman.

Above the hubbub, Senator Thaler proclaimed, "I am entirely in sympathy with these women. The law should be repealed in my opinion. We have had enough hearings."

With two or three women shouting together, Lent finally recessed the hearing, and moved the panel to another room. He posted policemen outside the door, and refused to allow the public inside. The women sat down en masse at the door while the panel continued to hear fourteen men and one nun. After the women had waited for seven hours, Lent allowed three representatives to speak. "We want to be consulted," one woman concluded.[22]

The constant pressure from referral services, arrests, public education, picket lines, demonstrations, and the anger of feminist cadres had a considerable impact on opinion polls. In the 1967 Gallup poll, 25 percent approved abortion for a woman who could not afford a child, 21 percent for a woman who did not want a child. By November 1969 the Gallup poll showed a marked increase in repeal sentiment. Forty percent now favored "abortion on demand" during the first three months of pregnancy. The swing toward repeal was even stronger on campuses. Eighty-three percent of over 180,000 freshmen at 275 colleges supported complete legalization of abortion, according to a survey by the American Council on Education.[23]

Repeal was also making its impact on medical societies which, except for psychiatrists and a handful of obstetrician-gynecologists, had been discouragingly reactionary. The American Public Health Association, more attuned to social responsibility than larger, hidebound organizations, broke through this apathy in 1968 when its governing board announced that, "restrictive laws should be repealed . . . ."

Planned Parenthood, with hundreds of chapters and clinics throughout the country, had been a particular disappointment. Legalized abortion, I insisted from the start, was the logical measure for contraception and an essential form of birth control. Under the leadership of Dr. Alan Guttmacher, the medical committee of Planned Parenthood-World Population proposed the "abolition of existing statutes and criminal laws regarding abortion" in 1968. After this plank was approved by the membership in 1969, PP chapters soon started abortion referrals, and even clinics, as "an integral part of medical care."

For the first time the repeal campaign also dominated two legislative struggles. Seven new laws, in addition to the three in 1967, were passed in 1968–1969.* All, unfortunately, followed the ALI formula, although Kansas and Maryland came startlingly close to passing repeal bills.

In Kansas, repeal passed the Senate and even the House Judiciary Committee, where its chief sponsor, significantly, was a Catholic physician. On the House floor, however, twenty Catholic legislators forced through an amendment that watered down the bill to the ALI formula.[24]

Maryland came even closer. In the House of Delegates, Allen B. Spector had sponsored an ALI-type law, which passed in 1968. He then submitted a new bill removing all state restrictions. It "treats abortion as a medical problem," the Washington *Post* declared editorially, "and puts the responsibility for making whatever choice is involved squarely where it belongs—on the individuals directly concerned and on those who taught them the moral standards by which they live." The General Assembly approved the bill early in 1970. But although his own poll showed 51 percent of the state wanted him to sign it against 42 percent for a veto, Governor Marvin Mandel vetoed the bill in May. The legislature could not even oppose the veto since

* In Arkansas, Delaware, Georgia, Kansas, Maryland, New Mexico, and Oregon.

the state constitution prohibits a new legislature in an election year from overriding the veto of a previous administration.[25]

Even more conclusive evidence of the demand for repeal developed in three states which had passed ALI-type laws in 1967. In Colorado, nineteen out of twenty women seeking abortion under the new law were rejected. By 1969, Rep. Richard Lamm, its sponsor, announced, "We're going to try to repeal it or overturn it."

"We tried to change a cruel, outmoded, inhuman law," Lamm observed, "what we got was a cruel, outmoded, inhuman law."

"Obviously we haven't made a dent in the problem," Dr. Harvey Cohen, a Denver obstetrician-gynecologist, pointed out. "It's a wonder anyone gets through."

The first obstacle was cost—a minimum of $500—which made it "a rich lady's law," as Cohen put it. The second obstacle was the technical hurdles. Only five of the state's fifty accredited hospitals (four of them in Denver) performed 81 percent of the abortions. Twenty-five did none at all. "A woman in Durango where the only accredited hospital is Roman Catholic cannot hope to get an abortion from her own doctor in her own hometown even if she were raped in broad daylight on the main street with the district attorney as a witness," Lamm noted wryly.[26]

Hospitals imposed complex requirements outside the law, refusing mental health grounds unless the patient had been under previous psychiatric treatment, setting up prohibitively small quotas, or making the approval machinery so difficult that a frantic woman gave up after a few weeks.

With 20,000 women forced to leave the state for illegal abortions elsewhere, the new law "made legal abortions so expensive, so difficult and so nerve-racking to obtain that it has actually driven some women to criminal abortionists, simply because the criminals work cheaper and faster," a reporter concluded.[27]

These obstacles particularly discriminated against the poor. Psychiatrists charged at least $50 for a letter of approval; some hospitals demanded two letters instead of the one required by law.

From April 1967, when the law took effect, until the end of 1968, Colorado hospitals performed only 616 abortions. "All the new law did was put a medical problem into politics, and make doctors and hospitals so nervous that in 1967 we did fewer abortions on medical grounds than we did before the new law," concluded Dr. Ben C. Williams, an obstetrician-gynecologist at the University of Colorado Medical Center.

After two years of the North Carolina law, its chief legislative sponsor, Arthur H. Jones, attacked it as the "perpetuation of a system that will continue to send 95 out of every 100 women to illegal abortionists or to self-induced terminations," and he came out for a complete repeal bill.[28]

In California, with an estimated 100,000 illegal abortions annually, hospitals performed only 2,035 in the first half of 1968. Even these came from a few hospitals—eight hospitals accounting for 40 percent. The San Francisco Bay area, with only 22 percent of the live births, accepted 63 percent of the abortions; Los Angeles, with 44 percent of the live births, did only 18 percent.[29]

The new law perpetuated traditional discrimination. Blacks received only 10 percent of the legal abortions. Medical and hospital fees ran $600 to $800, with psychiatrists often charging $100 for a single letter of approval. "This is not a poor woman's law," noted Dr. Keith Russell, chairman of the California Medical Association's committee on maternal and child health.[30]

All portents seemed ripe for repeal. With our political bases extended into Minnesota, Michigan, and other states, with religious denominations and other national organizations embracing repeal, with the rising anger of militant feminists reflected in opinion polls, a small group of radicals met at my New York apartment in August 1968 and agreed on a national conference to unite repeal forces in a permanent coalition. The National Association for Repeal of Abortion Laws was the turbulent outcome of that fateful decision.

NOTES

1. *People v. Belous*, 71 Cal. 2d 954, 458 P. 2d 194, 80 Cal. Rptr. 354 (1969), cert. denied, 397 U.S. 915 (1970).

2. Cleveland *Plain Dealer*, June 12, 1969, p. 1; National Council of Churches *Bulletin*, May 4, 1970, pp. 12–15.

3. Boston *Herald Traveler*, June 11, 1969, p. 6; NCC *Bulletin*, May 4, 1970, pp. 12–15; Cleveland *Press*, March 28, 1970.

4. This, and the preceding two paragraphs: Cleveland *Press*, June 24, 1969; Cleveland *Plain Dealer*, June 12, 1969, June 22, 1969, March 29, 1970.

5. Chicago *Sun-Times*, January 8, 1970.

6. Chicago *Daily News*, January 7, 1970, p. 1; Detroit *Free Press*, January 7, 1970, p. 1.

7. Chicago *Daily News*, January 7, 1970, p. 1.

8. Chicago *Sun-Times*, January 9, 10, 1970; Detroit *Free Press*, January 17, 1970, Letters to Editor; January 5, 1970, Sec. D., p. 1.

9. Detroit *News*, January 14, 1970, p. 21; Detroit *Free Press*, January 13, 1970.

10. This, and the preceding paragraph: Detroit *Sunday News*, January 18, 1970, p. 10; Detroit *News*, January 24, 1970, p. 3; Detroit *Free Press*, January 20, 1970.

11. Boston *Record American*, December 3, 1969; Boston *Evening Globe*, May 1, 1969.

12. Lawrence (Mass.) *Eagle Tribune*, January 21, 1970.

13. Boston *Sunday Herald Traveler*, June 8, 1969.

14. Boston *Record American*, October 18, 1967, p. 3; February 21, 1970.

15. Milford (Mass.) *News*, July 21, 1970; Framingham (Mass.) *News*, September 2, 1970; Boston *Globe*, September 22, 1970.

16. Boston *Record American*, February 21, 1970; Greenfield (Mass.) *Recorder-Gazette*, March 4, 1970.

17. Boston *Globe*, June 14, 1970.

18. Somerville (Mass.) *Journal*, February 26, 1970; *Christian Science Monitor*, April 3, 1970.

19. Boston *Globe*, March 17, 1970.

20. Sacramento *Union*, July 7, 1970.

21. Los Angeles *NOW Newsletter*, Vol. 1, No. 12, March 1970, p. 1.

22. *New York Times*, February 14, 1969, p. 42; *New Yorker*, February 22, 1969, p. 28.

23. *Studies in Family Planning*, The Population Council, New York, No. 30, May 1969; *New York Times*, December 8, 1969, p. 1, December 20, 1970, p. 42.

24. *NARAL Newsletter*, Summer 1969, Vol. 1, No. 1, p. 2.

25. Washington *Post*, March 13, 1970, Sec. C., p. 12; April 2, 1970, Sec. B., p. 1; May 4, 1970, editorial; *New York Times*, May 27, 1970, p. 43.

26. This, and the preceding three paragraphs: *New York Times*, December 8, 1969, p. 1; June 8, 1970, p. 1; Olga Curtis, "The Paradox of Colorado's Abortion Law," *Empire Magazine*, January 11, 1970, p. 14.

27. This, and the preceding paragraph: Curtis, *op. cit.*; *New York Times*, June 9, 1968, p. 33; *Current Medical Digest*, Vol. 36, No. 9, September, 1969, p. 761.

28. This, and the preceding paragraph: *New York Times*, December 8, 1969, p. 1; *Current Medical Digest*, Vol. 36, No. 9, September, 1969, p. 761; Curtis, *op. cit.*

29. "Third Annual Report on Implementation of California Therapeutic Abortion Act," Bureau of Maternal and Child Health, Department of Public Health, Berkeley, Calif., p. 2.

30. *New York Times*, June 8, 1970, p. 29.

CHAPTER SEVEN

THE BIG LEAP: FOUNDING THE NATIONAL ASSOCIATION FOR REPEAL OF ABORTION LAWS

It was a quirk of fate that touched off the national abortion movement. Any sane political strategist would have waited at least two more years. But there was a touch of insanity about the movement, always essential to its success. I had talked about a national organization often with Ms. Ruth P. Smith, former executive director of the Association for the Study of Abortion. We were already laying plans for a press conference in late 1968 to introduce New York State's first repeal bill. Then Dr. Lonny Myers arrived in New York, and the three of us met at my apartment on July 30, 1968, to construct, in an hour or less, a wild and soaring strategy that would consume our lives for years.

Myers had conceived the idea of a Chicago meeting, "The First National Conference on Abortion Laws." It would bring together every abortion group in the country—religious, political, feminist, medical—for a three-day conference whose ultimate purpose would be to swing moderate reformers to complete repeal. We needed the cohesion of such a gathering, but I had always been leery of conferences. They required huge amounts of effort and money and their results soon evaporated. Why not use the last day of the conference to build a permanent national organization? With hundreds of delegates in contact for the first time, we had an unequaled opportunity to put together a national association that would unify the movement at last.

It would give us new power—eventually the combined forces of over seventy national and state organizations—that could concentrate our campaign on the most likely targets. We could plan our strategy as a unit. If we decided to push a repeal bill in New York or the Midwest, we could harness all national affiliates and fund-raising for selected priorities. We would, above all, have a centralized clearinghouse for repeal literature and research, for legal and political tactics.

Myers and Smith quickly agreed to my suggestions. We set the date of the Chicago conference for February 14–16, 1969, and formed a coordinating committee with Prof. Garrett Hardin as West Coast cochairman, Myers in the Midwest, and myself in the East. It was an inspiring blueprint. All it would need was six months of grinding labor.

There must be logical reasons why I, who never spent a dollar gambling on cards or horses, took on the most frantic gambles of the abortion movement. The referrals I started in 1965 had already decimated my work as a writer. It was not only a risky business in terms of the law, but emotionally exhausting. Still, I had insisted the abortion laws were unconstitutional, and had made a commitment to women to refer them to physicians when abortion became necessary. Why then assume a larger gamble? A national association that would consume at least half my time without pay for years? It was the worst form of a gambler's disease. The stakes were much higher than money: the possibility of transforming an idea, first enunciated in a book, into an actual social reality.

Perhaps psychiatrists would call it the "impossible challenge." A mountain that had to be moved, a political and social revolution waiting for creation. It was like the slogan that students had scrawled on the walls of Paris during the riots of May 1968: "We must be realistic and strive for the impossible."

Perhaps I was also trying to prove a point about the apathy infecting our society in the last decade. There was a pall of helplessness hanging over all of us, an asphyxiation of will that seemed to crush the individual and his belief that he could bring about any constructive changes. If we could make a national association, and succeed in overthrowing the tyranny of abortion laws, it could offer a vision of action and accomplishment at the most fundamental democratic level. It seemed to me the country needed this desperately; that if the present social order, or any order, was to survive, the individual had to prove to himself once again that a revolution was still possible. The whole abortion movement, in effect, was an act of faith. And the national association was certainly for me an act of personal faith.

So we started building what politicians like to call the "power base." We needed influential honorary officers. The perfect choices for honorary president and vice president were Congresswoman Shirley Chisholm of New York, and former U.S. Senator Maurine Neuberger of Oregon. Chisholm, the first black woman in the House, and first black woman candidate for President, had already become an aggressive feminist. Neuberger, a respected legislator, had increased her stature with her abortion plank for the Presidential Advisory Council.

We needed prestigious organizational sponsors: American Baptist Convention, American Civil Liberties Union, Physicians Forum, Unitarian-Universalist Association, Women's City Club of New York. We lined up fifty individual sponsors: General William H. Draper, chairman of the Population Crisis Committee; Gordon Sherman, the Chicago industrialist; Marya Mannes, the author; a long list of physicians like Walter C. Alvares, and Edwin M. Gold of the University of California School of Public Health.

We had to find luncheon and dinner speakers, expert in their fields, and eminent enough to draw delegates from all over the country. The first acceptances came from Borough President of Manhattan Percy Sutton, always a devoted ally; Betty Friedan; and the Rev. Joseph Fletcher of the Episcopal Theological School in Cambridge, Massachusetts, the foremost philosopher of repeal. Dr. Lester Breslow, president of the American Public Health Association, and Dr. Alan Guttmacher, president of Planned Parenthood-World Federation, provided national status and the involvement of two influential medical groups.

A torrent of meetings, phone calls, and letters kept these five months in tumult. I sent memos on our progress in the East both to the West Coast and to Chicago, where our Midwest cochairman, Myers, and the Rev. Canon Don Shaw had hired a professional manager, "J.B.," to run the conference. But after one visit from J.B. in New York, our memos went unanswered. "The Tragedy of the One-Way Memos," Myers called it. "We honestly feel this is crisis time," I finally wrote Myers.

"I was pacing the floor from 2 a.m. on last night . . . but that doesn't help get the program printed," Myers wrote back. "It is now 3 a.m. . . . another night without sleep," she wrote a day later. "I sat on J.B. as no one has sat on anyone before. I did everything but snatch the paper from his hand and take it to the printer myself." Although shackled by a heavy hospital schedule, Myers worked furiously at each crisis, confessing, "When my eight-year-old asked me to play something last night, it was all I could do not to scream and have a tantrum, and then she patted me on the head and said, 'There, there, mother, it's all right'."

By Christmas, programs, press releases, and literature were in the mails, and we started to concentrate on fund-raising. Chicago had collected the first "seed money," and Smith and I promised to equal it. Our strongest support came from old allies—Stewart Mott; Hugh Moore of the Hugh Moore Fund, where I had worked a few years back as executive director; a group on the executive committee with me at the Association for Voluntary Sterilization, particularly Ms. Beatrice McClintock, her sister, Dr. Helen Edey, Ms. Ellen Brush, and Ms. Louise Mills. We raised $3,500 for the conference and $6,000 for the national association.

The returns from our mailings were pouring into Chicago, and after the early chaos, we could expect a turnout of 350 delegates, representing over fifty organizations. I kept on the phone, prodding repeal cadres across the country to send delegations—Minnesota, Wisconsin, Connecticut, even states like Massachusetts where an old friend put together a new organization from scratch in a few weeks. The only simple step in that period was the agreement on a name for the coalition: the National Association for Repeal of Abortion Laws (NARAL).

In December, our concentration on Chicago was interrupted for a week by a crucial priority—the launching of New York State's first repeal bill. The radical strategy had always been to press the decisive act even before the ideal moment, to use that act to educate voters and legislators. If we were going to create a national movement in Chicago, we needed a political symbol around which our forces could gather. We had to make a break with the past, and show the futility of years of bickering and compromise over a moderate and worthless bill that obscured the real issues of women's rights.

New York was a pivotal state for this test, and Assemblywoman Constance Cook and Assemblyman Franz Leichter, highly qualified as cosponsors. An upstate Republican, close to the inner circle of Albany power, and chairwoman of key Assembly committees, Cook at first supported and then rejected the old reform bill. "The Assembly debate over reform in 1968 disgusted me," she announced. "It made me an out-and-out feminist, and converted me to repeal." Leichter, a prominent liberal Democrat from Manhattan, the center of our repeal strength, adroitly balanced Cook's upstate influence.

The launching of the bill had the backing of our new National Association, the New Yorkers for Abortion Law Repeal, and feminist and political groups. I accepted responsibility for the December 16 press conference. The obvious hurdle was that the press had become so immured to reform debate for years, they had no grasp of the meaning or potential of repeal. To make matters worse, I came down with Asian flu and had to campaign by phone from bed. On December 16, with a 104-degree fever, I managed to stagger to a taxi through a heavy crust of snow and freezing wind. Somehow, I kept on my feet for an hour to chair the press conference in Ruth Smith's towering living room.

We had a respectable turnout considering the obstacles to repeal —two of the three major New York papers and the important Long Island press, two television and two radio stations. The real bonus came when I got back home, for the phone rang with wire services and upstate press and radio calls. While hardly a triumph, the coverage gave me reasonable assurance that repeal could stir some excitement in the press. It was a matter of relentless pounding, but in six months or a year, I was sure, we could ignite the country.

My first study of the results of abortion referral appeared in *Look* in early January and added more momentum to the repeal campaign.* "First Exclusive Survey of Non-Hospital Abortions" was based on poignant letters, revealing the medical, social, and psychological factors behind each case, from five hundred women who had applied to me for abortion help. To amplify this material, I sent a lengthy questionnaire,

* January 21, 1969, issue, but on newsstands two weeks before.

prepared with the help of sociologists and psychologists, to each woman. Since previous medical papers only had access to a handful of cases, this was the first in-depth study of a large sample. Its special impact, I believe, was that it combated most of the persistent myths and misconceptions that had plagued abortion literature.

Even medical reports (always a slim number of cases) had stressed the physical and psychological danger of abortion. Yet my study of hundreds of cases—their frank appraisals guaranteed by anonymity—clearly showed that abortion could be a safe and simple procedure.

Eighty-two percent of the women stated they had suffered no damage from abortion—and these were procedures performed secretly or semi-secretly in doctors' offices! The remainder cited only minor, emotional aftereffects.

With half the women receiving medical checkups, only one percent of their physicians called the abortion "poor." Seventy-eight percent of the women concluded they would have another abortion if faced with the necessity again. Only one case "regretted abortion," and that involved a physician of the woman's choice whom I had not recommended.

The article, therefore, gave us documentary evidence of the high medical standards of in-office abortion, and proved the referral system an essential tool of the movement. It also sparked, at the opportune moment, a new wave of publicity (and hundreds of additional applications from women). I was interviewed on a dozen radio and television shows before leaving New York, three more after arrival in Chicago.

The First National Conference on Abortion Laws met at the Drake Hotel from February 14 to 16, 1969. Large delegations came from the Midwest and California; from New York, Pennsylvania, and most of the East Coast. There were staid officials from the YWCA, ebullient students from Women's Liberation, law professors, sociologists, physicians, and legislators who would soon introduce new bills in their own states.

The core of the conference was the "workshop" panels: "How to Start a Repeal Group," "Legislative Action," "Public Education." The Rev. Howard Moody, director of the Clergy Consultation Service, and I addressed an open meeting on referral. At the debate on resolutions a day later, the battle began. The "activists" introduced a plank that would bind the new National Association to support all free referral services, and doctors, clergymen, or anyone involved in their operation. The conference, of course, included a broad range of moderates who attacked the plank. They were afraid of conflict with the law, of arrests, of bad publicity; the endless reservations that had always split the militants from the dilettantes of reform. Speaker after speaker took the microphone on both sides of the issue, with the militants solidly behind my thesis that only referral services could rouse the country for repeal. It was the basic issue on which the movement would rise or fall and there could be no retreat. After two hours of debate, the delegates approved our plank.

The luncheon and dinner speakers—Friedan, Sutton, Dr. Breslow—continued to push the conference toward an unshakable repeal position. "Only if the decision is freed of legal encumbrances, liberating both patient and physician to exercise their combined best judgment on health interest alone, can we expect to combat criminal abortion and its appalling ramifications," Dr. Breslow concluded. "The health of American women and their families is despoiled by anti-abortion laws. I join with those seeking repeal."

At eleven on Sunday morning, we reached the ultimate test: organizing the National Association for Repeal of Abortion Laws. The conference, in my view, had been a remarkable achievement, developing a blueprint that would guide the movement for years. The militants were in control. Reporters had come from as far as Los Angeles and Washington, and the *New York Times* gave a detailed analysis of repeal for the first time.

All these gains, and six months of labor, could be dissipated, however, if we could not unite hundreds of delegates into a permanent coalition. As chairman of this session, I presented the planning committee's report. We had met over the last two days with state leaders and open caucuses. Our report offered a tight organizational structure that would place NARAL in immediate operation—a slate of officers with regional vice presidents, the outline of a constitution, and a membership plan that emphasized organizations and state and local groups, rather than individuals.

The report raised a furious debate. Each delegate seemed to have his own formula. There seemed to be no unanimity on any point, and the meeting often went completely out of control. Perhaps it had been an illusion to expect hundreds of divergent philosophies and temperaments to fuse their interests in a few hours.

The struggle went on through lunch and into the afternoon. I tried to stress that we had to reach agreement, that the money and energy in this conference could never be repeated again. Eventually we hammered out what seemed a weak compromise: the selection of a twelve-member "planning committee" for NARAL that would meet in New York within a month. The committee was authorized to draw up a constitution, nominate a board of directors, call the first board meeting to elect officers, and get NARAL "functioning." It seemed to me we had strangled ourselves in organizational details and postponed the essential objective of launching repeal campaigns throughout the country. I went back to New York, exhausted by months of work for the conference, depressed by our lack of decisiveness.

When the planning committee met in New York, I was elected chairman, and subcommittees moved ahead on writing the constitution, renting a small office on West 57th Street, and hiring a salaried executive director, Ms. Lee Gidding. The tensions of Chicago, however, soon reasserted themselves. The majority, or "activists" as we were labeled, refused to be bound by "housekeeping" details. As spokesman for this group, led by Constance Billé, Friedan, Dr. Bernard Nathanson, and Borough President Sutton, I insisted that the organizing process could not prevent the start of national programs.

The minority wanted a board and elections before anything else. Their leadership, mainly McClintock and Smith, were women of wealth, accustomed to the disciplines of more conservative organizations, often ruffled by our flamboyant tactics. We called them "go-slowers," which was perhaps unfair. They never wavered in their commitment to repeal, and despite our differences over the years, all factions stayed together. We argued at meetings, and drank together afterwards.

The activists now pushed through a plan to get repeal groups into the streets—"a new day expressing the anger of women across the country," as we wrote in the blueprint. With a series of national demonstrations on May 8, 1969, to coincide with Mother's Day, we called for picket lines and sit-ins at many hospitals to expose the cruelty and hypocrisy of hospital boards in approving abortions, and their prejudice for private patients over the poor.

This ambitious plan produced "days of anger" in eleven cities, including Atlanta, Los Angeles, Milwaukee, New York, and Philadelphia. In New Haven, Connecticut, a Catholic priest joined the picket line. In Philadelphia, women chanted, "No more Lysol, soap, arsenic or coat hangers." Dr. George Wilson, president of the Medical Committee for Human Rights, demanded that "outdated abortion laws be brought into the twentieth century." A new group, Mothers for Abortion Law Repeal, wheeled their baby carriages before the Trenton, New Jersey, state house, with a soft drink and cookie stand for children in the center of the picket circle, and signs that proclaimed, "Illegal Abortions Support the Mafia." [1]

Almost 200 pickets—including a uniformed delegation of nurses and medical students—marched in front of Lenox Hill Hospital in New York City. Rev. Moody carried a placard, "You don't have to be a woman to know this law is wrong." Borough President Sutton told the press, "Failure of the reform bill at this session will build strength for the repeal bill." The press turned out strongly in every city (three TV cameras in New York alone), and NARAL had suddenly become a national force.

Despite this success, the planning committee clashed again shortly afterwards over the most critical issue in the movement. On May 23, the Bronx district attorney and police raided the Riverdale apartment used by Louis Brown and his medical group for abortion, arrested him, a physician, and two nurses. This was the busiest group in the East, particularly since Dr. Vuitch's indictment. It took the bulk of my referrals, and many from the clergy and feminists. Coming so shortly after the Baird case in Boston, and the arrest of clergy and doctors in the Midwest, it threatened the whole referral system, and numerous NARAL members, myself included.

The activists insisted that NARAL had to support anyone involved in the Bronx arrests "whose case would forward the objectives of NARAL." The go-slowers, however, opposed us. Even Dr. Myers, a longtime militant who, in this case, seemed to misjudge the threat of nationwide arrests, supported the go-slowers, and concluded in a memo that "a close alliance with referral services provides a target for our enemies."

When the activists pushed through our motion on the Bronx arrests, the split in the planning committee widened further. On the official slate of officers, Councilwoman Carol Greitzer, a vigorous advocate of women's rights in New York City, had been nominated for president. I had been put up for chairman of the executive committee, and Friedan and Phelan for vice presidents, East and West.

Now the go-slowers nominated their own slate with Myers as candidate for president. The resulting campaign was hard, sometimes bitter. But behind this struggle for every vote lay the realization that the outcome would affect the direction of the movement for years to come.

The board of directors met on September 27, 1969, at a New York Hotel, and Greitzer, I, and most of the activist ticket were elected, giving us a clear majority on the executive committee. In a move for solidarity among all factions, Myers agreed to run for vice president, Midwest, and was elected by acclamation. Despite the months of pain after Chicago, we had finally created a disciplined national movement set on an uncompromising course of militancy.

Admittedly, there were risks in this early clash, and the movement might have split irremediably. But I believed then, and in a few later cases, that issues came first, and that NARAL was meaningless unless it adhered to its fundamental radical stand. I always found that a 2 to 1 majority of the board supported the activists' program; and that the high character of the opposition could stand such tests without malice or resignations.

"How it was achieved is unknown, but you people have an assembly of enthusiasm, drive and hard sense which is remarkable," Dr. Lalor Burdick of Delaware's Lalor Foundation wrote. "The ability to give and take in matters of strong argument and still come up smiling and with no rancor impressed me no end."

At our first national press conference on September 29, before an overflow crowd of reporters, Congresswoman Shirley Chisholm announced, "We consider it a national disgrace that these referral services have been forced to operate in a twilight zone. We pledge ourselves to support them openly through newspaper ads, radio and television, and direct action." NARAL had taken its stand on the Bronx arrests, and the immediate battleground would be the Bronx County Courthouse.[2]

NOTES

1. Philadelphia *Tribune*, May 9, 1969; Trenton *Evening News*, May 8, 1969; Newark *Evening News*, May 9, 1969.

2. New York *Daily News*, September 30, 1969, p. 12; New York *Post*, September 29, 1969.

CHAPTER EIGHT

THE BRONX ARRESTS (1969): THE CLIMACTIC ASSAULT ON REFERRAL SERVICES

At about 4:30 p.m. on Friday, May 23, 1969, my telephone rang. Louis Brown, administrator of the largest abortion group in the East, a jovial, pink-cheeked, former hospital executive, not inclined to panic, begged, "Get me a lawyer. I'm in jail at the Bronx County Courthouse." *

It was the first time in years of referrals that I had an immediate feeling of fear. The possibility of arrest had always been there, but somehow I had learned to ignore it. You rationalized the risks, balanced your gamble against the cumulative benefits for dozens, then hundreds, of women. The process of referrals became routine. You built an immunity by making referrals as much a part of your structured life as the typewriter or classroom. Then, with one phone call, all defenses collapsed. Brown and his wife, Margaret, were behind bars. You were alone, knowing that your letters and phone messages might have been seized by the police, that a detective might ring your bell at any moment.

It took a while that warm May afternoon to find a lawyer still at

* The names "Louis and Margaret Brown" have been substituted for real names at their request.

his office, but David Ellenhorn, who had advised NARAL skillfully on previous problems, agreed to go to the Bronx and raise bail. (The others arrested had retained their own lawyers.) By the time he reached the Courthouse, however, the Browns were on their way to Manhattan jails—the Bronx court not being open on Saturday. Almost twenty hours passed before Ellenhorn could get them released.

Around midnight on Friday, Ellenhorn came back to my house and pieced together the events. The police had raided the Browns' first-floor, two-bedroom apartment at 5800 Arlington Avenue in the wealthy Riverdale section of the Bronx not far from the Hudson River. A 17-year-old high school student was on the operating table, her mother in another room, when detectives broke in at 3:05 p.m. In addition to the Browns, authorities arrested the doctor and nurse. Two women recuperating from abortion in the second bedroom, and four or five others in the waiting room, including a college professor of thirty and her husband, also a professor, were arraigned as material witnesses.

The raiding party seized stacks of documents and files from the Browns as well as letters and notes from a search of the patients' handbags. "The assistant district attorney mentioned your name a few times," Ellenhorn told me. "You'll certainly be hearing from him." [1]

"As several men and women rushed into the apartment," Margaret Brown described the scene later, "I asked, 'What do you want?' One answered, 'Just keep quiet and sit down. I have a gun and badge.' One detective flashed a badge. Several men rushed into the clinic and began taking pictures of the doctor and the young woman on the table. The mother became hysterical, and cried, 'Let the doctor finish helping my duaghter. Don't stop him. Don't do this to her.' The daughter also became hysterical, and pleaded with them to let the doctor finish. They did not.

"As they questioned women in the waiting room, a detective would say, 'You're not cooperating. You're going to be arrested.' Then he would turn to another man, ordering, 'Place her under arrest.' After fifteen to twenty minutes of questioning and threatening, one woman suggested we be informed of our rights. A detective quickly read the law, stating the right to remain silent."

Louis Brown recalled, "I was standing in front of my car in the basement garage, when suddenly four men approached, and asked if I were Brown, and one said he was from the Bronx District Attorney's office. As he flashed a badge, a man grabbed me from the back and put handcuffs on my wrists. Then another went through my pockets, removing keys, wallet, and other personal items. One said, 'Here are the keys to the apartment. Let's go.' Two stayed with me; the others left.

"A young woman came to the car next to mine and greeted me. One detective asked if she had been in my apartment, and when she said yes, he told her she would have to testify against me and the doctor. She said, 'I will not. He saved my life.' The detective grabbed her purse, and emptied the contents, and found a card showing she was a registered nurse in New York State. He said, 'You'll cooperate with us, or I'll report you to the State Medical Association, and have your license revoked.' I told her to ask for her right to remain silent, and get a lawyer. The detective pushed me into the car, and closed the windows, shouting, 'Shut up, you son of a bitch'."

Once Ellenhorn had reported back to me, I knew I had to dispose of boxes of letters, questionnaires, and notes from my *Look* article that could incriminate hundreds of women if found by the District Attorney. I called a friend a few blocks away and she agreed to store the files. Packing them in two suitcases, I hauled them through the streets, glancing occasionally over my shoulder to be sure no one followed me in an absurd replica of a dime-novel chase. Our lawyers eventually insisted that the files be destroyed.

On Saturday, the Bronx District Attorney, Burton Roberts, announced the raid at a press conference—a circus of accusations and inferences obviously intended to create an orgy of headlines. Red-haired, stocky, with freckles that even seemed "pugnacious," a reporter noted, Roberts jabbed a stubby finger at the television cameras as he painted the Brown group as an "abortion mill" and "ring" in his growling, threatening voice. His figures conjured up a flood of plunder—"$1 million abortion mill" with prices ranging from $400 to $1,500, one newspaper reported. Each sentence built the image with vivid overtones of sex and money—a group "catering chiefly to college girls," an apartment-clinic, "plush and luxurious."

The final touch of sensationalism was the involvement of the clergy. "We will reveal at the proper time that many of the referrals were made by clergymen," Roberts announced. When a reporter asked if clergy referrals constituted a crime, Roberts snapped, "That is an offense and will be prosecuted."

"Toughest District Attorney in New York," one magazine called Roberts in an article. Now he had produced the most publicized abortion case in a decade, riding like the plumed knight of the Bronx against clergy, coeds, and sex. "NAB 4 IN BRONX ABORTION MILL," cried the *Sunday News* in front-page, 1½-inch headlines. "Clergymen Sent Coed To Ring," the subhead reported. The *New York Times*, in a more conservative, inner-page story, called it the "Riverdale Raid." [2]

No one investigated the discrepancy between Roberts' accusations and reality. The actual fee charged by the Brown group for the clergy, myself, and other referral agencies was $300. At least a tenth of the cases were accepted without charge, some for only $50. New York hospitals asked far more for "legal" abortions—$600 to $800. None of the referral agencies I checked knew of a case at $1,500 (or more than $300), nor would Roberts ever substantiate this higher figure.

The "luxurious" apartment that Roberts described actually rented for $275, a moderate figure then for a good New York neighborhood. (Roberts himself, ironically, lived only a few blocks away.) The emphasis on "coed patients" was also exaggerated. At most they made up a third of the clergy and my referrals.

The District Attorney's most damaging inference was the repetition of "mill" and "ring"—words that always connoted the worst underworld butcher shops of abortion. Actually, the medical outcome of Brown's cases had been exceptional. Not one complaint ever reached me or the clergy I worked with. In fact, scores of letters and phone calls in cases we checked attested to the skill and compassion of the clinic. Pressed by a reporter, Roberts admitted, "The overwhelming percentage of patients suffered no ill effects." [3]

One of Brown's doctors (not present at the raid, but indicted months later) practiced at a large New York hospital, and after passage of New York's repeal law in 1970, became a highly rated staff member at the city's leading abortion clinic. The other doctor arrested in the raid, was licensed in the Dominican Republic, but not in New York State. This was the one serious flaw in Brown's administration. He had interviewed the doctor's medical colleagues in private practice and was so impressed by their recommendations that he failed to check the doctor's license. Nor had an inspection team of Philadelphia clergy who visited the clinic and approved it some months before done so.

Except for this licensing flaw, the clinic's standards gained additional strength from its emphasis on therapy and personal care. Brown and his wife not only met arriving patients at the airfield to counteract the loneliness and stigma of the procedure, and housed and fed those short of money; they treated abortion as a dignified, feminine right. This was a decisive break with the past. Even in hospitals, women had generally been made to feel degraded. As a result of his own professional background, Brown was equipped to reverse the trauma of abortion, long instilled by society and medical tradition, and deal with the problems and fears of each woman.

Brown had only recently retired as chief of corrective therapy at a Veterans Administration Hospital after a distinguished record of thirty years. A former president of the Association for Physical and Mental Rehabilitation, a retired Lieut. Colonel in the U.S. Army Reserve, he had pioneered in the development of driver-training programs for the disabled. Both he and his wife, an educational therapist at the same hospital, had master's degrees from New York University. "Few people had done more to help other people who have been disabled," observed a professor of education at Northeastern University, "One of the finest men I've ever met." An officer of the American Corrective Therapy Association concluded that Brown "helped to build one of the best Physical Medicine departments in America."

The Bronx raid had a devastating impact on the whole referral system. By closing down the most expert clinic on the East Coast, it left us without a major outlet of recognized standing. One doctor in the South, handling only a few cases, doubled his quota in the emergency. But the search for new physicians became so desperate that I turned to a New York man on the slimmest of recommendations. On his second case, he failed to complete the abortion and the patient had to be hospitalized for a day for further curettage.

Poverty cases, which could hardly afford the plane fare to the South, were particularly penalized. Even women of means became panicky after weeks of delay in appointments and resorted to inferior sources. With thousands of women now forced to backstreet, high-risk abortionists, the Bronx raid seriously crippled abortion standards and health care so carefully maintained by the referral system.

In an interview with District Attorney Roberts two years after the raid, I asked why he had singled out the Brown clinic. "The police had been tipped off. The law is the law—that's all there's to it," he responded. But with dozens of backstreet abortionists in the Bronx, why hadn't he gone after the hacks and incompetents? Why close down the one clinic of proven standards? "Look, we don't go searching out abortionists," Roberts insisted. "We investigated a tip, and we made arrests." [4]

Since no law enforcement agency can investigate every tip, and the prosecution of gambling rings and even dope peddlers in crime-heavy urban areas becomes a highly selective process, the motivations for the raid seem more complex. There are always religious pressures in a strongly Catholic city. The publicity potential of a clinic linked to the clergy must have been tempting. Above all, the involvement of the repeal movement's leadership offered a promising target for a D.A. of acknowledged political ambition. "Burt's ego is tremendous," a lawyer who had opposed Roberts in court told a *New York Magazine* reporter. "Anything that will feed that ego, he will do." After court appearances, Roberts would ask associates how he had done. They would say, pretty good. "Then Burt would storm at you, 'What do you mean, *pretty* good!' " a former colleague noted. "He wouldn't take that. He was seeking unreserved love and unquestioned admiration."

After his election as District Attorney, a friend told Roberts, "Hey, Burt, in four years you'll be Governor, huh?" Roberts replied, "Governor? What's the matter with emperor?" [5]

A forty-seven-year-old bachelor, Roberts kept a pile of seven scrapbooks on his coffee table filled with newspaper clippings about his career. Eating dinner recently with a woman friend, he asked the waiter where he lived. The waiter replied, The Bronx. Did he know who was the District Attorney of The Bronx? The waiter shook his head. "It's Burton Roberts," the D.A. shouted. "You're waiting on him right now."

If Roberts' hunger for publicity required a direct assault on the repeal leadership, he could now parade three prominent ministers and myself before the Bronx grand jury with a serious threat of indictment. Rev. Howard Moody was not only head of the New York Clergy Consultation Service, but the catalyst of all other services throughout the country. Although not a NARAL board member, his organization was an affiliate. Rev. Jesse Lyons of the Riverside Church, a NARAL board member, and Rev. Finley Schaef of the Washington Square

Methodist Church, who sponsored the Chicago conference, had long been aggressive participants in referral. My own position as NARAL chairman implicated the whole movement.

Combined with recent clergy arrests in the Midwest, the indictment and trial of any of us would go far to stifle the referral system. Or, at the very least, it could intimidate our associates to the point where referrals might be cut to a trickle. One lawyer, in fact, urged us to halt referrals until the grand jury investigation was completed—a concession rejected unanimously. The division within the NARAL planning committee over support of the Bronx case, however, indicated the paralysis that could grip the movement if the District Attorney pressed for indictments.

Once we had arranged for the Browns' defense (Ellenhorn would represent Brown, and Leonard Sandler, later a Civil Court judge, his wife), we had to formulate our strategy. The weak link was the Dominican doctor. Because he lacked a New York license, we could not base the case on the constitutional grounds of a woman's right of medical care from a licensed physician, used by Dr. Vuitch and Dr. Belous. Our only recourse was to rally public support through massive confrontation, and the clergy became pivotal in this approach.

Lyons and Schaef announced they would reject the authority of the grand jury. They would simply refuse to be interrogated on the basis of the First and Fifth Amendments and the clerical privilege of privacy for the penitent (the woman seeking abortion counsel). The District Attorney then could take them before a judge and ask their indictment. "But if Roberts forced an indictment," explained Prof. Cyril Means, who represented Lyons and later became NARAL's legal counsel, "it would mean the greatest confrontation between church and state since Thomas à Becket."

To expand this confrontation, we started to line up legislative allies in the Bronx. We drafted a newspaper ad: "Women of America! How long will you let your D.A. force you to bear a child against your will?" Women's Liberation and NOW chapters were alerted for picket lines around the courthouse—all contingent on whether the D.A. would press for indictments.

The web seemed to be drawing around us as the grand jury summoned its witnesses. From Brown's files, seized at the time of the raid, the D.A. had the names of scores of women referred by the clergy and myself. I was constantly receiving calls from people I had helped, obviously terrified by the prospect of interrogation. After their appearance, they would describe tearfully, how they had been forced to reveal the link between my referral and the Brown clinic. "The D.A. kept asking what you were paid, and what you were getting out of this," the father of one young woman told me. "They're definitely gunning for you."

Lyons and Schaef were subpoenaed to appear in late August. Schaef caused a flurry of excitement by arriving in shorts and sandals, and when Roberts entered the lounge where witnesses were waiting, Schaef refused to stand up or shake his hand. Neither clergyman was asked to testify that day. On July 16, I received a call from the D.A.'s office, setting a date for my appearance. Since my lawyer, Ephraim London, was on vacation, I secured a postponement.

When London returned, he urged me to testify under the immunity of the Fifth Amendment, which the D.A. would probably offer. I agreed, provided that no answer would incriminate any patient who had not already testified to her involvement. On September 15, two detectives appeared at my door with a subpoena—that inoffensive piece of white paper whose reality I had tried to deny for so long. The next few days of waiting moved by numbly, as if hours, and day and night, had been eliminated.

Yet on the morning of September 19, the numbness was replaced by a strange exaltation. I met Schaef at his church (he had been subpoenaed again, but was dressed more formally this time) and we took the subway to the Bronx County Courthouse—a white pile of stone and marble hovering like an enormous box-tomb over the rundown streets nearby. From the ornate, bronze entrance doors and the towering main floor, we rode upwards to the grand jury floor, a scruffy contrast of chipped paint and unwashed walls.

The waiting room was already filled—Moody and his assistant, Arlene Carmen, Lyons, Means, Roy Lucas who was Schaef's counsel, and surprisingly, Paul Krassner, editor of *The Realist*, jauntily attired in a black leather jacket. We sat on rickety chairs, talked perfunctorily, and then as an hour dragged by, forced ourselves to produce listless jokes to break the tension. We had all been called for noon. At one-thirty Krassner told a startled assistant district attorney he would wait no longer unless served lunch. Coffee and sandwiches soon appeared. A few minutes later, a clerk summoned the first witnesses.

When my turn came, I felt as if years of struggle had built to this moment, and everything hinged on my performance. It was like opening night. The grand jury, in fact, sat on rising tiers of seats—a theater of twenty-three, about evenly divided between men and women, with intense, intelligent faces, seemingly devoid of antagonism. I was placed on a small platform before them, standing. The foreman, sitting at my right, offered me immunity under the Fifth Amendment. I took it. Hopefully, I could say the things I had to say. If they asked a question that incriminated others, I still had a chance to force the confrontation into court.

An assistant district attorney, in charge of questioning, started by showing the jury a copy of my *Look* article, and asking me to describe my book and referrals. It was the perfect cue; I might have written it myself. I told them how women had called me after my book, desperate, lonely women who wanted something better than the risks of underworld abortion. I told how I had found medical outlets like the Brown clinic, and how the referral system had gradually raised health standards across the country and roused people against the old laws. I told how legislators had begun to catch up with their constituents, first with moderate new laws in Colorado and California. Now the campaign had reached the point in New York where dozens of legislators were sponsoring a bill to wipe out the old law entirely.

Just a week ago—I wasn't sure whether the District Attorney had explained this momentous step to the jury—the California Supreme Court had declared its old law unconstitutional in the Dr. Belous case.* I read the essential lines, that the right of a woman to choose whether or not to have a child, whether by contraception or abortion, was a basic right that could not be infringed by church or state. Dr. Belous, who had referred a woman for abortion, was exonerated. Since the New York law duplicated the old California law, were not our referrals a clear parallel with the California case?

I stressed the rapidity of change. With the California decision and New York's repeal campaign, the issues today could be meaningless in

* See Chapter Nine.

a few months. Perhaps I had gone too far, inferring that the Brown clinic and referrals would soon be honored history in the march toward repeal. But they let me talk for ten or fifteen minutes, interrupting occasionally with questions.

Then the assistant district attorney sharpened his tone. Had I ever made any money from referrals? "Not a penny," I said. Whenever a woman had enclosed a dollar or five-dollar bill with her letter, I returned them immediately. One man in New York had even sent a one-hundred-dollar bill, and I had asked him to come to the house and returned it in person. In fact, my costs in stamps and other expenses had probably run to $500 a year. And if I included the time taken from professional writing, my referrals had cost me $20,000 a year.

At the end, the District Attorney raised the only dangerous questions. Reading from a list in his hand, he asked whether I had sent Mrs. X or Miss Y to the Brown clinic. The names were unfamiliar to me. He read a dozen more, still unfamiliar. I explained that by now I had referred at least a thousand women to many doctors, and purposely blocked out the memory as soon as I had made the referral. He finally gave me two names I knew—one a student at the university where I taught, the other a relative of a friend. Both had previously testified that I had sent them to Brown, so my identification was pointless.

I left the grand jury room exultant. None of the questions had forced me into a judicial confrontation. They had listened well, perhaps even understood the absurdity of the Bronx raid in the total context of the abortion campaign. Lyons, Schaef, and Krassner held fast to their positions, refusing to testify. We waited, but no indictments were handed down that afternoon. We went home and waited for a month, nervously at first, but increasingly confident that Roberts had pulled back from his attack on NARAL and the clergy.

On October 16, the grand jury announced its indictments. The only charges made were against the four principals at the raid—the Browns, the Dominican doctor, and the nurse; and against two others supposedly implicated in the clinic, a New York doctor and a Maryland man whose status had never been defined.

Significantly, Roberts did not even bring the case to trial. The defendants settled for trivial penalties—a misdemeanor charge and $500 fine each for the Browns. Only the charges against the New York doctor remained unsettled by 1972.

It had turned into a stalemate. The carnival of propaganda at the raid, the television histrionics, all had evaporated. Once the referral system had stood up against the threat of prosecution, once the California Supreme Court, and a Federal Court decision in the Vuitch case in October, had defined a woman's right to abortion, once the New York campaign showed a tide of public support for repeal, the whole point of Roberts' case became ludicrous. It was the last serious assault on the referral system. The growth of the movement had passed Roberts by.

The final irony was that Roberts would eventually claim a part in the New York repeal law, passed in 1970. A year later, I went up to see him at the Courthouse. Brash, exuberant, chomping on a cigar, he announced, "I was the first D.A. in the city to say that the old law was not serving the community. That statement was an important factor in passing the law. It had a real influence on Bronx legislators."

Startled, I went back to clipping files to find his statement at the time of the raid. Buried in his oratory on "rings," "mills," and "college girls," the New York *Post* had quoted him as saying, "I'm by no means advocating a completely permissive attitude, but some consideration should be given to reform that takes account of the pragmatics of the situation." I asked Roberts which Bronx legislators this statement had persuaded to vote for the repeal bill. He refused to name them.[6]

I didn't ask him about the small type on the back of my subpoena to the grand jury, which said that a witness was entitled to fifty cents for his appearance, and eight cents for each mile of travel. The District Attorney still owed me about $1.30.

NOTES

1. *New York Times*, May 25, 1969, p. 34; New York *Post*, May 24, 1969, p. 2; New York *Sunday News*, May 25, 1969, p. 1; Riverdale (N.Y.) *Press*, May 29, 1969, p. 1.

2. This, and the preceding two paragraphs: *New York Times*, October 17, 1969, p. 28; New York *Daily News*, October 17, 1969; also see Footnote 1, above.

3. New York *Post*, October 16, 1969.

4. Personal interview, October 29, 1971.

5. Nancy Mayer, "The Toughest District Attorney in New York," *New York Magazine*, May 19, 1969, p. 24.

6. New York *Post*, October 16, 1969.

CHAPTER NINE

BREAKTHROUGH IN THE COURTS AND LEGISLATURES (1969–1970)

They came, almost like miracles, at one of our grimmest hours. While the Bronx grand jury threatened indictment, and we struggled to line up the first mass legislative support for the New York State repeal bill, two momentous court decisions in the fall of 1969, followed by two new laws in Hawaii and Alaska, swept the movement forward with exhilarating speed. Suddenly, the referral system, the prosecutions, the years of lonely organizing were producing a coherent pattern. We had reached a new stage of development: a national mandate for repeal.

The first breakthrough came in the California Supreme Court. On September 5, 1969, by a 4 to 3 decision, the court declared the old state law unconstitutional, and exonerated Dr. Leon Belous. For the first time, a high state court defined the rights of a woman over her own procreation, and accepted the constitutional issues as we had promulgated them in 1965—even citing the work of Zad Leavy, the Los Angeles lawyer; Dr. Christopher Tietze of the Population Council; myself, and others in its decision. "We couldn't have written a better decision ourselves," Professor Means observed.

"The fundamental right of a woman to choose whether to bear children follows from the Supreme Court's and this court's repeated acknowledgment of a 'right of privacy' or 'liberty' in matters related to marriage, family, and sex," the court announced.

Its decision struck hard at the vagueness of the old state law. Since a woman could only secure abortion when "necessary to preserve her life," and these words had no "clear meaning," the court agreed she would virtually be at the point of death before getting a physician to act. This, in itself, created a "great and direct infringement of constitutional rights . . . ."

But the physician was equally endangered by the old law. Since a "physician acts at his peril if he determines that the woman is entitled to an abortion," the court agreed that he would invariably refuse abortion rather than take the risk. Both doctor and woman, therefore, were denied their rights. "A woman whose life is at stake may be as effectively condemned to death as if the law flatly prohibited all abortions," the court concluded.

The decision became a revolutionary precedent for a score of forthcoming challenges to similar state laws—cited just two months later in the Federal Court opinion on Dr. Vuitch, for example. "A landmark decision," observed Dr. Keith P. Russell, clinical professor of obstetrics and gynecology of the University of Southern California School of Medicine. "This is the first State Supreme Court decision in the history of the nation which declares unconstitutional any anti-abortion statute."[1]

In California itself, the decision had little impact at first. It applied only to the old law under which Belous had been tried—not the moderate 1967 law. This new statute, as we have seen, hardly altered the conservative practices of California hospitals. In 1967, they approved only 5,000 legal abortions—a minuscule increase. Even its legislative sponsors considered the new law a failure.

But with the Belous decision in 1969, the new law was suddenly infused with surprising flexibility. By frequent inference that it, too, might be unconstitutional "because it contains uncertainties similar to those in the repealed statute," the California Supreme Court provided an opening for broad hospital interpretation that was quickly exploited by pragmatic strategists. Charles T. Munger, a wealthy Los Angeles lawyer who had helped finance supporting briefs in the Belous case, organized a campaign, with Ms. Elizabeth Canfield, Dr. Jerome Kummer, Dr. Russell, and Joseph Sunnen, the St. Louis philanthropist, to demolish the rigidity of hospital abortion practices. They concentrated on Los Angeles County Hospital, largest in the state, through personal meetings and community pressure, and expanded their attack with lengthy memos to every accredited California hospital. After convincing Los Angeles County and others to "revolutionize previous barbarous procedures," as Munger put it, the abortion approval rate climbed rapidly.[2]

The Rev. Hugh Anwyl's Clergy Consultation Service manipulated further sweeping gains. Its huge volume of applicants gave the service an advantageous bargaining position. In addition, profit-motivated proprietary hospitals were eager for clergy referrals. This combination enabled Anwyl to force radical changes—trading off one hospital against another to secure a soaring approval rate, low costs, and high quality care. By establishing permanent hospital agreements all over California, Anwyl eliminated the cruel and cumbersome system of abortion committees and processed almost every case in less than two days, mainly for "mental health" and usually without the cost of psychiatric approval letters.

Once these gains had been secured, new hospitals and clinics began to open up solely for abortion. Dr. Belous himself, at first "crushed by the long, gruelling, persecution and harassment of our so-called civilized society," as he wrote, left for an extended European trip, and returned in late 1971 to open his own hospital and "do battle all over again."

California thus became a unique example of an unworkable law that was made to work through the inferences of a court decision and hard-fisted medical politics. By 1972, California hospitals performed in 135,000 legal abortions a year—the second highest total, behind New York, of any state in the nation.[3]

The same process now began in Washington, D.C., as a result of a second crucial breakthrough. On November 10, 1969, just two months after the Belous decision, Judge Arnold Gesell of the Federal District Court declared the District of Columbia law unconstitutional, and exonerated Dr. Milan Vuitch. For its immediate impact alone, this decision exceeded the importance of California. It made Washington the first area in the country where abortion was completely legalized. The Gesell decision neither required in-hospital treatment, nor committee approval. Any licensed physician could perform abortion according to his best medical judgment—even in office if his equipment met medical standards.

This decision, affirming the constitutional rights of the woman and physician, gained further impressive support when retired Associate Justice of the U.S. Supreme Court, Tom C. Clark, wrote in the *Loyola University Law Review*, "I submit that until the time that life is present, the State could not interfere with the interruption of pregnancy through abortion performed in a hospital or under appropriate clinical conditions." [4]

The reopening of Dr. Vuitch's practice relieved the pressure on the referral system, which, for five months since the Bronx raid, had been critically short of medical outlets. Vuitch established an expensively equipped clinic—four treatment rooms, laboratory, recovery room with emergency facilities, and pine-paneled waiting room and offices—at 1712 I Street, a few blocks from the White House. Soon he was taking a hundred abortion cases a week.[5]

While the California breakthrough required years to exploit, the Gesell decision offered the chance for instant confrontation. It had been my policy in NARAL to grasp any opening quickly and to expand it on a national scale. As a result of my relationship with Vuitch, I asked him to come to New York for a national press conference which would demand immediate application of all rights under the Gesell decision. We would strengthen our forces with two influential physicians—Dr. Dorothy Ferebee, the black president of the District of Columbia Commission on the Status of Women, and Dr. Laura Morrow, president of the American Medical Women's Association.

At the press conference on December 10, 1969, which produced the largest turnout of reporters and television cameras since the start of the abortion campaign, I challenged the District of Columbia Health Department to comply with the Gesell decision. The judge had ruled that the poor must have equal rights to abortion with the rich. The Health Department, I insisted, must open at least five free abortion clinics. Otherwise, NARAL would launch a new confrontation. We would bring a lawsuit against the Department's hospitals, or even open our own free clinic.

In his statement, Dr. Vuitch hammered further at the medical profession's obligations. "I urge that scores of physicians volunteer their services, and I have already made a written pledge to the Health

Department that I will donate at least half a day a week so that the medical profession can achieve, in Gesell's words, 'principles of equal protection under our Constitution.' "

The unfortunate reality, however, was that the Gesell decision proved a paper breakthrough at first. Although a few psychiatrists, working with Women's Liberation counseling services, rubber-stamped applications to get through the old hospital boards, the medical profession generally ignored the Federal court. The city's three leading voluntary hospitals together performed only about 400 abortions a month at prices from $600 to $800. Their abortion committees rejected most applicants, particularly nonresidents. "The ruling has had little effect on abortion practices of Washington hospitals," the Washington *Post* concluded on February 23, 1970.

The chief sufferers, as always, were the poor. The city's principal public hospital, D.C. General, maintained its longstanding virtual blockade, and in the first two months of 1970 took only ten abortion cases.[6]

The NARAL Executive Committee decided the time had come for confrontation—taking D.C. General to court. We asked American Civil Liberties Union to handle the case with NARAL putting up part of the costs, and Women's Liberation and the Medical Committee for Human Rights joining in the complaint. On March 20, 1970, the U.S. Court of Appeals in the District upheld our suit and ordered the hospital to accept abortion cases on mental health grounds after certification by one or two psychiatrists.

Still, D.C. General evaded the order. We had to go back to court, insisting the rights of the poor were being denied. Again, the Appeals Court ruled in our favor, and on May 23 with a front-page, banner headline in the Washington *Daily News*, D.C. General finally agreed to accept 1,000 abortion patients a year on mental health grounds and to set up a special unit to accommodate them.[7]

At the same time, NARAL pushed ahead with its own Washington clinic. We wanted to develop a model for other states where abortion would soon be legalized and to demonstrate that abortions in early pregnancy could be performed on an out-patient basis safely and efficiently. This approach had little appeal to the medical hierarchy which preferred the procedure under their control in-hospital—naturally, at higher profits with anesthesia, bed-care, and nursing. Except for my own analysis in *Look*, there were few statistics to support the out-patient position.

We had no trouble lining up financial backing, nurses, and equipment for the clinic. But to find one or two physicians was another matter. After weeks of telephoning medical contacts in Washington, I could get no commitment from a single physician besides Vuitch who was willing to stand up against the medical hierarchy. Dr. Bernard Nathanson, chairman of NARAL's medical committee, would have volunteered himself but lacked a District license. He agreed to commute to Washington weekly to supervise the clinic, and wrote every obstetrician-gynecologist in the city, asking them to give a few hours a week. Only one affirmative response came in, and that soon reneged.

The pressures against a physician were too intense. Anyone who cooperated with us could lose his hospital privileges. If the police closed the clinic, another Federal judge could reverse Gesell's decision and expose the doctor to indictment. Above all, the Catholic Church sought to block the effect of the court. "Nothing any judge can say could make truly just the slaughter of innocents that would be unloosed by abortion on request," Patrick Cardinal O'Boyle announced. The "Sons of Thunder," militant Catholics dressed in khaki shirts, red berets, and rosaries, assembled at Washington Circle to seize and baptize aborted fetuses and "take the bodies to an appropriate place after their execution—to a cemetery." The rally took place near two of the city's principal hospitals. The obvious threat dissipated our last hope for medical volunteers.[8]

With Dr. Vuitch taking an increasing number of cases without charge, NARAL abandoned its plan for a free clinic. It was simply too early for such a revolutionary concept. The medical profession would adjust in time to the Gesell decision and to the radical shift in public opinion demonstrated by repeal laws in Hawaii, Alaska, and New York in early 1970. Other physicians gradually joined Vuitch in performing in-office abortion. But the critical step came a year later—the opening of an out-patient clinic at Washington Hospital Center, and of the Preterm Clinic at 1726 I Street by a nonprofit coalition of prominent citizens.

The U.S. Supreme Court in the Vuitch decision added essential props to these clinics. After the case was argued by Joseph Nellis and

Prof. Norman Dorsen of New York University Law School, the Supreme Court on April 21, 1971, handed down a quixotic opinion. It upheld the constitutionality of the old law by 5 to 2 (two justices not voting). This decision might have damaged abortion rights in the District. Actually, it strengthened them by broadening two existent rights.

Although the law already allowed abortion to save a woman's "health," the Court enlarged its definition to include "psychological as well as physical wellbeing." Even more important to a medical profession terrorized by the possibility of proving an abortion necessary, the Court emphatically placed the burden of proof on the prosecution. "It would be highly anomalous for a legislature to authorize abortions necessary for life or health and then to demand that a doctor, upon pain of one to ten years' imprisonment, bear the burden of proving that an abortion he performed fell within that category," the Court concluded. "We are unable to believe that Congress intended that a physician be required to prove his innocence." [9]

With this definitive ruling on mental health and the physician's right of medical decision, which had been our position from the start, Preterm Clinic became an integral part of the medical community. Its charge as a nonprofit service was $150, one of the lowest in the country. Its patients, mainly referred by Planned Parenthood chapters and physicians, were largely residents of Washington, Virginia, and Maryland, with a handful from as far as Texas and Florida. Once Preterm and Washington Hospital Center had proved the safety and efficiency of out-patient cases, two other clinics opened in the city. Washington's abortion facilities soon ranked among the busiest in the country, with 20,000 patients in 1971.

The momentum generated by the Belous and Vuitch decisions radiated through every legislative campaign at the start of 1970. It was particularly evident in Hawaii, the first state to pass a virtual repeal bill. Hawaii's geopolitical structure made the Legislature acutely sensitive to its constituents. Although the Hawaiian islands are widely scattered, three-fourths of the population live within fifty miles of the capital at Honolulu and can exert constant pressure on its representatives. The abortion campaign sprang from a popular groundswell—the product of a radical shift in public opinion that even astute legislators underestimated. It was the first proof of NARAL's thesis that repeal would excite far more support than half-hearted compromise. Hawaii concentrated on repeal from the start, and pushed it through within six months.

Ms. Joan Hayes, legislative chairman of the American Association of University Women, focused the campaign on State Senator Vincent Yano. Although a Catholic, Yano opposed government controls in matters of private conscience, including abortion. Equally important, he was chairman of the committee on public health, welfare, and housing, which would introduce the bill. With the University of Hawaii's School of Public Health, Hayes prepared a questionnaire on abortion, and a covering letter from the president of the Hawaii Medical Association, that was sent to all physicians on the islands. Of the two specialties most concerned with abortion, 80 percent of psychiatrists, and almost every obstetrician-gynecologist, supported repeal.

Hayes then sent invitations to more than one hundred organizations for a Citizens Seminar on Abortion, which produced a broad coalition of repeal groups. Impressed both by the medical poll and the coalition, Senator Yano announced on September 10, 1969, that he would back repeal.[10]

In the growing coalition, the most significant additions were the Chamber of Commerce, the AFL-CIO, and the International Longshore Workers Union—organizations that had never openly supported abortion in other areas. The Government Employees Association, Council of Churches, National Association of Social Workers—almost every important group in the state—joined the campaign. Zero Population Growth started a petition drive for 10,000 signatures. Arriving on a lecture tour, Bill Baird, a NARAL board member, organized a student march which resulted in the University Abortion and Birth Control Committee.

By the time of the Senate hearings in February, the coalition had sent dozens of teams to talk with every legislator at the capitol, and Senator Yano's committee was clearly favorable. Both principal newspapers in Honolulu, the *Star Bulletin* and *Advertiser*, supported the bill editorially, and their polls showed that 90 percent of their readers had swung to repeal.

The campaign had accelerated so rapidly that the Catholic opposition, channeled through the Knights of Columbus and parochial school students, proved ineffective. In a last desperate effort to stop the bill, Bishop John Scanlan requested time to address a special joint session of the legislature. He was refused, but given a private hall at the capitol—a privilege that stirred a backlash in the press. "It seemed as if the opposition did not believe the repeal bill could possibly be passed until it was already too late to stop the momentum of the groundswell," concluded Drs. Patricia Steinhoff and Milton Diamond of the University of Hawaii.[11]

In late February, the House approved the bill 31 to 20, the Senate by 15 to 9. Governor John A. Burns, a Catholic who, like Senator Yano, considered abortion a matter of individual conscience, let the bill become law on March 13 without signing it.[12]

It was a remarkable triumph, the first in a series of increasingly important legislative breakthroughs in 1970. While the bill fell slightly short of NARAL's concept of repeal, it allowed a completely free choice in abortion between a woman and her physician of a "nonviable" fetus, generally interpreted by the medical profession to mean about twenty-four weeks of pregnancy. The bill also required that the procedure be done in a hospital—not a burdensome limitation in a moderately populated state where hospitals could meet the demand—and that a woman be a resident of Hawaii for at least ninety days. Even the residency requirement might not remain an obstacle since the U.S. Supreme Court had already ruled that health care could not be denied on a geographic basis.[13]

In Alaska, at the same time, public opinion had been building so precipitously that even State Senator John Rader of Anchorage, the first legislative convert, was startled by its strength. "When I introduced the original abortion bill, I could not get a single cosponsor, and honestly did not think it would pass in any form," Rader observed. "I did better than my colleagues in estimating the public desire for a new abortion law, but as it turned out, I grossly underestimated the depth."

The momentum of recent court decisions, but particularly the furious debate in the press since 1965, had built a mood of revolt that made the abortion movement a social phenomenon. "We rode the crest of something I still can't define—but that something was clearly changing attitudes on the part of the American public, assisted by coverage of the basic issues in magazines and newspapers," explained Ms. Helen Nienhueser, chairman of Alaska's Alliance for Humane Abortion.

Rader, as well as Nienhueser and four other women who organized the Alliance, represent another aspect of this phenomenon—the ability of a small but committed leadership to mold a popular groundswell into a major political force. The number of organizers, whether in Alaska, Hawaii, New York, or in NARAL itself, was always minuscule. But the unique gift of the movement was to grasp and harness the demands of the public at a moment when they were ready to erupt.

Rader, a graduate of the University of Kansas Law School who had lived in Alaska since 1951 with his wife and three children, had seen the first ALI-type abortion bill expire in the legislature without rousing any public interest. After his election to the Senate, following service as City Attorney of Anchorage and State Attorney General, he discussed the repeal issue with his family physician, Dr. Rodman Wilson. As it happened, Wilson was also legislative committee chairman of the Alaska Medical Association. Both agreed that abortion should become a purely medical choice between a woman and her physician, and Wilson presented a resolution to this effect to the Association. The resolution passed. By contrast with the conservative bureaucracies in the District of Columbia and New York, organized medicine in Hawaii and Alaska became early converts to the repeal position.

Rader's first bill allowed for free choice in abortion in the first twenty weeks of pregnancy, after that by approval of a hospital committee on mental and physical health grounds. Still, he could not get a single Senator to cosponsor the bill with him. His family provided the campaign staff at first—his brother, a psychiatrist, working with the medical profession; his wife, clipping magazine and newspaper articles; his oldest son, who had just become a page at the State Capitol, researching other laws. Once Rader's bill was publicized, Nienhueser's Alliance, headed by Ms. Jan Erickson, Evey Ruskin, Pat Soll, and Primula Babcock, made it the focus of their mounting drive against the old abortion law.

Ms. Nienhueser, a graduate of Rhode Island's Pembroke College in 1957, recognized that the progressive stand of the Alaska Medical Association would be wasted unless the Alliance brought enough grass roots pressure on the legislature. The support of organizations like the State Nurses Association, the Commission on the Status of Women, and the Alaska Conservation Society was essential. But the vast distance between cities and towns in Alaska required a predominantly local campaign. The women started a petition drive aimed at each wavering legislator. Their special techniques became the telephone "chain" and "writing klatch." Each of their fifty hard-core workers were assigned a list of telephone contacts which were persuaded to call a similar list of their own. Each of the fifty gave regular coffee parties for their friends where hundreds of letters were written on the spot to local legislators.

The Alaska Council of Churches proved the backbone of the campaign—the Rev. John Shaffer of Juneau's United Methodist Church rallying clergymen across the state, and conferring with Nienhueser and Rader almost daily. Student groups concentrated on polling. A class at Anchorage Community College, sampling a cross section of 400 city voters, found that 85 percent favored repeal. At Juneau-Douglas High School, 71 percent of 444 students supported the bill.

By March 4, 1970, Rader decided that the campaign had grown strong enough for his first test in the Senate. With an overflow crowd in the galleries watching "the most dramatic floor action of this legislative session," as a reporter described it, Rader's bill failed by a one-vote margin, securing 10 votes to 9 (with eleven needed for passage, and one Senator ill). In a second attempt, adding provision for a popular referendum if the law passed, Rader lost by the same count.[14]

Undaunted, Rader walked into the press room a few minutes after his defeat and announced that he would introduce a new bill. Hawaii had just passed the first repeal act in the nation, and Rader decided to use it as his model. He telephoned the Attorney General of Hawaii, who read him the act word by word. The new Rader bill became even more radical than the first. Instead of free choice in abortion in the first 20 weeks, the time span now included the "nonviable" fetus, or about 24 weeks of pregnancy.

Rader's bill went to the floor again on April 1. The crucial vote was a new member, Senator Kay Poland of Kodiak, who had replaced her husband, absent because of illness on the previous tally. In the midst of angry debates Senator Poland announced her support for the bill. When a Catholic Senator attacked her, she replied, "I am a Catholic. I am adopted. I am, of course, a woman. I don't feel I can sit here and make a decision for my fellow women."

This time, the bill passed by 11 to 9. When the Senate agreed to reconsider it, two votes switched to make the count 13 to 7. The Senate had been torn apart for months by the abortion issue; now the House acted quickly. On April 9, it approved the bill by a comfortable 29 to 10 margin.

The momentary celebration collapsed a week later when Governor Keith Miller, a Methodist, married to a Catholic, vetoed the bill, reversing the objective policy of Hawaii's Catholic governor who had let his bill become law. Urging the legislature to override the veto, the Anchorage *Daily News* called Miller's "nineteenth century mentality . . . incapable of grasping one of the tragic realities of the twentieth century." [15]

Rader and the Alliance worked feverishly to rally votes against the veto. With Alaska's Constitution requiring two-thirds of both houses, or 40 votes, to override, Rader feared that previous votes could melt away under gubernatorial pressure. On April 30, however, both houses stood firm. The veto was overturned 41 to 17 with one vote to spare.

Alaska had joined Hawaii—two frontier states where the radical tradition had asserted itself with astonishing speed—as the third repeal state. In New York, the second repeal state, a volcanic struggle (to be described in the next chapter) would climax the most fruitful campaign in the movement's history.

To symbolize this revolt, "Lysistrata Day" under NARAL's sponsorship was celebrated in cities across the country—a picket line around the American Medical Association building in Chicago, a demonstration before D.C. General Hospital in Washington, the invasion of legislative hearings on abortion in Boston. Adapting to abortion the Lysistrata theme of Aristophanes which rallied Grecian women against war with a boycott on sex, a Greek chorus at the University of Pennsylvania, in flowing white robes and garlanded ivy, satirized the medical profession and distributed hundreds of Women's Lib armbands to the audience. "I will abstain from love and love's delights," they chanted in the original Lysistrata oath.

"Even though this is only a symbolic gesture for one day," announced Constance Billé of NARAL's Executive Committee, "it dramatizes the fact that our bodies are not our own as long as the law can dictate that we must bear unwanted children." [16]

NOTES

1. *People v. Belous*, 71 Cal. 2d 954, 458 p. 2d 194, 80 Cal. Rptr. 354 (1969); Letter of October 28, 1969, to signers of Physicians' Brief in Belous case.

2. *People v. Belous, op. cit., n.* 15; Personal letter, Charles T. Munger to author, February 28, 1972.

3. Personal letter, Dr. Leon Belous to author, December 10, 1971; *New York Times*, January 30, 1972.

4. *United States v. Vuitch*, 350 F. Supp. 1032 (D.D.C. 1969); *New York Times*, November 12, 1969, p. 46; *Loyola University Law Review*, Vol. 2, April, 1969, p. 1.

5. Washington *Post*, February 23, 1970, Sec. C, p. 2.

6. This, and preceding paragraph: Washington *Post*, February 24, 1970, Sec. B, p. 1; February 23, 1970, Sec. C, p. 1.

7. Washington *Daily News*, May 23, 1970, p. 1.

8. *New York Times*, December 10, 1969, p. 110; Washington *Post*, June 5, 1970, Sec. C, p. 2.

9. *United States v. Vuitch*, 402 U.S. 62 (1971).

10. Roy G. Smith, "Changing Hawaii's Abortion Laws," *Pacific Health*, Vol. 3, 1970, pp. 2–4.

11. Patricia Steinhoff and Milton Diamond, "Freedom of Choice: Abortion Politics in Hawaii," Population Council, N.Y. (unpublished).

12. *New York Times*, February 25, 1970, p. 1.

13. Roy G. Smith, Milton Diamond, Patricia Steinhoff, and Norma Brown, "Abortion in Hawaii: The First 124 Days," *American Journal of Public Health*, Vol. 61, No. 3, March 1971, pp. 530–542.

14. Anchorage *Daily News*, March 5, 1970, p. 1.

15. This, and preceding two paragraphs: Anchorage *Daily News*, April 1, 1970, p. 1; April 9, 1970, p. 1; April 20, 1970, p. 4.

16. Philadelphia *Tribune*, March 17, 1970; Philadelphia *Plain Dealer*, March 28, 1970, Vol. 1, No. 7, p. 2.

CHAPTER TEN

NEW YORK: THE IMPOSSIBLE VICTORY (1970)

After Assemblyman Albert H. Blumenthal's moderate abortion reform bill failed in 1968 ("We had four votes we needed and they backed out," he explained), the portents for 1969 appeared dazzlingly good. Assembly Speaker Perry Duryea supported the bill. While Senate Majority Leader Earl Brydges, a Catholic, was personally opposed, he conceded, "I will do nothing to keep it from coming to the floor." The recent Oliver Quayle poll had shown that 75 percent of New York State residents (72 percent of Catholics) supported a reform law on physical and mental health grounds, and Blumenthal had 82 votes—with 76 needed for passage—"firmly promised." On the day of the vote, April 17, 1969, the affirmative count lined up with unfaltering precision, and passage seemed assured, until Assemblyman Martin Ginsberg of Nassau County rose to his feet to deliver one of the most quixotic speeches in the history of abortion debate.[1]

A Republican, considered pledged to the bill, Ginsberg now attacked it in terms of his own physical affliction. Crippled by polio since infancy, and dependent on heavy braces and cane, he argued that a law allowing abortion for a malformed fetus could set a frightening precedent. "If we are prepared to say that a life should not come into this world malformed or abnormal," he told the Assembly, "then tomorrow we should be prepared to say that a life already in this world which becomes malformed or abnormal should not be permitted to live."

Concluding that perhaps "God saw fit to let me live in this form and condition . . . so I could be here on April 17 to speak on this specific bill," Ginsberg was received with frantic applause. Legislators rose to their feet, crowding around him, shaking his hand. After three minutes of gavel-pounding by the Speaker, Blumenthal tried to explain that the bill, which allowed abortion in proven cases of fetal abnormality, had nothing to do with victims of polio or other abnormalities after birth. His floor leaders, however, reported that 14 pledged votes (13 of them Republican) had melted away. The bill was soon defeated, 78 to 69.[2]

Ginsberg's speech, as it turned out, simply provided an excuse for this last-minute switch—a defection partly due to Catholic pressure on suburban counties. "An incredible debate, a big fairy tale," Assemblywoman Constance Cook, who had just introduced the first sweeping bill repealing all abortion laws, called it. "The arguments on both sides of the aisle were so incredibly unreal . . . that obviously the truth wasn't even forming the basis of political action that was going on."[3]

What was more significant about Ginsberg's speech, however, was that it unleashed a storm of protest among his own constituents. Ms. Sylvia Fields, mother of three children and a nurse teaching maternal health, criticized the speech in a letter to *Newsday*, and a group of neighbors in Plainview, a predominantly Jewish area, met at her house to organize the Nassau Committee for Abortion Law Repeal. Ginsberg found himself flooded with letters, telegrams, and phone calls from doctors, nurses, clergymen, and hundreds of other professional leaders in the area. He even received a voodoo doll pierced with pins. Two of the Committee's principal allies, Anita and Alan DeLorenzo—he was the legislative director of the local United Automobile Workers—employed the Union's extensive mailing list to put further pressure on Ginsberg to support the Cook bill.

After Protestant churches and synagogues in his district insisted that Ginsberg address their congregations to explain his abortion stand, the Assemblyman executed an amazing reversal. An astute politician who saw where the votes lay, he announced, on August 14, 1969, that he had really been for repeal of abortion laws after all. He had only attacked the Blumenthal bill for making the State the "moral denominator"—setting up hospital committees and other legislative criteria for abortion approval. The repeal bill, on the other hand, "leaves the moral justification to the individuals and not to the State, and I have no right to infringe upon that," he explained.[4]

Whatever the semantic twists behind Ginsberg's reversal, the immediate result was that public pressure had converted him to repeal and made him a staunch supporter of the Cook repeal bill in 1970. "It became obvious that if he hadn't switched to repeal," a lobbyist observed, "he would have been slaughtered at the next election."

This same pattern of grass roots pressure appeared in two neighboring Long Island districts. State Senator Norman Lent, a Republican whose district included a sizable number of middle-class Catholics, mailed out a questionnaire, eventually returned by over 7,000 of his constituents, and was startled to find that 65 percent favored "complete repeal" of the abortion law. Lent, Chairman of the Senate Health Committee, thereupon swung to the repeal bill—a route soon followed by the late State Senator Edward Speno, a Nassau Republican and Catholic. Speno's conversion had special impact since, as chairman of the Senate Codes Committee, he was instrumental in deciding which bills could be approved quickly for floor debate.

"Speno and many other legislators learned that public demand for abortion repeal was at a point where they couldn't vote No," concluded State Senator Manfred Ohrenstein, a Manhattan reform Democrat and early repeal leader. "The eventual vote on the bill was a remarkable triumph of grass roots pressure."

While New York State, with its 6.5 million Catholics about 40 percent of the population, and its potent Catholic lobby in Albany, appeared an impossible gamble for repeal, the conversions on Long Island had been going on elsewhere for the past year. One vivid manifestation was an increase in legislative sponsors. While Ms. Cook and Franz Leichter of Manhattan were the only names on the bill in 1969, they quickly found twenty-four Assemblymen to sponsor the 1970 bill. The list covered a broad spectrum—blacks, Puerto Ricans, three of the four women in the Assembly, even a few Catholics, and perhaps most significant of all, the Democratic Minority Leader, Stanley Steingut of Brooklyn, who worked tirelessly rounding up votes. It obviously fell short of the 76 votes needed, but still made an impressive core.

The National Association for Repeal of Abortion Laws decided that the risk of concentration on New York was well worth taking. Even a reasonably close vote could build a successful drive in 1971; a victory now could produce an immeasurable boost for the rest of the country. There were other advantageous factors—the momentum of the recent court decisions in California and the District of Columbia and the repeal campaign in Hawaii which would soon push through the first bill.

The early radicals had built the movement in New York State carefully. The basic step since 1965 had been education—an incessant flow of articles, speeches, and radio and television shows that had convinced most people repeal was the feasible solution. Our second step was to confront the law through abortion referrals by the clergy, Bill Baird, and myself, galvanizing women into militancy. "I knew that women didn't want reform, at least not enough to go out and work for it, whereas I suspected they would work for repeal, and they did," Cook observed.[5]

Politically, New York was organized from the precinct level. After Percy Sutton and I addressed the Yorkville Democratic Club in 1965, repealers converted club after club until almost every Democratic district in New York City (and many Republican clubs) had lined up behind repeal. The aggressive campaign in Nassau and Suffolk Counties was the turning point. Upstate New York remained the critical unknown in our gamble.

State and national organizations in New York—religious, social, medical, political—were the final building blocks. Starting with the New York Civil Liberties Union and the Unitarian-Universalists in 1965, repeal gained the backing of most Protestant denominations in the State Council of Churches, many Jewish groups like the National Council of Jewish Women and the American Jewish Congress, the Liberal Party, Americans for Democratic Action, National Organization for Women, American Public Health Association, American Medical Women's Association, Physicians Forum, National Association of Social Workers, Citizens Committee for Children, and the New York Women's Bar Association, among others.

By January 1970 over fifty such organizations, with millions of members, supported repeal. The question was whether this sprawling framework could be turned into a disciplined force—into letters, telegrams, phone calls, and delegations to Albany—that would produce enough legislative votes.

Perhaps our greatest asset was the quality of legislative leadership. Ms. Cook, an influential upstate Republican, not only held the chairmanships of the Education Committee and Republican Program Committee, but worked closely with Governor Rockefeller and the Republican hierarchy. Even before her election in 1962, when she startled neighbors by campaigning in a shimmering 1927 Packard, she had served as counsel to numerous legislative committees, and had mastered political infighting.

Born in Cleveland in 1919, schooled in New York City, she was a handsome, poised, and literate woman with a motherly sweetness overlaying an unbending will. After Cornell College and Law School, she joined the Manhattan law firm of Shearman and Sterling, served as confidential law assistant to Governor Thomas E. Dewey, and took a year off for graduate study at the University of Oslo and The Hague Academy of International Law.

"The only mother in the legislature," as she called herself, she joined the National Organization for Women in 1967 and supported its female rights plank at the Constitutional Convention. "Every woman is a feminist if you ask her the right questions," she observed. An early sponsor of the Blumenthal bill, she concluded, "The reason why they could never get any votes for reform is that reform is a terrible approach. When you pull in the State in any way—establishing grounds or hospital committees or any of that stuff—women are not interested. They'd rather go to an illegal abortionist." When an opponent told her, "The next thing you'll want is abortion on demand," she retorted, "Naturally—the need is clear." [6]

Ms. Ruth Cusack of NOW, a Ph.D. in nutrition, organizer of Suffolk County's repeal movement, and NARAL board member, wrote Cook on July 19, 1968, to ask her to sponsor a repeal bill. Cook immediately agreed. "I talked to my best friend and she said, 'Gee, you're quitting politics,' " Cook recalled. The fact that at least a third of her district was Catholic never dissuaded her. In 1968 she ran ahead of the winning Congressman, and two years later rolled up a plurality of 14,000 votes.

Her Assembly cosponsor, Franz Leichter of Manhattan's preponderantly Jewish West Side, made an ideal balance for an upstate Protestant. A graduate of Swarthmore and Harvard Law School, Leichter had been a respected district leader among reform Democrats who won election to the Assembly in 1968. Other sponsors furthered this balance. Vincent Balletta, Jr., of Nassau, William Passanante of Manhattan, and Mary Anne Krupsak of Amsterdam-Schenectady were Catholics; Charles Rangel of Harlem, a black Catholic soon to be elected to Congress. Denouncing Catholic attacks on abortion, Rangel told legislators, "Those who would now protect life have done nothing when the mortality rate of black mothers is four times higher than of whites, when the Negro infant mortality rate is 58 percent higher, and when the death rate within one month [of birth] is three times higher."[7]

In the Senate, Basil Paterson, a black Catholic from Harlem and prime sponsor of the repeal bill, and Manfred Ohrenstein, both liberal Democrats, balanced Clinton Dominick and Thomas Laverne, who were upstate Republicans. Paterson would run as Lieutenant Governor on the Democratic-Liberal ticket in 1971. Ohrenstein, the first reform Democrat elected to the Senate in 1960, was chairman of the Senate Mental Health Committee. Consistently, the Civil Liberties Union gave him its highest rating in the Senate.

Dominick was elected to the Assembly in 1954, the Senate in 1958. "A strong, gentle, courtly private man who could manage controversial legislation without hysteria . . . looking like a college professor, oozing respectability but without affectation," a repeal aide described him. Although chairman of the Education Committee and linked to the Republican leadership, he frequently championed social legislation for the Democrats. Laverne, a Senator since 1960, refused to allow his Catholic faith to interfere with legislative decisions, but came under such pressure on abortion he was said to have thrown a badgering priest out of his office.

Another optimistic factor for repeal in 1970 was that the inflexible opposition of the Republican leadership had been considerably diluted by public pressure. Governor Rockefeller in 1968 could go no further on abortion than admit "a great deal of human tragedy [is] involved here, and I think a lot could be done to alleviate it." To ease the squeeze on his own neck, he appointed a distinguished "Governor's Commission" that spring to study the abortion law. Adroitly balanced between three repealers, four moderates, and four Catholics, the Commission could come up with no stronger recommendations than the standard Blumenthal bill, and one slight innovation approved by a 7 to 4 vote—abortion on request for a woman after four children.[8]

By January 13, 1970, however, when the Governor was asked at the Women's Legislative Forum whether he would approve a repeal bill, he replied, "I think I'd probably say Yes." [9]

There was an explosive issue behind the Governor's hesitant shift. Few political analysts, including the Catholic lobby in Albany, thought the Cook bill had a chance. The real Catholic target in 1970 was to abolish the "Blaine amendment" to the New York State Constitution, which spelled out separation of church and state more stringently than the First Amendment to the U.S. Constitution.

With Catholic schools in desperate need of public funds barred by the Blaine amendment, Rockefeller may have assured Senate Majority Leader Brydges of his opposition to Blaine while giving lip service to the Cook bill. This in no way approximated a deal—a common theory, which responsible insiders characterized as "baloney." It simply meant that Catholic legislators like Speno (or others with a heavy Catholic vote) could support abortion and balance this risk with a vote against Blaine. One upstate assemblyman was heard to remark to another, "This abortion thing doesn't mean a thing. It's how you vote on parochial aid that counts."

Brydges himself may have accepted this balancing act between Blaine and abortion, for on February 18, 1970, he "indicated today that his stand [on abortion] was easing and that he might support some form of liberalization." [10]

The third member of the Republican trinity, Assemblyman Perry Duryea, had become Assembly Majority Leader in 1969 and represented the increasingly populous and affluent eastern end of Long Island. Gray-haired and aristocratic, he approached controversial issues as a statesman rather than local politician, possibly preparing for a gubernatorial race whenever Rockefeller left Albany. Two years before, Cusack had written Duryea, her assemblyman, and received his assurance for repeal. Somewhat startled at this far-out stance, she exchanged more letters until she knew he understood the difference between reform and repeal. ". . . I feel confident I could support a repealer introduced by Assemblywoman Cook," Duryea wrote her on September 19, 1968.

After the Cook bill was introduced in 1970, Cusack, a modest but dogged campaigner, asked whether he would sponsor the bill. He refused, but promised in case of a tie vote (almost the only time a Speaker casts a ballot) that he would support repeal. This commitment, repeated in the press until it became gospel, turned out to be the cornerstone of Assembly strategy.

One more issue had to be worked out—the conversion of Assemblyman Blumenthal from reform to repeal. As prime sponsor of the reform bill since 1967, and a central figure in Democratic policy since his selection as Assistant Minority Leader, he had shown unflagging energy in promoting his bill. Unless he dropped it and supported Cook, however, the campaign would be dangerously fragmented. "It would be a tragedy for New York to be saddled with a Blumenthal-type bill," the Suffolk Committee for Abortion Law Repeal insisted in its October 16, 1969 newsletter. "It covers perhaps 5 percent of the women now getting illegal abortions."

Cusack had already tried to move him toward repeal in a 1968 memorandum, but he called his bill the "only feasible approach." [11] When I appeared with Blumenthal on a radio show on December 15, 1969, I stressed the rising tide of public and legislative support for the Cook bill, but he insisted that only his bill could get through the legislature. We continued this debate on the sidewalk outside the studio, and Blumenthal finally put his arm around my shoulder and concluded, "You're a good guy, but you just don't understand politics."

Blumenthal's long devotion to a moderate bill had given him a personal stake that was hard to shake. Ms. Barbara Gelobter, an influential black politician in his area, later a NARAL board member, visited Blumenthal with her coleader to tell him that his constituents demanded repeal. "But he refused to budge even though all his clubs might line up against him," she recalled.

Gelobter, along with Ms. Lucinda Cisler and James Clapp, who had recently formed New Yorkers for Abortion Law Repeal as a NARAL affiliate, decided on direct confrontation. On election day that November, they set up tables with over sixty workers at many polling places in Blumenthal's district, and collected over 6,000 signatures on petitions demanding that he give up reform and support the Cook bill.

Blumenthal finally yielded to political reality. On January 28, 1970, he announced, "I am giving full support to the Cook bill which calls for total repeal of New York's law on abortion." He quickly became a persuasive voice in every floor debate. "He worked just as hard as anybody else to get that bill," Cook concluded.[12]

The bill that Cook and Leichter, with twenty-two other Assemblymen, introduced on January 7, 1970 was slightly different from their 1969 version. Instead of removing abortion completely from the criminal code and leaving its control to medical regulations, the new bill kept abortion in the code but with no limitations except that it must be performed by a licensed physician. The sponsors considered this change essential to gaining legislative support. "We couldn't have gotten five votes without it," Leichter stated.[13]

The change, however, caused a bitter crisis within the movement. The extremist faction of New Yorkers for Abortion Law Repeal, headed by Cisler (NARAL's secretary) and Clapp, had just won control from Ms. Arlene Emery Brown, Emily Moore, and Ruth Smith (NARAL's treasurer). The extremists opposed the licensed physician requirement, insisting that abortion could only become completely available to women if performed by "paramedicals"—nurses, medical technicians, and others trained in the procedure. Holding out for all or nothing, they pushed their boycott of the Cook bill through the "New Yorkers" board and general membership, although the Smith faction claimed both meetings had been packed and votes unfairly counted.

NARAL's Executive Committee now faced a torturous decision. Although most members favored paramedicals (and NARAL would back this stand at its annual convention in the fall), we recognized that no legislature would accept paramedicals in the immediate future, and voted to intensify our campaign for the Cook bill. This left NARAL with a New York affiliate in conflict with its policy. Meanwhile, the seceding faction of "New Yorkers" established a new organization, the Committee for the Cook-Leichter Bill, with Ms. Ruth Frey and Ruth Smith as cochairmen. NARAL agreed to support them, offered a small loan, and placed a few officers on the new board.

The Cook-Leichter Committee now had to build a political machine almost overnight—focusing the pressure of fifty cooperating organizations on legislators. At the first meeting, on February 5, seventy-five delegates from these organizations agreed on a campaign of letters, telegrams, phone calls, and personal visits to Albany. The Committee, as well as NARAL, got out an immediate mailing. Each affiliate sent their own mailings—as well as constantly prodding members to write personal notes. It was a rare morning when a legislator's desk wasn't piled with repeal literature.

This strategy was implemented by on-the-spot lobbying. The Committee frequently sent its officers to Albany. The Abortion Reform Association, which had swung from reform to repeal, hired Ms. Elizabeth Elkind, a vivacious lobbyist with long experience on Blumenthal's staff, to work in Albany for the session. The New Democratic Coalition, Civil Liberties Union, and Council of Churches, among others, kept representatives circulating the Capitol.

The Albany command post was Cook's office. Each day legislators and lobbyists caucused briefly to evaluate strategy, pinpoint legislators that needed particular attention, and assess the wavering votes. Cook kept a small book with notes on every legislator. No one was included in the "Yes" column until unshakably committed.

The prime objective of our strategy was building upstate support. Our resources were scanty at first—the clergy, NOW chapters, and Women's Liberation campus groups. Buffalo women concentrated on Assemblyman Arthur Eve, a crucial vote. Syracuse women helped gather 2,000 signatures to persuade Assemblyman Kenneth Bartlett. The Citizens Committee for Abortion Law Repeal in Watertown staged an abortion forum at Trinity Episcopal Church, where one Assemblyman, a shaky vote, pledged himself to the Cook-Leichter bill before 300 constituents.

The backbone of our upstate forces were dozens of Unitarian-Universalist churches and their Women's Alliances. At a political workshop on November 8, 1969, led by the Rev. Robert Eddy of Schenectady and Rev. Nicholas Cardell of Albany, a NARAL board member, the women agreed to work in five neighboring Assembly districts, setting up tables at all churches on Sunday with stationery and literature to encourage letters to legislators. Ms. Kay Dingle and others lobbied at the Capitol, and special "lobbying days" were scheduled for women across the state, who were fed and housed overnight by the Alliance and taken in groups to visit their legislators.

NARAL focused on our metropolitan political base. I asked Eugene Nickerson, a college classmate and Nassau County Executive, to support the Cook-Leichter bill, and he produced a ringing statement. Since Mayor John V. Lindsay of New York City had just been re-elected with considerable reform Democratic support after losing the Republican primary (his party then), I wrote Borough President Sutton, "Now that he owes so much to you and other reform leaders, I wonder if this isn't the time to exert real pressure on him to take this [repeal] stand." Councilwoman Carol Greitzer, NARAL's president, introduced a Council resolution in favor of the Cook bill, sponsored by over half the members. On March 8, 1970, the *New York Times* announced, "MAYOR ENDORSES ABORTION REPEAL." [14]

The most damaging gap in our coalition of supporting organizations was the Medical Society of the State of New York, which met on February 3. We put together a packet of literature and covering letter signed by Dr. Bernard Nathanson, NARAL's medical committee chairman, and hand-delivered it to two hundred delegates. Despite the swing toward repeal in medical polls, and some fervent allies among the psychiatrists and New York City and Nassau delegations, we failed to budge the Society's leadership, which harassed the Cook-Leichter bill through the final roll call.

In late February the campaign received a startling boost. Senator Brydges, the slight, ruddy-faced, bustling Majority Leader, whose approval was virtually mandatory for floor debate, announced he was ready to consider a Senate bill. By holding Senate debate first, the Assembly might avoid the furious bloodletting that had characterized its struggle in recent years. Another advantage was that the Senate Codes Committee chairman, Edward Speno, favored repeal, while Prescott Huntington of Assembly Codes remained an implacable enemy and could keep the bill bottled up.[15]

Brydges's strategy became an insoluble riddle in an increasingly tangled campaign. He ordered his staff to prepare his own bill to replace the Paterson bill, the Senate replica of Cook-Leichter. Amazingly, it turned out to be the ideal, "pure" repeal bill—removing abortion from the criminal code and eliminating all restrictions, including the licensed physician requirement.

During those frantic days of drafting, Senators tried to uncover the final wording of the bill. "We thought we were being taken down the garden path," confessed Ms. Ross Graham, Ohrenstein's legislative assistant.

When the bill emerged in printed form as pure repeal, the accepted explanation of Brydges's strategy was that the Majority Leader had hatched the ultimate plot—a bill so radical and shocking it would be overwhelmingly destroyed in the Senate. "It's a hoax, a conspiracy by the archenemy of reform," cried Senator Seymour Thaler, Democrat, of Queens. One lobbyist overheard Brydges remark in the Senate restaurant, "I have the votes to beat it." Cook observed, "I would say nobody expected that bill to pass." [16]

"Brydges and his staff were just playing games," Graham insisted. "They didn't realize both the public and Senate were ready for this bill."

"I think that Brydges just miscalculated, and that had he not made this miscalculation, we wouldn't have this bill now because there's no question he could have stopped it in committee," Leichter concluded.

Senator Clinton Dominick, who worked energetically lining up Republican votes, rejected the conspiracy thesis. "I think Senator Brydges felt that as leader of the Senate and as a Catholic, and that as someone personally opposed to abortion reform or abortion repeal, he should do nothing to use his power as majority leader to impede or block the bill in any way," he commented, "so he bent over backwards not to block the bill." [17]

Whatever Brydges' motivation, he was undoubtedly caught off guard by rising Senate support. Even the Catholic lobby remained unconcerned through early March.

The Cook-Leichter Committee and NARAL, on the other hand, went after the Catholic lay vote. On February 25 and March 6, we sent lengthy telegrams to every Senator, signed by the New York State Catholic Women for Abortion Repeal and over 75 community leaders, emphasizing that "Many of us oppose abortion for ourselves but believe our church should not impose its will on our non-Catholic neighbors." This theme, voiced by Senators Laverne and Paterson from the start, obviously influenced other Catholic legislators. Senator Ralph Marino of Nassau-Suffolk, a Republican Catholic and uncommitted vote, announced, "I'm not going to foist my religious beliefs on others."

Freedom of choice in abortion, unfettered by religious dogma, eventually swung the votes of a number of upstate Protestant Republicans like Senator Dalwin Niles who were "big on freedom of the individual," as a legislative aide put it. Niles concluded that "A large proportion of women were in favor of this bill even though many were of the Roman Catholic faith." [18]

Another crucial vote, dependent partly on religious influence, was Senator Paul Bookson, an Orthodox Jew with a considerable Orthodox constituency in his lower Manhattan district. The Orthodox (by contrast with conservative and reform Jews) often opposed abortion. To offset this opposition, the American Jewish Congress and local Jewish groups produced a flood of letters and telegrams for the Cook bill. A second factor was that Bookson, an old-line Democrat, had a large bloc of reform Democrats in his area. Ohrenstein told him bluntly, "Abortion is a reform issue, the only issue that will infuriate reformers in your district if you vote No. It's not a threat but a political reality—if you vote against the bill, we'll fight you in a primary and beat you."

When the Senate took up the bill on March 18, Dominick and Paterson counted 29 sure votes with 29 needed for passage out of 57. "Barring a few shaky votes, we had a pretty good count," Graham noted. Every Senate seat was filled in the vaulted chamber, the mood strangely hushed. Dominick led off the debate, speaking quietly. Since no woman sat in the Senate, he offered his wife's personal thoughts—a startling approach for this reserved man. He explained that he and his wife had agreed to have no more children. His wife had sworn that if she ever became pregnant again, she would go to any lengths for an abortion—even the worst underworld abortion—if the Senate couldn't guarantee women their health and safety by passing this bill today. Here was the crux of the bill—the right of a woman to good medical care in place of underground butchery.

On the first vote, Bookson passed. "We were really worried," Graham recalled. Sitting on the side of the chamber, near Bookson's seat, she announced to an associate, loud enough for Bookson to hear, "We'll have to run a primary against him." Assemblyman William Passanante, a proabortion Catholic from the same district, came down the aisle and talked fervently with Bookson.

When Senator Theodore Day, who had never revealed his position, voted Yes, there were gasps throughout the chamber. "I remember Brydges spun around, really shocked," Leichter reported. Then James E. Powers, a Rochester Democrat, voted Yes, and the whole chamber stirred with excitement. "It was a lovely free gift," Graham explained. "We never knew his vote, but he came from a poor district and grasped the need for abortion." [19]

Lieut. Governor Malcolm Wilson, a Catholic strongly opposed to abortion, "really blew his cool," one Senator described it. "When he saw this thing, he just didn't believe it." [20]

On the second roll call, Bookson voted Yes. Brydges, who supposedly had been told by Bookson the day before that he would pass, turned ashen white. "Brydges never thought it could happen," a lobbyist concluded.

At the twenty-ninth and winning vote, a ripple of applause, the only demonstration of the evening, broke out in the chamber. The final tally was 31 for the bill (18 Democrats and 13 Republicans) and 26 opposed. Calling the passage "historic," even the *New York Times* was jolted by a victory that "may seem like too sweeping a reform of too restrictive a statute." Brydges himself, the next day, apparently dispelled the thesis that he could accept a "pure" repeal bill, and told reporters "he would consider further legislation to modify [it]. . . ." [21]

The Senate vote electrified the state. Many people took repeal seriously for the first time, and our organization mounted a campaign of letters and telegrams to the Assembly that dwarfed anything in recent decades. The Catholic Church, too, swung into furious action, with pastoral letters from all dioceses urging parishioners to a final stand. With the Assembly bill bottled in Codes Committee by chairman Prescott Huntington, the next week became a maze of backstage maneuvering.

A tall, aristocratic, sixty-three-year-old Republican, a graduate of St. Mark's and Harvard, who favored yachting as much as he disliked abortion, an Episcopalian although his brother had become a Catholic priest, Huntington ruled Codes majestically. Of twenty members, eleven were Catholics. Twelve votes were needed to pass a bill to the floor. Ironically, Cook, as chairman of the Education Committee, shared an extensive Capitol office with Huntington. "It got very complicated," an aide recalls. "We tried to stay hidden in an inside office when we were planning strategy."

Although Senate passage, as well as Duryea's pressure on Codes, ensured the bill would come out of committee eventually, Huntington and the conservative bloc demanded severe restrictions on the Senate version. Committee repealers like Stanley Fink and Joseph Dowd of Brooklyn refused to budge, but Milton Jonas of Nassau and Kenneth Leasure of Endicott, who were close to Cook, informed her of the need for compromise. Two changes were proposed: first, that abortion be legalized only up to 24 weeks from the commencement of a woman's pregnancy (after that, only to save her life); second, that abortion only be performed "with her consent" (a phrase requested by Huntington, concerned about pressure on teenagers; and by black militants, fearful of possible genocide).

Although Cook, Leichter, and other sponsors agonized over the 24-week limit, they decided it was the only way to save the bill. Cook called me in New York for NARAL's opinion. It plunged the Executive Committee into a two-day crisis. To accept 24 weeks would mean the first retreat from our repeal position. It was a compromise, perhaps slight, but still a wrenching compromise for a movement founded on the right of abortion without restriction.

On the other hand, the compromise would affect only a handful of women. In practice, almost all applicants would seek abortion within 24 weeks, most within 12 weeks when the procedure was safest. The few that delayed until after 24 could probably be accepted under the "life" provision of the bill—an assumption that proved accurate over the next few years.

The NARAL Executive Committee debated back and forth in hour-long telephone conversations. The decision became even more painful when a few trusted advisers opposed the compromise. But Cook and Ohrenstein, in whom NARAL had unstinted confidence, insisted that the bill was dead without the 24-week clause. It was a matter of weighing NARAL's philosophic stand against the reality of almost unrestricted abortions for thousands of women—over 200,000 a year in New York, as it turned out. Reluctantly, fully aware that a pure repeal bill might be even harder to get now in another state, we agreed to the compromise.

The bill came out of Codes with the necessary 12 to 8 vote, but Dowd and Fink also accepted the compromise at the last moment, to make it 14 to 6. On March 23, the new version was printed and sent to the Assembly.

The next week started with rising tensions—an angry rally of 2,000 feminists in Manhattan's Union Square on March 28, a squabble in Queens when thirteen members of the American Jewish Congress accused Western Union of "deliberate deception" in changing the wording of telegrams to their assemblyman from support of the bill to opposition. These were essentially flyspecks in the last stages of a campaign that depended on a score of uncommitted or shaky Assembly votes. Every organization in the movement now concentrated on a final strategy to win them.[22]

A Brooklyn assemblyman, for example, who wanted to support the Cook bill, was threatened with a fight in the Democratic primary, as well as with Catholic reprisals. One influential politician saw to it not only that the majority of political clubs in the district pledged the assemblyman their support, but also convinced his primary opponent that the abortion issue should not be injected into the upcoming campaign. The assemblyman also depended on the endorsement of the Liberal Party, which made it clear its help was linked to his abortion stand. He voted for the bill, and eventually won his primary easily.[23]

Assemblyman Arthur Eve, a Buffalo Democrat and the only black member outside New York City, had been harassed by black militants on the genocide issue. NOW's Buffalo chapter asked a group of black associates to survey black opinion, and Barbara Gelobter convinced Eve from the survey that three out of four blacks supported the Cook-Leichter bill. Paterson, Sutton, and other black leaders stressed the demand of low-income blacks for abortion, and the necessity of black unanimity in the Assembly. Every black member but one, as it turned out, voted for the bill. Still, at the first vote on March 30, Eve was absent with a "splitting headache." At the final roll call on April 9, he switched to Yes at the last minute, one of four crucial votes.

No legislators suffered a worse ordeal than Catholics who backed the bill from the start. Mary Anne Krupsak, an original sponsor, came from a devout Catholic family. Her father's pharmacy, already hurt by the depressed economy of the area, suffered even further when neighbors—including her own sister-in-law—picketed the premises against abortion. Ostracized at home, she was singled out by a Catholic demonstration on the Capitol steps, authorized by the Bishop of Albany, in a day of mourning for legislators supporting "murder." [24]

At the first roll call on March 30, she voted No. "We just couldn't believe it," an associate recalled. "When I ran into her in the corridor, I couldn't even talk to her. Her husband told me, 'Leave her alone. Don't push her. She'll come around.' A few days before the final vote, she called me and said, 'Don't worry. I'm okay.' She switched back to Yes, one of the critical switches."

Despite a final drive by Catholic bishops, who ordered a pastoral letter against the bill read in all churches on Easter Sunday, March 29, Assemblywoman Cook was confident of 76 votes when she brought the bill to the floor the next day. In the cavernous Assembly hall, with the sun seeping through the cathedral-like stained glass windows, Cook told legislators, "I submit to you we are not considering here today abortion on demand—we have that already. The only question is how abortions are to be had. Right now, if you have $25, you get an abortion in a back alley under the most abominable conditions, but if you have $2,500, then you can go elsewhere and get a proper abortion. . . . We now have abortion on demand. . . . What we are here to do is to put the illegal abortionist out of business."

Three attempts were made to amend the bill from the floor, but Cook had the forces to defeat them by voice votes. At 5 p.m. Speaker Duryea announced that 42 members still wanted to speak on the bill. Blumenthal described the scene as "total confusion." Between 10 and 11 p.m., Hulan Jack of Manhattan, a black and a Catholic, and Herbert Miller of Queens left the hall, but first recorded their votes as Yes with the teller—votes that have been traditionally counted throughout Assembly history. It was not until 1 a.m. the next morning that the roll call began.[25]

With the Assembly in an uproar, the teller announced 73 votes for the bill, 71 against. The Miller and Jack votes already recorded, and Speaker Duryea's pledge to provide the 76th vote if needed for the majority would have carried the bill. At this hectic moment, Duryea announced he would not count the two absent votes. The bill was defeated. Acting quickly so that the bill could be brought up again, Cook moved to have it tabled.

It was the first time in the memory of political experts that votes recorded prior to the roll call had been rejected. "I thought I had the bill," Cook observed. "Miller made an impassioned speech in favor of it, and everyone saw Jack vote and heard him." Miller, whose district was overwhelmingly behind the bill, burst into tears the next day when he heard this unprecedented decision and accused Duryea of "altering the tally sheet and changing the outcome of the vote." [26]

Still, Duryea had probably acted within his parliamentary rights. If he had cast the deciding vote on top of two absentee ballots, he might have been subject to sharp attack, even legal challenge, from his own Republican party, predominantly opposed to passage.

The first week of April was a struggle to protect every affirmative vote both from extremists in the movement and the Catholic Church. The New Yorkers for Abortion Law Repeal, which had been sniping at the bill from the start, attacked it on radio and in a press conference, insisting, "We feel that what we are likely to get through court action is actually *better* than what we will have if the Dominick-Cook bill becomes law."

Church pressure on six or seven Catholic assemblymen became intense. "The tales I got of the pressures were unbelievable," Cook recalled. "We had nuns and priests walking the floor of the session, and that was a horrifying thing—it turned my stomach," a Bronx Senator observed. Within two days, Cook knew that three Catholic Assemblymen—Joseph Lisa, Democrat of Queens, Anthony Stella, Democrat of the Bronx, and possibly Hulan Jack—would switch from Yes to No.[27]

Stella, a veteran reform Democrat, had been largely influenced in his first, affirmative vote by an almost unanimous bloc of reform legislators and leaders in his area working for repeal. But the counterpressure from the Catholic Church in his strongly Catholic district built up steadily before the second vote. "He almost had a breakdown from the pressure," an associate commented. "The priests were calling him 'murderer,' and his friends were saying, 'You're not even an Italian any more.' He was in tears the day of the final vote."

Lisa was a regular Democrat from an Italian district, almost a fiefdom, inherited from his father. Although the growing influence of reform Democrats persuaded him to vote Yes at first, the Catholic counterattack switched him to the opposition. Later he claimed he might have stayed with Cook-Leichter if the bill had offered more protection for freedom of conscience for Catholic hospitals. (No Catholic hospital, however, has since reported being forced to perform abortion.) Another assemblyman from the area insisted, "I think it boils down pretty much along religious lines, and if people deny it, I think they're putting their head in the sand."

"My monsignor raised Cain with me; he practically lives with me," Jack admitted.

"My church saw fit to have my name called as one who acted improperly. And had it printed in the parish newspaper," Rangel, who still refused to change his affirmative vote, told the Assembly. "But I am hurt and disappointed that the clergy did not so act when we tried to stop the welfare cutbacks, or get decent housing, or get basic health care and hot water for our people."

Like Rangel, Anthony Mercorella, a Catholic and Bronx Democrat, withstood church pressure. His polls showed that constituents favored the bill 3 to 1 (including 60 percent of Italians, the most sizable bloc; and almost all Jews). Still, the protest directed against him after his first affirmative vote was harsh. Pastoral letters were read in all parishes. When he attended church on Sunday, April 5, with his family, the priest cited him by name as promoting "murder." His wife and children cried, and his twelve-year-old kept asking if he really committed murder. That afternoon, three priests visited him, but he refused to change his stand. In addition to a barrage of calls from prominent Catholic laymen, Mercorella received petitions signed by 600 parents. The petitions had been distributed at parochial schools (without authorization, as it turned out), and the children instructed to bring them home to their parents for signing.

"It was very tough pressure," concluded a Brooklyn Catholic legislator who was attacked in his church while a young daughter sat at his side, "but I think the lay Catholic is far ahead of the church on this issue." [28]

Rather than let the pressures build further, on April 8 Cook suddenly presented a motion to take the bill from the table. This would usually have been accomplished by a voice vote, but with twelve members absent from the chamber, an upstate Republican opponent of the bill demanded a "slow roll call," requiring a recorded Yes or No tally. Smarting from criticism of his ruling on March 30, Speaker Duryea ordered that absent members be brought to the chamber "by whatever force necessary"—a ruling the *New York Times* called "unique in the memory of the oldest member of the Legislature." The motion passed 92 to 52, but it was hardly indicative of a swing to Cook-Leichter since many opponents voted Yes in annoyance at the roll call.[29]

The mood of the repeal forces was grim on the morning of April 9. We had definitely lost Lisa and Stella—that had been confirmed by their vote against the motion the day before. If Eve and Krupsak switched to affirmative, we could balance that loss. If all other commitments held firm, we would still need one vote to reach 75, and Hulan Jack remained a remote possibility.

Meeting in the corridor outside Cook's office, Gelobter and I ran over a list of black leaders in New York City who could exert some final pressure on Jack. I called Borough President Sutton's office, but he had left early that morning, driving to Albany specifically to talk with Jack. We dashed back and forth to the phones as if motion itself could relieve our panic, then returned to a small, eddying circle of associates, afraid that to stand still for a moment would be an admission of defeat.

The floor of the Assembly began to fill at noon. The galleries, a wave of heads craned toward the stage below, had waited for hours. Legislative aides and lobbyists crowded the edge of the floor. The debate began, not in the reasoned mood of the Senate, but with angry, rasping speeches. "It's all window dressing for the cameras," a legislative aide observed.

Amendments came one after another—to change the time limit from 24 to 15 weeks, to confine abortions to hospitals and clinics. All were beaten down. Calmly, holding the floor like a patient headmistress, Cook insisted, "It's just a matter of deciding that you can't sit here and decide when and how an abortion is to be performed—they are being performed now."

Supporters of the bill emphasized that their districts demanded repeal. An upstate Republican cited 2,000 petition signatures at his office. A Bronx Democrat spoke for "thousands of blacks who died in back rooms because they could not afford a good abortionist."

"Murderers!" screamed an elderly woman from the galleries. "You are murderers, that's what you are." Police quieted the woman, and Speaker Duryea warned against further demonstrations.

Opponents hammered at this theme. "I point my finger at every member who votes for this bill and say, 'You, sir, killed these innocent children,' " cried a Queens Republican. "It will permit a mother to kill her child for whatever reason strikes her fancy," added a Suffolk Republican. "It will put our civilization back to the days before Moses," an upstate Republican observed. "Abortion is the invention of the middle class who don't know what to do with affluence," concluded Manuel Ramos, Bronx Democrat, the only Puerto Rican voting against the bill.[30]

At 4:30 p.m. Cook called for the vote and there was a sudden hush throughout the chamber. The moment had come after five years of incessant campaigning. Once I would have been lucky to draw a few dozen listeners at a political club. Now the legislators of the most powerful state were ready to revolutionize the social and political traditions of a nation. This was the ultimate test—no hospital or residence requirements as in Hawaii, no boards, no restrictions in the first 24 weeks of pregnancy.

The slow roll call began, each member recording his Yes or No vote, an Assemblyman occasionally rising to interrupt the count and speak for his limit of two minutes to explain his vote. There was a mood of resigned desperation as the votes followed their expected pattern. We lost Lisa and Stella, gained Eve and Krupsak. When Jack voted No amidst gasps of anguish from the rim of the floor, defeat seemed certain. The vote would end in a 74 to 74 tie unless we could pick up one switch in the final, fading moments of the count.

Just seconds before the clerk would announce the tally, with all television cameras focused on Speaker Duryea's proclamation of defeat, Assemblyman George Michaels, Democrat of Auburn, rose to his feet. His first words were lost in the hubbub, but he seemed to be referring to an appointed position on a state commission that had been promised him. In a faltering voice, his face drained of color, his hands shaking so that he could hardly hold the microphone, Michaels said, "I am releasing Speaker Duryea from any commitment." Now the television cameras swung toward him. Those sitting nearby saw his face contorted, his eyes filled with tears. He fumbled with his thick black-framed glasses. His hair, too, is black with only edges of gray. A prosperous, reserved, 59-year-old lawyer, Michaels seemed to be talking about his firm. "My law firm may suffer from what I am doing," he mumbled. His sentences were fragmented, coming in bursts. Still, everyone had finally realized that Michaels was about to switch his vote, and a slow rumble of whispers, like a flood dammed too long, began to build throughout the chamber. "I just burst into tears. It was unbelievable," Elizabeth Elkind recalled.

Michaels was talking about his family, his three sons, a devout Jewish family whose second son was a student at Hebrew Theological Seminary and had served as Assembly chaplain one day earlier in the session. "My own son called me a whore for voting against this bill," he explained, his voice breaking with sobs. "He said for God's sake don't let your vote be the one that defeated this bill. I can't go back to a family seder and say I defeated the bill. I must keep peace in my family."

His words slurred and broke. Often it seemed as if he could not go on. "I had nothing prepared," Michaels recalled. "I had only a few minutes to think what I was doing. I had spent thirty-seven months in the Marines in World War II, much of it in combat in the Pacific, under mortar fire. This was worse than anything. It was the summit of my life."

Michaels, representing a heavily Catholic district, addressed his last words to Speaker Duryea: "What's the use of getting elected if you don't stand for something. I realize, Mr. Speaker, that I am terminating my political career, but I cannot in good conscience sit here and allow my vote to be the one that defeats this bill—I ask that my vote be changed from 'No' to 'Yes.' "

The Assembly seemed to break up in chaos. Repeal leaders, legislative aides, secretaries, some with tears streaming down their faces, pushed their way onto the floor, shouting, embracing each other or anyone they could find. A few of us reached Constance Cook and kissed her, still unruffled, aloof from the turbulence around her. Almost no one noticed that Duryea had asked that his name be called so that, as Speaker, he could cast the essential vote and make the count 76 to 73.

Michaels remained slumped in his chair. A Staten Island Republican stood over him, shouting, "In other words, vote your family and the hell with your constituents." Other legislators intervened, slapping Michaels on the back, shaking his hand. When he took the freight elevator to his office, tears still wetted his face. Those who came to congratulate him found him bent over his desk, his head in his hands, sobbing.

The next day, April 10, the Senate took up the Assembly version of the bill with the 24-week limitation. Except for a few Catholic Senators, the debate was short and calm. Majority Leader Brydges read the fantasied thoughts of a fetus about to be aborted from an article in a Catholic magazine and apologized for his fervor, "I'm sorry, Mr. President. I try to keep myself under control." An upstate Republican Catholic pleaded, "Kill this bill and you will please the people of New York. What's more, you will please God."

As a Catholic himself, Laverne retorted, "I have been told that I am obviously not a good Catholic . . . even that I am a phony. . . . But many do not support the church on this issue; sixty percent of the Catholics in my district don't agree with the church on this issue. I don't think I have the right to force my morality on anyone else."

The Senate then approved the bill, 31 to 26, the same vote recorded for its own version. Although Cardinal Cooke called on the Governor to veto it, Rockefeller promptly signed it into law on April 11 (to take effect on July 1, 1970). "Women's liberation played an important part in the passage of this bill," he noted, also crediting "the wives of the Senate and the Assembly [who] put this bill through." As a political afterthought, Rockefeller called the bill a Republican measure. Despite the crucial role of Republicans like Constance Cook and Clinton Dominick, 49 Republicans in the Assembly voted against the bill, with 30 for it; 20 Republicans in the Senate opposed it, with 13 supporters.[31]

George Michaels' last-minute switch converted an obscure legislator into a national hero whose vote helped produce a social revolution. At the same time, he became a political pariah in his own district.

Born in New York City, a graduate of Cornell and Brooklyn College Law School, Michaels started his law practice in Auburn in 1933, involving himself in Democratic politics. With the area traditionally Republican, he was a frequent sacrificial candidate until election to the Assembly in 1960, the first Democrat in fifty years to represent Cortland and Cayuga Counties. With a constituency about 65 percent Catholic, he automatically opposed Blumenthal's moderate abortion bills. His political associates considered him such an implacable enemy of Cook-Leichter that his sudden reversal intensified the hatred of his own party.

Still, at least two years previously Michaels had begun to agonize about his political stance. An admirer of President John F. Kennedy, he recognized that his voting record—support of welfare cuts, for example—often contradicted his beliefs. "My family and friends kept harping on these conservative votes," he admitted. "I could see the hypocrisy eating away at me."

None of the abortion repealers, except Cook, who was an old friend, spotted him as a potential convert. Even on March 23, when he addressed a meeting of medical societies in his area and opposed any abortion bill without "essential safeguards to the mother," no one considered this small crack in his opposition worth investigating. "Once he claimed he wanted to vote for the Cook bill but was scared to death of it," a legislative aide recalled.

The inner turmoil that Michaels suffered in late March had been accelerated by his family. His twenty-three-year-old son, Jim, grasped the urgency of abortion while working as a rabbinic urban intern in the ghettos of Cincinnati, and kept telling his father, "You're prostituting yourself, voting constantly with the conservatives." None of his family called him a "whore," as Michaels said in his Assembly speech. "I just insisted it would be disastrous if his vote defeated the bill," Jim recalled.

Michaels's twenty-nine-year-old son, Lee, now his law partner, is married to a gentle woman with strong social convictions, a Unitarian by birth who insisted on converting to Judaism and drove eighty miles a day for religious instruction. The Sunday before the final vote, Michaels visited Lee and Sarah, whom he particularly admires and loves. "She said I had to vote Yes on abortion," Michaels recalled. "I told her the bill would pass anyway in a year or two, and I didn't see an immediate crisis. She looked at me for a long time and said, 'In the meantime, thousands of women will be butchered in underworld abortion.' I thought about that often in the next days."

Despite his Catholic constituency, Michaels received a dozen phone calls a day before the final vote, and was stopped frequently on the streets of Auburn by voters insisting on his support for Cook-Leichter. He was jarred when an old friend, a Lutheran minister, told him he would work for Michaels' defeat at the next election if he didn't vote Yes. Assemblyman Eli Wager, a Nassau Democrat who shared an office with Michaels at the state capitol, pressured him to switch in the last week. "This thing was tearing me apart," Michaels said.

Assemblyman Stephen Hansen, a Manhattan Republican supporting the bill, rode down in the Capitol elevator with Michaels and his wife after the first vote on March 30. Unseen by the Michaels, he heard Helen Michaels ask, "What are you going to do if there's a tie on the final vote?" Michaels responded, "I wish to God I knew."

Michaels obviously hoped he would never have to face this crisis. "I was counting on Jack, Lisa, and Stella," he admitted. "On the day of the final vote, I was horrified when they switched to No. Wager left his seat and sat next to me. 'It's going to be a tie,' he said. I told him he was crazy. But after Stella's switch, I went into a panic. Everything my family had told me kept pounding in my head."

Hansen, who must have hoarded the memory of that elevator conversation, came over and sat next to Michaels. "He looked at me steadily—he's got very penetrating eyes—and said, 'George, you're our only hope,' " Michaels recalled. "I really panicked then. I was jumping around in my seat. With only a few minutes left, I was so shaken I couldn't rationalize what I'd do. I managed to get to my feet. If I'd had time to think, I wouldn't have mentioned the Duryea appointment—it was to the State Crime Commission. Somehow I thought I had to release him from this commitment so my District didn't consider the appointment a payoff for my switch. I wouldn't have made so much of my family either. But it was all scrambled in my mind, and everything came out jumbled. All I really meant to say was, 'What's the use of getting elected if you don't stand for something.' That's what my vote was really about."

Every element of irony and retribution from classic Greek tragedy coalesced at the end—the irony of a legislator who dreaded a bill and became its salvation, the vengeance heaped on a politician by his own district after the climactic act of his career. Within weeks after passage of the abortion bill Michaels was branded a traitor by his party. With two Auburn priests organizing a scurrilous campaign against him, the Cayuga County Democratic Committee, mainly Catholic in membership, rejected him by 72 to 53 for another term. Michaels had to compete in a primary without organization or money. Although NARAL, Planned Parenthood, and others raised a small campaign fund, the abortion movement had no framework of clergy or campus militants in his area. The opposition goaded him constantly—a typical ad headlined: "Can you trust this man?" The *New York Times* concluded, "The obvious retaliation by the Cayuga Democrats against a respected attorney and Assemblyman is a horrow show of machine politics at its worst." [32]

Overwrought, traveling by himself on a speaking tour, Michaels ran his car into a bridge abutment on May 28 and was hospitalized—eleven days in intensive care alone—with his right leg shattered and seven fractured ribs. Unable to complete his campaign, he was beaten in the primary, and running on the Liberal line in the general elections, defeated again.

"Perhaps it spells the end of George Michaels' career," he wrote, "but I know for a fact that this measure [the abortion bill] will be a landmark in American history. It will settle once and for all the limits of legislative interference with private family life."

Here was the final political irony—the unknown legislator who had struggled for years to emerge from mediocrity catapulted into history by forces far beyond himself. While the abortion movement concentrated on a dozen crucial votes, and it was Krupsak, Eve, and others who had wrestled publicly with abortion and gone through months of torment, Michaels, seemingly in spite of himself, had become the margin of victory, and at the same time had found peace with himself. "He's a much better, a much happier man for what he's done," Jim Michaels concluded.

Destroyed by his local party, Michaels gained larger honor beyond his political horizons. He received 10,000 letters from all over the country thanking him for his vote. The American Ethical Society gave him its Humanist of the Year award. Recently, two women about forty years old, both accidentally pregnant and vehemently opposed to further childbearing, came to Michaels's house. One, a Catholic with five grown children, told him, "I suddenly realized—how wonderful! I can do something about it at last." After they had thanked Michaels, they added, "We're starting a new club—the 'Thank God for George Club.' "

NOTES

1. *New York Times*, April 4, 1968, p. 1; January 30, 1969, p. 22; January 10, 1968, p. 1.

2. This, and preceding paragraph: *New York Times*, April 18, 1969, p. 1.

3. Research study on New York campaign (unpublished), The Population Council, New York, Chap. V, pp. 9–10.

4. *Newsday*, August 15, 1969; Speech on Assembly floor, March 30, 1970.

5. Population Council study, *op. cit.*, Chap. V, p. 26.

6. *Ibid.*, Chap. V, p. 26.

7. *New York Times*, April 4, 1968, p. 1.

8. *New York Times*, January 10, 1968, p. 1.

9. New York *Daily News*, January 14, 1970.

10. *New York Times*, February 19, 1970, p. 51.

11. Personal letter, Assemblyman Blumenthal to Ms. Cusack, February 19, 1968.

12. New York *Daily News*, January 19, 1970.

13. Population Council study, *op. cit.*, Chap. V, p. 15.

14. New York *Post*, February 17, 1970, p. 14; *New York Times*, March 8, 1970, p. 38.

15. *New York Times*, February 19, 1970, p. 51.

16. *New York Times*, March 11, 1970, p. 1; Population Council study, *ibid.*, Chap. V, p. 24A.

17. Population Council study, *op. cit.*, Sen. Dominick interview, p. 4.

18. Research project on New York campaign, Center for Criminal Justice at the University of Chicago Law School (unpublished), p. 3.

19. Population Council study, *op. cit.*, Chap. V, p. 24.

20. Chicago Law School project, *op. cit.*

21. *New York Times*, March 20, 1970, pp. 46, 52; March 22, 1970, Review of Week, p. 8.

22. *New York Times*, March 29, 1970, p. 35; April 7, 1970, p. 72.

23. Chicago Law School project, *op. cit.*

24. *New York Times*, April 11, 1970, p. 17.

25. *New York Times*, March 31, 1970, p. 1; April 5, 1970, Review of Week, p. 4.

26. *New York Times*, April 9, 1970, p. 46.

27. Chicago Law School project, *op. cit.*, p. 33.

28. *New York Times*, April 11, 1970, p. 17; April 10, 1970, p. 42.

29. *New York Times*, April 9, 1970, p. 1.

30. *New York Times*, April 10, 1970, p. 42.

31. This, and seven preceding paragraphs: *New York Times*, April 10, 1970, p. 42; April 11, 1970, p. 17; April 12, 1970, p. 47.

32. *New York Times*, April 23, 1970, p. 36.

Special Reference:

Background material has been drawn from the Research Project of the Center for Criminal Justice at the University of Chicago Law School under the direction of Prof. Hans Zeisel, for which the author is greatly indebted.

CHAPTER ELEVEN

THE SECOND CRISIS: MAKING THE NEW YORK LAW WORK (1970–1972)

The jubilation over passage of the New York law had hardly begun to fade when we were plunged into a new crisis. "Battle due on abortion guides," the New York *Post* announced on June 10, 1970. "Administrators at public hospitals turned down interviews saying, 'There is nothing to talk about. We don't know what we're going to do,' " a reporter described the chaos.

On July 1, the first day the law took effect, over 350 applicants telephoned the Family Planning Information Service to plead for appointments. One fortunate case, forty-four-year-old Mary S., who had two grown-up sons and was "too old to start again with a baby," checked into Flower and Fifth Avenue Hospital where her abortion and overnight stay cost her $750. By contrast, Eleanor P., a nineteen-year-old college student, fifteen weeks pregnant, was shuffled from hospital to hospital for weeks before she got an appointment. Kathy D., an eighteen-year-old Boston student, who came to New York with $300 painfully saved, was told at her doctor's office for the first time that she needed $275 more for overnight hospital costs. "I was crying so much I couldn't see the buildings," she recalled. Of 2,000 women who registered that first day, less than 100 received abortions.[1]

The chaos began to build from the moment the law was passed. Senator Brydges and other Catholic legislators threatened amendments that would cut the time limit of abortion to pregnancies of 12 weeks.

Dr. Hollis S. Ingraham, the State Health Commissioner, announced "guidelines" to restrict abortion to hospitals or clinics, compounding the danger of an increasing jam-up of applicants. Dr. Mary McLaughlin, New York City's Health Commissioner, established further "guidelines" for the city on May 21, with such complex and costly requirements that small clinic or medical-group abortion would be virtually eliminated.

The financial exploiters and privately owned or proprietary hospitals rushed into this vacuum, buying up facilities where early abortion would cost $800. It was a wave of madness. The electorate had secured an epochal law. Now the politicians, the Catholic hierarchy, and old-guard medical factions were determined, as I told the press, to "cut the law to shreds." [2]

In a series of emergency meetings, NARAL agreed on a policy of confrontation. "PHYSICIANS URGED TO DEFY CITY AND STATE GUIDELINES ON ABORTION," the *New York Times* headlined our stand. Councilwoman Greitzer and I announced "A Radical Plan for Outpatient Clinics to Meet the Abortion Crisis." By limiting abortions to hospitals and their clinics, the "guidelines" not only contravened the law, but deprived hospitals of critically needed bedspace. Most applicants would be forced into high-priced hospitals, or in desperation would have to resort to underworld practitioners. Abortion would thus become "an unobtainable privilege," concluded Borough President Sutton.

The only rational solution was a network of freestanding, ambulatory clinics, using the new vacuum method of abortion under local anesthesia—a thin tube connected to a vacuum pump which quickly removes all fetal tissue. Women in early pregnancy could be admitted and released in three or four hours. The cost would be only a fraction of overnight hospital care—we proposed a limit of $300, preferably $200. With a skilled staff, such a clinic could process 200 cases a day—a prediction that our medical chairman, Dr. Nathanson, eventually fulfilled at his own clinic.

The medical advantages of clinic treatment had already been proved at the Johns Hopkins University Hospital and the University of California School of Medicine, San Francisco, where ambulatory abortions had long been performed "simply, efficiently, and effectively . . . with high medical standards," according to a pilot project study.

Supporting our demands, Assemblyman Leichter stressed, "The Legislature specifically rejected a requirement that abortions be restricted to hospitals. . . ." A *New York Times* editorial added, "To require that abortions be performed only in hospitals is to risk further crowding of those already overcrowded facilities, to the detriment of all patients." [3]

The core of our attack was an all-day training session for physicians on July 1, "The First Symposium on Non-Hospital Abortion Procedures," held at New York University Medical Center. A few days before, New York City officials backed down from their rigid "guidelines." "OK ABORTIONS IN DOCS' OFFICES," the *Daily News* announced in front-page headlines. The Board of Health would approve abortion in clinics and doctors' offices if "stringent requirements" were met.

That same day, the American Medical Association's House of Delegates reversed decades of inflexible opposition and voted to approve abortions in accredited hospitals with the consent of two consulting physicians. Another breakthrough followed—agreement by the Blue Cross and Blue Shield plans to cover abortions for single women and dependent children.[4]

NARAL's symposium—"a direct confrontation with the guidelines," I told reporters—drew an audience of over one hundred physicians and public health officials for lectures on every aspect of clinic and office abortion. With Dr. Nathanson as chairman, the panels presented experts on vacuum aspiration, the saline technique for late abortion, psychological counseling, and the rights of physician and patient under the law. At a luncheon for the press, Borough President Sutton urged "the greatest variety of abortion facilities . . . especially in ghetto neighborhoods where they can reach women who do not know they can obtain legal abortion or do not know where to go for one." My statement, reiterated, "We will use every form of action—law suits, demonstrations, sit-ins if necessary—to protect the meaning of the law, and insure it becomes a law for the poor as well as the rich." [5]

At that moment, the first freestanding clinic, the Women's Medical Center, started performing abortions at prices under $100. To develop a clinic "where the patient's dignity is paramount," the Center stressed counseling services, "designed to relax the patient and make her feel she is supported in her decision to terminate her pregnancy." In the first six weeks, the clinic handled 262 first trimester abortions. Dr. Irvin Cushner, associate professor of obstetrics and gynecology at Johns Hopkins, called its "total patient management . . . competent, compassionate and nonjudgmental" and its counseling "particularly commendable." [6]

The confrontation intensified throughout that summer. Determined to keep abortion under its control as a traditional in-hospital procedure, the medical hierarchy refused to "agree that the supermarket or freestanding clinic approach will meet the usual supervised hospital standards," as Dr. S. B. Gusberg, chairman of obstetrics and gynecology at Mount Sinai, put it. At the City Health Department's public hearings on guidelines on July 15, Women's Liberation pickets marched with signs, "Raped by the Medical Bureaucracy." One witness, who had just had a clinic abortion, testified, "This amendment [to the Health Code] would leave the woman open to the same kind of mental, financial, and social exploitation which she was subjected to in the old days." Dr. Nathanson stressed the health hazards of hospital chaos—waiting lists of at least five weeks were already forcing early abortion cases into the more risky period of late, saline treatment.

"Should anything short of abortion on demand be the result of the historic law, then we have perpetrated a fraud and a hoax," Borough President Sutton concluded.

The attack on hospital chaos was led by Rev. Howard Moody and Ms. Arlene Carmen of the Clergy Consultation Service, who had set up a new unit, Clergy and Lay Advocates for Hospital Abortion Performance. From hundreds of complaints that flooded their office each month, and constant surveillance by their staff, they presented a documented condemnation of the bureaucratic morass. By August 3, city hospitals had done only 2,343 abortions with a backlog of almost 3,000 cases. Women had to wait two weeks for their first examination, and four to five weeks more for an abortion. On September 18, at least three city hospitals stopped performing abortion. Another had a waiting list of eight to ten weeks. The majority refused all cases after the first trimester of pregnancy although the law allowed up to twenty-four weeks. Hospital officials often refused applicants living outside the hospital district, and demanded cash on the spot from the poor, uncovered by insurance or Medicaid. "A woman can spend days and weeks shoved from hospital to hospital before she finds one willing and able to assist her," Moody observed. "I see now changing the law doesn't mean much. You have to change the system." [7]

Another agency attacking hospital chaos was the Women's Abortion Project, an offshoot of the Women's Liberation center in a loft building on Manhattan's West 22nd Street. Specializing in assisting young, low-income, single women, it was a brash, radical group, working anonymously with no titles or officers. The only sign on its door was the Liberation symbol—the palm of a hand with four, raised fingers. Inside, its meeting room and nests of officers were lined with bulletin boards, where abortion meetings competed with NOW lectures, picketing lists, and karate lessons. As a result of its volume of applicants, almost one hundred calls a day, the Project had developed a network of doctors and small clinics at prices under $100. It campaigned for abortion price ceilings set by the City. "Women have been traditionally victimized by the archaic practices of the health establishment, paying with both their dollars and their lives," its representative told the hearings.

Despite massive documentation presented by Moody's committee and other agencies, the City's Health Services Administration insisted the waiting list had been reduced to a "manageable level of about 2,500" by September 16. Moody called it "a game of illusion." The illusion was obviously timed for the Board of Health's announcement the next day. We had lost the struggle. The guidelines would be incorporated into the Health Act on October 19, and thus have the force of law. It was a serious setback, particularly bitter since the Board had submitted no evidence that clinics or medical groups failed to equal hospital standards.[8]

NARAL demanded the medical statistics be brought to the public. We invited a panel—Congressman Ed Koch, Borough President Sutton, and other public officials—to examine evidence on October 16. We sent telegrams to all Board of Health members, inviting them to testify. Not one showed up or even answered the telegram.

At our hearings, Dr. John Holloman, past president of the National Medical Association, Dr. Jack Lippes of the University of Buffalo, developer of the intrauterine "loop" bearing his name, and Dr. Tietze of the Population Council all corroborated the advantages and medical proficiency of the clinics. The crucial statistics came from the

Women's Medical Services on East 73rd Street. It was the product of Rev. Moody's imaginative planning. Almost immediately after passage of the New York law, he visualized a nonprofit clinic of uncontestable medical standards, an outlet for Clergy Consultation referrals from the East Coast and Midwest. He asked Dr. Hale Harvey to organize it. A slim, intense, thirty-eight-year-old physician, a Ph.D. in philosophy with a Master's degree in public health, who had processed abortion referrals for the clergy in the South, Harvey quickly expanded his clinic from a suite of offices to a whole floor in his medical building. The top price was $200, with about 25 percent accepted free.

The cornerstone of its treatment was psychological counseling—one counselor for each patient. All counselors, who had previously gone through abortion themselves, and had a college degree or nursing training, spent at least an hour with the patient, discussing her reasons for abortion, explaining the procedure on models of reproductive organs, alleviating any fears and anxieties. Later, they explained contraceptive methods for subsequent use, and during the procedure, stayed with the patient as an assistant nurse.

When Dr. Harvey and the Rev. Moody presented their statistics to our panel, their clinic had performed 4,000 first trimester abortions. There had been no deaths (compared to three deaths in accredited hospitals by November, which the City's Chief Medical Examiner attributed to "extenuating circumstances"). Further, the complication rate —perforated uterus, infection, hemorrhaging—was only one-third of that in all New York City hospitals. And it was improving steadily—eight perforated uteruses in the first 2,000 cases, for example, with only one in the second 2,000.

Despite this evidence, the guidelines were incorporated into Article 42 of the Health Code on October 19, threatening to "make it even more difficult for women to obtain legal abortions here," as the *New York Times* reported. We were still determined to hold the clinics and medical groups. We had to test the meaning of Article 42, comply with it where possible, ignore it when necessary. We had to make the clinics so essential to medical care, and so invulnerable politically that they would become the dominant force in abortion. It took grinding pressure over many months to force the Health Department into a *modus vivendi* that preserved the scope of the abortion law within the requirements of Article 42.[9]

An influential factor was the incorporation of the Health Department into a new super-agency, the City's Health Services Administration. Its director, Gordon Chase, a devoted supporter of the abortion law, announced on November 24, that his policy was "to work with those services gearing up to comply with Article 42." HSA henceforth cooperated with clinics and medical groups that would meet reasonable medical standards, including laboratory, plasma supply, and resuscitation equipment, and sign a "back-up" agreement with an accredited hospital no more than ten minutes away to handle any emergency problem.

Most clinics met these standards. In fact, new clinics with considerable private capital, like Park Med Associates with a $500,000 investment and eight treatment rooms in a glossy, Park Avenue South office building, easily exceeded the City's requirements. Similarly, Planned Parenthood's nonprofit clinic on Second Avenue and 22nd, which opened in January, 1972, was a superbly equipped center requiring a heavy investment.

These two, along with Bronx Planned Parenthood and, of course, Women's Medical Services, were the giants. They quickly passed HSA inspection, and since the City had no licensing power (only the pressure of Article 42 to enforce standards), secured their licenses from the State Department of Health.

At least twenty other clinics and medical groups in the City, however, ignored the State's licensing authority. Many were essentially enlarged offices. Dr. Michael Truppin's Manhattan Women's Center of Fifth Avenue, for example, had three treatment rooms, two waiting rooms, and a counseling office where Truppin and another obstetrician-gynecologist performed 50 to 80 abortions a week. His top charge was $110, probably the lowest in the City. He had a laboratory, plasma, oxygen, resuscitation equipment, a large staff of registered nurses, and a social worker for counseling. After numerous inspections by State and City officials, he refused for two years to apply for a license, insisting, "The State only controls hospitals and clinics. We don't fit in either category. We're a medical group, an abortion service for Madison Avenue Hospital."

Here was the confusion in authority between State and City—the "gray area" that NARAL claimed protected Dr. Truppin and similar services. The Abortion Rights Association of New York, successor organization to the Committee for the Cook-Leichter Bill, inspected all facilities through its medical committee and included Truppin and others on its approved list. The heart of the confrontation was our insistence that such medically qualified groups at low prices must be maintained to prevent the abortion law from being decimated.

Women's Medical Services was the symbol of clinic achievement from the start. Performing more abortions per week than all municipal hospitals combined, it quickly outgrew its 73rd Street facility. Its administrative complexities, however, overburdened Dr. Harvey, who had the additional disadvantage, even as supervisor and not an active physician, of lacking a New York medical license. The clinic decided on a complete overhauling. Its name was changed to the Center for Reproductive and Sexual Health. It took a long lease on a vast floor-through on East 62nd Street, and constructed in the gutted interior often two-floors high, the most lavish and best-equipped clinic in the country, virtually a hospital.

For its new medical director the clinic selected Dr. Bernard Nathanson, NARAL's medical committee chairman, a shrewd, tough administrator as well as an eminent obstetrician-gynecologist, whose probing mind ranged in research studies from James Joyce to Russian political history. Nathanson enlarged his staff to thirty part-time obstetricians, signed an agreement with Lenox Hill as back-up hospital, and expanded his counseling and nursing departments so that he could handle two hundred patients a day.

One significant impact of the clinic was its price—the original $200 reduced to $125 by 1972. Soon drawing patients from other services, it forced down the price at other clinics and hospitals, and within a year most ambulatory abortions in the City averaged about $150.

An equally important statistic was to bolster NARAL's original position that all first trimester abortions should be done on an ambulatory basis. Although seven inflexibly conservative chiefs of obstetrics-gynecology clung to in-bed abortion in municipal hospitals, by mid-1971 80 percent of early abortions in the City were performed on an ambulatory basis.[10]

The crowning achievement of the clinic was its low complication rate. In Dr. Nathanson's study of its first 26,000 cases in the *New England Journal of Medicine*, not only were no deaths reported, but the complication rate proved equal to or better than the most sanguine statistics in the United States or Europe. Uterine perforation, for example, ran only 1.4 per 1,000 cases; incompletes requiring further curettage, 3.5 per 1,000; hemorrhages, 2.1 per 1,000.

After Dr. Tietze's similar study of about 73,000 abortions, he found, "The rate of complications, repeat curettage and admission to hospital for inpatient care, reported by Nathanson, are significantly lower than those ascertained by the Joint Program for the Study of Abortion (JPSA) for outpatients in teaching hospitals." Dr. Tietze rated Nathanson's clinic "not only the largest but also one of the best of its kind," concluding, "There is no doubt in my mind that a freestanding clinic under competent leadership can provide abortion services of high quality, at a reasonable price, during the first trimester of pregnancy, in a setting that is more acceptable to many women than a hospital." [11]

By mid-1971, we had emerged from the crisis. With the pressure of Rev. Moody's committee and other agencies, and HSA's determination to make the New York law a model for the country, the administrative morass had been virtually eliminated. Waiting lists at municipal hospitals were cut to one or, at most, two weeks. Only one clinic, generally recognized as far below standard, had been closed. NARAL's confrontation policy had not only produced a remarkable adjustment between health officials and the public's demands, but eventually guaranteed a successful balance between the City's medical standards and unobstructed availability of low-cost abortion.

This achievement hinged, above all, on the increasing dominance of freestanding clinics and medical groups. In the last half of 1971, their case load soared to 52,000 (almost all first trimester) out of a total of about 110,000 abortions in the City. Municipal hospitals, by contrast, performed only a little over 12,000.[12] But, while the main crisis was now almost solved, a crass political deal threatened to destroy Medicaid abortions for the poor.

Pressed for votes to pass his budget in April 1971 Governor Rockefeller was blocked by five, upstate Republican Senators, led by James H. Donovan of Chadwicks, all violently opposed to the abortion law. If the Governor agreed to eliminate Medicaid payments for abortion except when a woman's life was imperiled, the *New York Times* reported, they would support his budget. The Governor got his votes, and on April 8, his Commissioner of Social Services announced the Medicaid ban.

Calling the deal "a vicious, inhumane thing to do," the *New York Times* pointed out that "medically indigent women, who may already have several children and not want any more, could be denied the opportunity to have an abortion," and be deprived of "the equal protection of the laws to which they are clearly entitled."

HSA predicted that thousands of children each year would be added to the welfare rolls. In contrast with the average abortion cost of $64 at municipal hospitals, city and state agencies would now have to fund a pre- and postnatal expense of $800, and an average relief cost of $624 annually.[13]

The further irony of this deal was that Senator Donovan and his supporters had consistently attacked rising welfare costs. Yet the obvious result of the Medicaid ban would be to increase such costs. Donovan's only logic was that if he hated welfare, he hated the abortion law more.

After New York City opposed the ban in court, supported by Planned Parenthood and a score of health and welfare agencies, the State Supreme Court declared the ban unconstitutional on May 18, 1971, and the Appellate Division supported this decision on July 1. Unexpectedly, since these rulings were mainly based on the equal protection clause of the Fourteenth Amendment, the Court of Appeals reversed both favorable decisions and upheld the Medicaid ban by a 4 to 3 vote on February 10, 1972.

It was a shocking discrimination against the poor, "a double standard of justice . . . perpetrated by the highest state court," as the *New York Times* pointed out. While the City pressed its appeal to the Federal court, HSA's Gordon Chase promised, "Our municipal hospitals will not turn away any city resident, regardless of whether she can pay." In effect, the City continued to treat every Medicaid case as if her life was imperiled.[14]*

* On August 24, 1972, adopting much of State Supreme Court Justice Samuel A. Spiegel's original reasoning, a three-judge Federal court in the Eastern District of New York overturned the Medicaid ban, ruling that it denied indigent women equal pro-

The Medicaid ban, however, was only a peripheral glow in Donovan's vehement offensive, backed by Majority Leader Brydges, to overthrow the new law entirely. They pulled together an increasingly potent coalition—not just the Catholic hierarchy and satellite "Right to Life" organizations, but a sizable percentage of Republicans elected with Conservative Party backing. The Conservatives, rooted in the Catholic electorate, had made impressive gains in 1970.

This counterattack began in the fall of 1970 when two Long Island assemblymen and supporters of abortion were "accused of being 'Hitlerites' and 'murderers'," according to the *New York Times*, and "subjected now to a scurrilous political attack far exceeding any bounds of fair campaign comment." Such demagoguery influenced few voters; both were reelected. Assemblywoman Cook also won that fall by 24,000 to 10,000. Assemblywoman Krupsak, a Catholic and Democrat in a usually Republican district, and Senator Laverne, also a Catholic, were both harried by opponents for their strong abortion stands, but still reelected easily. On the negative side, Senator Dominick was defeated, more likely for his liberal record in a conservative district rather than his abortion vote—an assemblyman in his district, for example, winning despite his support of abortion. The only real defeat that could be attributed to abortion was a Republican Catholic, whose Conservative opponent split off enough votes to elect a Democrat who, as it happened, stood solidly behind the abortion law.[15]

The counterattack now moved to another level—the passage of local ordinances in counties, villages, and townships, which prohibited small clinics and medical groups, and almost wiped out abortion in many areas. The drive was aimed particularly at suburban counties on Long Island and in Westchester, where the Catholic opposition was organized and "almost hysterical . . . as if they are hunting witches," Ms. Helen Gurley Brown, editor of *Cosmopolitan*, observed.

After the Orangetown Council in Rockland County prohibited his medical group by local ordinance, Dr. Young W. Kim went to the

---

tection of the laws. With the only possible appeal to the U.S. Supreme Court (not taken at this book's publication date), it appeared that the Federal court order would be accepted throughout New York State.

State Supreme Court, where Justice Leonard Rubenfeld enjoined the ordinance, and ruled that a local municipality could not preempt the function of the state on health legislation.

The Albany County Legislature went even further—prohibiting both nonhospital abortion and the establishment by any hospital of a satellite clinic. As one member pointed out, the ordinance not only contravened the state law, but created "a virtual monopoly" for the few local hospitals practicing abortion.[16]

In Nassau and Suffolk Counties on Long Island, a stronghold of Right to Life groups, Hempstead, Huntington, Babylon, and other towns rushed through ordinances to outlaw freestanding clinics like Bill Baird's Parents Aid Society. Six of the eight Hempstead board members were Catholics, and a Catholic at the hearings cried, "One day you will have to stand up before God in judgment of your souls, and give an accounting of the souls you allowed to be killed." The ordinance was upheld by a State Supreme Court Justice although Baird insisted, "he should have disqualified himself because he is a Roman Catholic." Baird appealed to the Appellate Division of the State Supreme Court, which, as in the Orangetown, N.Y., case, overturned the ordinance, ruling, "The regulation of the practice of medicine, and there can be no doubt that such is the effect of this ordinance, is not a matter of an inherently local nature and has never, as far as we can perceive, been considered to fall under the authority of the village level of government." [17]

The Suffolk Board of Health compounded this assault with its own countywide ban on January 28, 1971. The impact on poor patients was particularly harsh. Few Suffolk hospitals accepted abortions, and then at a prohibitive cost, as the Health Commissioner himself admitted—as much as $600 with Medicaid paying only $85 of the doctor's fee. As a result, Planned Parenthood officials testified that two-thirds of their patients had to be sent 100 miles to low-priced New York City clinics—transportation costs and baby-sitting fees adding to the burden.

The plight of the poor became even harder after the Medicaid ban. With Nassau Medical Center the only public hospital in Nassau and Suffolk counties, the County Executive outlawed all Medicaid abortions (in contrast to New York City), and closed the Nassau hospital on February 28, 1972, not only to the poor but even paying abortions.

The struggle over local ordinances was finally resolved by the Court of Appeals on June 1, 1972, when the state's highest court upheld the Appellate Division in the Baird case, and ruled that local governments could not interfere with the practice of medicine, including abortion.[18]

Meanwhile, Baird's Boston University case of 1967—his arrest for distributing contraceptives at a lecture—finally reached the U.S. Supreme Court.

Exonerating Baird, the Court, in a 6 to 1 decision on March 22, 1972, declared unconstitutional Massachusetts' ninety-three-year-old law which forbade selling or giving birth control devices to unmarried women. Although the decision only applied to birth control laws in two states (the abortion referral charge had been dropped along the way), Justice William J. Brennan, the only Catholic on the Court and author of its opinion, gave strong constitutional sanction to the freedom of decision regarding parenthood. "If the right of privacy means anything," the Court declared, "it is the right of the individual, married or single, to be free from unwarranted intrusion into matters so fundamentally affecting a person as the decision whether to bear or beget a child." The crucial issue, which the Court would soon decide in other cases before it, was whether "bear and beget" applied to abortion as well as contraception.[19]

The Catholic counterattack against the abortion law and political candidates supporting it reached a peak of hysteria in 1971 and 1972. "Could you be a murderer? You could be if you believed in legalized abortion," cried the headlines of a *New York Times* advertisement for the Mt. Vernon, N.Y., "Committee for Life." Speaking at St. Patrick's Cathedral in New York, Archbishop Humberto S. Madeiros of Boston called the law "a most horrendous situation crying to heaven for vengeance." An Albany rally on the Capitol steps, addressed by Senator Donovan, constantly applied the "Nazi" label to abortion supporters.

Such language was hardly accidental—"Right to Life" committees from thirty-seven states met in Illinois in the summer of 1970 to coordinate their campaigns. The Church's official campaign handbook against Washington State's abortion referendum, supported by Archbishop Thomas A. Connolly of Seattle, and directed to a compulsory training session for priests, instructed, "We want the clergy to stop talking about abortion and start talking about killing . . . to force the use of such words as 'killing babies'. . . ." Billboards across the state, showing a human fetus in the palm of a hand, admonished voters in blazing type: "KILL Referendum 20, not ME!" [20]

This ferocity of language reached the point where a coalition of Protestant and Jewish organizations in New York City issued a statement on May 6, 1971, protesting, "We resent this implication of being murderers." Rev. Moody attacked "the Church's decision through its Cardinals and Bishops to . . . go for emotional outburst and frenzied labeling of the opposition as 'baby killers' and 'wanton murderers'—what is new is the call for *all out* religious warfare. . . ."

This warfare was often waged illegally through tax-exempt church funds. In the 1971 fall primaries, priests in at least six churches at Sunday mass opposed the reelection of R. Bradley Boal, a prominent member of the Westchester legislature and chairman of the Committee for Legal Abortion—and "substantially contributed to his narrow, unexpected defeat," according to the *New York Times*. "A bad precedent and a very dangerous thing when any church gets this involved with politics," observed the assistant Republican county chairman.

At 14 of 29 Catholic churches in Orange County, California, at Sunday mass in August 1970, voter registration tables were set up outside. The priests then asked their congregations to switch registration from Democratic to Republican parties in protest against the "abortion on demand" plank passed by the California Democratic convention. In one church alone, 530 members became instant Republicans.[21]

The threat came not just from the political use of the Church's far-flung structure, but the channeling of tax-exempt funds and facilities into the fight against abortion. The Washington State anti-abortion campaign cost an admitted $300,000—the amount from untaxed church funds could never be pinned down because the courts refused to intervene.

Our own resources were minuscule. NARAL's national office in New York, consisting only of a paid executive director, secretary, and part-time assistant, existed on $30,000 in 1970, not reaching $50,000 until 1972. As a non-tax-exempt political organization, we could get no help from foundations except Prynce Hopkins in San Francisco and Joseph Sunnen in St. Louis.

Another Catholic offensive came in the courts. Prof. Robert Byrn of Fordham University Law School, a forty-year-old bachelor who headed the Metropolitan Right to Life Committee, devised an audacious strategy. Byrn went to the State Supreme Court to get himself appointed legal guardian of "Infant Roe," a fictitious fetus symbolizing all unborn fetuses between four and twenty-four weeks of gestation scheduled for abortion. Then he petitioned for an injunction to halt all abortions in municipal hospitals while his guardianship claim went through the courts. With Justice Francis Xavier Smith on the bench, Byrn secured both the injunction and a favorable decision on guardianship on the grounds a fetus constituted a human person.

With the future of the abortion law hinging on a clear-cut definition between fetal "life" and a living *person,* Prof. Means published an exhaustive study of all legal precedents, submitted to the court as an *amicus curiae* brief for NARAL, and concluding:

> What neither the original Constitution nor any amendment ever did was to call or treat a fetus as a person. Although the Enumeration clause commands each decennial census to count "the whole Number of . . . Persons"—a command repeated in the Fourteenth Amendment—no census-taker from 1790 to 1970 has ever counted a fetus. The reason is that at no stage has the Constitution ever treated a fetus as a person.

The Appellate Division of the State Supreme Court agreed. In the first decision of a higher court on this crucial point, it ruled that the unborn fetus was not a "legal" person, and upheld the constitutionality of the state abortion law. Overturning Justice Smith in a 4 to 1 decision on February 25, 1972, the court declared, "In our opinion, the extent to which fetal life should be protected is a value judgment not committed to the discretion of judges but reposing instead in the representative branch of the government." [22]

Another danger to the abortion law was the torrent of commercial referral services which made staggering profits from the anguish and ignorance of women. This sleazy exploitation required only a secretary, a telephone, and a splurge of advertising. Linked to a few profit-hungry hospitals and clinics, the commercial services simply booked an applicant for abortion at $300 to $500, and kept from $100 to $150 of the fee themselves. Often they increased their kickbacks with "packaged" deals for hotel space, overnight deluxe hospital rooms, and similar unnecessary frills.

The plunder from such referrals was revealed by the U.S. District Court which estimated that in six months the Abortion Information Agency on Manhattan's West 86th Street "had a gross income of $5,500,000, of which $1,200,000 represented fees charged to clients."[23]

The system itself was a fraud. The same referral that cost a woman $150 could be secured free from a battery of nonprofit agencies—Family Planning Information Service, Clergy Consultation's forty branches, the Women's Abortion Project, and scores of NARAL, Planned Parenthood, and ZPG affiliates across the country. Unfortunately, desperate women, particularly the young in rural areas, were gulled by high-pressure advertising (billboards, matchbook covers, even banners drawn by a blimp along Miami Beach) before they consulted a nonprofit agency.

NARAL, which had supported only *free* referral services at its 1969 convention, now issued a position paper, "NARAL Wants Commercial Referral Services Outlawed." After an investigation of Abortion Information Service and other profiteers by the State Attorney General and State Senate Committee on Health in February 1971, the Attorney General closed down AIS. Upholding the ruling, the State Supreme Court declared, "The law which sought to emancipate women from servitude as unwilling breeders did not intend to deliver them as helpless victims of commercial operators for the exploitation of their misery." The Appellate Division supported this opinion. Meanwhile, the Legislature acted on its own, and on July 1, 1971, outlawed all profit-making referrals within the boundaries of New York State.[24]

The most disturbing problem remained abortion in late pregnancy. Originally, it was performed by hysterotomy requiring an incision in the lower abdomen and surgical removal of the fetus—the disadvantages including scarring and the possibility that a future birth might have to be delivered by Caesarean section. This technique had recently been discarded for saline induction or "salting out." A woman who delayed past the 12- or 13-week deadline for vacuum aspiration, had to wait till the 16th week, at which time saline becomes effective. Part of the amniotic fluid surrounding the fetus was drawn out by needle in the abdominal wall, and then replaced with an equal amount of saline, or salt solution, which brought uterine contractions and expulsion of a nonliving fetus 12 to 48 hours later.

Saline abortions in the first months of the law turned into a nightmare for most applicants. Municipal hospitals frequently rejected them. At the few performing saline up to eighteen or twenty weeks (each made their own rules, none allowing up to twenty-four weeks despite the law), physicians were poorly trained. Salines at Bellevue during the first year, for example, were almost always done by young resident physicians. Nurses frequently shunned these cases, or treated them with spite and cruelty. Even by 1972, only three municipal hospitals specialized in the procedure.

As a result of medical inexperience, the saline technique led to an early calamity that threatened the continuance of post-thirteen-week abortion. When performed correctly, saline ended all signs of fetal life before expulsion. Any error—the wrong amount of saline injection, for example—could result in a brief flash of fetal life, like a muscular twitch. On December 19, 1970, HSA reported that in the first five months or so of the law, twenty-six fetuses had remained alive for a few minutes or hours. One case (which turned out to be a twenty-eight-weeks pregnancy and should never have been approved for abortion) was actually resuscitated and became a living child.

The problem had to be met bluntly. After NARAL asked Dr. Nathanson to investigate, he studied the twenty-six cases and reported that "none of these live births should have occurred." Citing a series of 400 salines at New York City's Women's Hospital, and 900 at Stanford University Hospital, with not one live birth, Nathanson concluded that the twenty-six cases "resulted from inexperience." [25]

There were two obvious solutions. The first was to launch a campaign, through subway-car cards, leaflets, and other public announcements, to convince women to take early pregnancy tests and increase the number of first trimester abortions, a campaign that proved successful within six months.

The second solution was to train more gynecologists in the saline procedure. An expert saline unit at Manhattan's Park East Hospital under Dr. Thomas Kerenyi, assistant professor, Mt. Sinai School of Medicine, quickly eliminated most saline complications. In a medical paper analyzing the first 530 consecutive patients, he listed only minor complications—ten instances of fever, six of hemorrhage; and retained placenta for four hours or more, removed by instrument, curettage, or spontaneous expulsion, in about 10 percent of all cases. Intensified training at medical schools and municipal hospitals would soon make saline what Dr. Kerenyi called a "relatively simple technique." [26]

Despite almost two years of struggle against the Catholic hierarchy, political wreckers, and medical reactionaries, the New York law had proved a phenomenal success. The annual total of abortions reached over 200,000. In terms of improved maternal health, the complication rate had been cut sharply—from 12.4 per 1,000 in the first six months of the law to 6.3 per 1,000 in the nine months ending in March, 1972.

More important, the complication rate for first trimester abortions had been cut to 2.8 per 1,000 in the last six months of 1971, a reduction of more than half since the start of the law. The first trimester rate for freestanding clinics was even lower, averaging about 1.1 per 1,000. As a result of early pregnancy detection and the elimination of waiting lists, over 80 percent of applicants now received abortion in the first trimester.[27]

Another measure of success was the drop in the death rate—maternal mortality ratios in New York City dropped by two-thirds the year after passage of the abortion law. Significantly, of four recent deaths, none occurred in the first trimester. The New York figure of 4.2 per 100,000, therefore, compared favorably with England and Wales where the death rate ran 25.5 per 100,000 (1968–1969), and with Sweden, where the rate was 18.1 in the mid 1960's. It even approached the impressive statistics of Eastern Europe (2.2 per 100,000 in Czechoslovakia, for example, from 1962 to 1966), which kept deaths to a minimum by confining almost all abortions to the first trimester.

A further advance in maternal health was achieved by a sharp reduction in "incompletes"—the bungled cases rushed to emergency wards, maimed by self-abortion or underworld operators. Ten municipal hospitals had to treat an average of 480 a month at the start of the law, but only 199 in the last six months of 1971.*

Out-of-wedlock births—often having a detrimental impact on health rates since unmarried women usually receive the poorest prenatal care—declined for the first time in twenty years of official record-keeping. Legalized abortion, therefore, was not only destroying the old underworld system, but was ending pregnancies that formerly would have become unwanted births.[28]

An essential factor in maternal health gains was an almost equal distribution of abortion among all ethnic, racial, and economic groups. Of New York City residents, 43.4 percent of abortion cases were non-white, and 10.4 percent Puerto Rican in the first fifteen months—proving that the early opposition of black militant men had little effect on black women.

With 600,000 *legal* abortions performed throughout the country in 1972, a stunning increase from 8,000 in 1966, New York was not only meeting the demands of its own residents but of many Eastern and Midwestern states. New York City abortions for nonresidents (including upstate) now exceeded those for residents by over 2 to 1. The demand, moreover, imposed no strain on facilities, most clinics in 1972 having a greater weekly capacity than applicants. Calling New York's abortion law "very, very clearly a progressive piece of legislation" and "terribly important," HSA's Gordon Chase urged, "I would like to see other states with this kind of legislation." [29]

NOTES

1. This, and preceding paragraph: *Manhattan Tribune*, May 2, 1970, p. 3; New York *Post*, June 10, 1970, p. 7; Testimony of Women's Abortion Project at NARAL hearings, October 16, 1970; *New York Times*, July 2, 1970, p. 1.

2. This, and preceding paragraph: *New York Times*, May 13, 1970, p. 37; May 21, 1970, p. 34; May 22, 1970, p. 33; May 30, 1970, p. 1.

3. This, and two preceding paragraphs: *New York Times*, June 10, 1970, p. 7; April 11, 1970, p. 17; June 3, 1970, p. 44; June 11, 1970, p. 18.

* After the liberalization of California's abortion law, the number of women treated for bungled, illegal abortion or self-abortion dropped from 800 to 100 at Los Angeles County-University of Southern California Medical Center.

4. This, and preceding paragraph: New York *Daily News*, June 26, 1970, p. 1; *New York Times*, June 26, 1970, p. 1; June 27, 1970, p. 1.

5. *Long Island Press*, July 2, 1970, p. 2.

6. *New York Times*, July 2, 1970, p. 43; "Procedures for Women's Medical Center" (unpublished), August 23, 1970; Personal letter, Dr. Cushner to Dr. Christopher Tietze, September 11, 1970.

7. This, and two preceding paragraphs: *New York Times*, June 25, 1970, Letters to Editor; July 16, 1970, p. 24; July 28, 1970, p. 35; *Village Voice*, October 15, 1970, p. 1; Rev. Moody, *et al.*, "The Unmasking of Hospital Abortion Performance in New York City, July 1–October 1, 1970" (unpublished).

8. *New York Times*, September 17, 1970, p. 43; September 18, 1970, p. 1; *Village Voice*, October 15, 1970, p. 1.

9. This, and preceding paragraph: *New York Times*, November 18, 1970, p. 75; October 25, 1970, News of Week, p. 12; H. Hale Harvey and Barbara Pyle, "On the Healthiness of 4,000 Abortions in a Free-Standing Abortion Service" (unpublished).

10. Jean Pakter and Frieda Nelson, "Abortion in New York City; The First Nine Months," *Family Planning Perspectives*, Vol. 3, No. 3, July 1971, p. 5.

11. Bernard Nathanson, "Ambulatory Abortion: Experience with 26,000 Cases (July 1, 1970 to August 1, 1971)," *New England Journal of Medicine*, Vol. 286, No. 8, February 24, 1972, pp. 403–407, 432; Christopher Tietze and Sarah Lewit, "Joint Program for the Study of Abortion (JPSA)," *Studies in Family Planning*, Population Council, New York, Vol. 3, No. 6, June 1972.

12. Health Services Administration, New York City, February 21, 1972.

13. This, and two preceding paragraphs: *New York Times*, April 2, 1971, p. 44; April 9, 1971, p. 28; April 3, 1971, pp. 26, 28; February 18, 1972, p. 34.

14. This, and preceding paragraph: *City of New York v. Wyman*, 66 Misc. 2d 402, 321 N.Y.S. 2d 695 (Sup. Ct., N.Y. County 1971), affirmed, 37 App. Div. 2d 700, 322 N.Y.S. 2d 957 (1st Dep't 1971), reversed, 30 N.Y. 2d 537, 281 N.E. 2d 180, 330 N.Y.S. 2d 385 (1972); *New York Times*, July 2, 1971, p. 8; February 18, 1972, p. 34.

15. This, and preceding paragraph: *New York Times*, April 28, 1971, p. 51; May 6, 1971, p. 1; November 2, 1970, p. 46.

16. *Kim v. Orangetown*, 66 Misc. 2d 364, 321 N.Y.S. 2d 724 (Sup. Ct., Rockland County, 1971); New York *Post*, May 1, 1971, p. 24; *Knickerbocker News*, December 30, 1971, p. 1; Albany *Times Union*, December 29, 1971, p. 1 B.

17. *Robin v. Hempstead*, 66 Misc. 2d 482, 321 N.Y.S. 2d 20 (Sup. Ct., Nassau County, 1971), reversed, 38 App. Div. 2d 758, 329 N.Y.S. 2d 678 (2d Dep't 1972), affirmed, 30 N.Y. 2d 347, 285, N.E. 2d 285, 334 N.Y.S. 2d 129 (1972); *Newsday*, June 16, 1971, p. 16; Long Island *Press*, June 16, 1971, p. 3; August 11, 1971, p. 1; *New York Times*, February 1, 1972, p. 34; 167; *New York Law Journal* No. 23, February 2, 1972, pp. 1, 4.

18. This, and two preceding paragraphs: Long Island *Press*, January 29, 1971; February 1, 1971; February 9, 1971; March 10, 1971; *New York Times*, March 24, 1972, p. 45; June 2, 1972, p. 41; *Newsday*, March 20, 1972, p. 23.

19. *Eisenstadt v. Baird*, 405 U.S. 438, 31 L. Ed. 2d 349 (1972); *New York Times*, March 23, 1972, p. 22; March 25, p. 30.

20. This, and preceding paragraph: *New York Times*, July 5, 1971, p. 17; April 28, 1971, p. 51; "The Who-When-How of the Campaign," by Wessels-Strachofsky, Inc., for Catholic Church training session of May 13–14, 1970.

21. This, and two preceding paragraphs: *Village Voice*, May 13, 1971; *New York Times*, September 16, 1971, p. 28; Lawrence T. King, editorial, *Commonweal*, October 9, 1970.

22. This, and two preceding paragraphs: *Byrn v. New York City Health and Hospital Corporation*, 38 App. Div. 2d 316, 329 N.Y.S. 2d 722 (2d Dep't 1972); *New York Times*, December 4, 1971, p. 29; January 7, 1972, p. 26; March 17, 1972, p. 40; Cyril C. Means, Jr., "The Phoenix of Abortional Freedom," New York Law Forum, Vol. XVII, No. 2, 1971, pp. 336–410.

23. This, and preceding paragraph: *State of New York v. Abortion Information Agency, Inc.*, 69 Misc. 2d 825, 323 N.Y.S. 2d 597 (Sup. Ct., N.Y. Cty., 1971), affirmed 37 App. Div. 2d 142, 330 N.Y.S. 2d 927 (1st Dep't 1971), affirmed 30 N.Y. 2d 779, 285 N.E. 2d 317, 334 N.Y.S. 2d 174 (1972); *New York Times*, February 10, 1971, p. 47; February 12, 1971, p. 38.

24. *New York Times*, May 14, 1971, p. 1; July 1, 1971, p. 40; July 2, 1971, p. 8; NARAL position paper, February 11, 1971.

25. This, and two preceding paragraphs: Susan Edmiston, "A Report on the Abortion Capital of the Country," *New York Times Sunday Magazine*, April 11, 1971, p. 10; *New York Times*, December 20, 1970, p. 15; Arnold Roufa, John Mackenzie, Harold Tovell, "Experience with Four Hundred Cases of Saline Induction," *Clinical Obstetrics and Gynecology*, Vol. 15, No. 1, March, 1972.

26. Thomas Kerenyi, "Technique of Late Abortion," S. Lewit, ed., *Abortion Techniques and Services: Proceedings of the Conference* (Amsterdam: Excerpta Medica Foundation, in press).

27. This, and preceding paragraph: New York City Health Services Administration release, February 20, 1972; April 25, 1972; Jean Pakter and Frieda Nelson, "Abortion in N.Y.C.," *Family Planning Perspectives*, Vol. 3, No. 3, July 1971, p. 10.

28. This and preceding paragraph: *New York Times*, March 17, 1972, p. 18; HSA release, February 20, 1972; Tietze and Lewit, *op. cit.*

29. HSA release, February 20, 1972; *New York Times*, September 27, 1971, p. 27.

CHAPTER TWELVE

WINNING THE WEST, TESTING THE MIDWEST (1970–1972)

"At some point, the tide favoring abortion legislation has got to be stopped," an official of the "Voice of the Unborn," the Catholic Church's political arm in Washington State, announced in early 1970. After its unexpected defeat in New York, the Church planned to make Washington its prime battleground. The repeal movement there had started slowly. After organizations like the Council of Churches formed a Citizens Abortion Committee, headed by Dr. Samuel Goldenberg, a University of Washington psychologist and NARAL board member, a coalition of feminists decided to make the abortion bill a test of radical power. Their demonstrations at the capitol in Olympia in March 1969, "blasted the abortion bill into a high priority item," the Seattle Radical Women concluded.[1]

Washington was almost torn apart by a campaign that exceeded New York's in bitterness. It was, in fact, two campaigns. First, the Legislature struggled with a bill that only passed with a referendum provision. Then the real campaign followed—the long months to convince the electorate to approve the bill at the polls on November 3, 1970.

The Catholic hierarchy had the best financed and organized lobby ever thrown against an abortion bill. Its strategy depended on conservative rural Protestants dominating the Senate far out of proportion to their numbers. Consequently, the Senate Rules Committee, made up mainly of conservatives from safe districts, buried the bill without hearings or debate in 1969. "The Washington State Senate is the only legislative body in the nation where a bill can be killed behind closed doors in an absolutely ironclad secrecy," a Senator noted.

The feminist coalition, Abortion Action Now, sent a delegation of fifty women to the capital on March 12, 1969. With churches across the state announcing the rally, the coalition brought almost 2,000 people to Olympia two weeks later, parading with signs and posters proclaiming "The Flying Fickle Finger of Fate Award to the Rules Committee." A police lieutenant tried to stop a delegation from entering the capitol building, scuffling with a few women until the State Attorney General approved their admission. They kept their abortion armbands on, leaving their signs outside.[2]

"The idea that poor and working women would make such a vociferous and angry demand on the august real estate dealers, lawyers and petty businessmen who run the state's government was stunning to the all-male Senate," a Seattle Radical Women newsletter commented.

The bitterness over the killing of the abortion bill without public hearings or debate was reflected in leading newspapers. A columnist for the Seattle *Post-Intelligencer*, Lorenzo Milam, bluntly attacked "the seven Catholics who help run our state from the comfort and power of the Senate Rules Committee in Olympia . . . two more who are married to Catholics, and a handful of others who quiver every time they get a call from the local representative of El Papa [the Pope]." Milam's column added, "Maybe someday the disciples of El Papa—at least those who sit on the Senate Rules Committee—maybe someday they'll realize that their God may not be the god of the rest of us . . . that the voice of their celibate 70-year-old Papa sounds like a curse to the rest of us." It was getting close to all-out war, compounded by the threatened boycott of the *Post-Intelligencer* by Catholic churches. Milam refused to retract, and left or was fired from the paper.

By 1970, the pressure for an abortion bill had reached the point where a large bloc of Senators threatened to force it out of Rules Committee from the floor—an expedient not used for eighteen years. Analyzing the bill's support, Dean Dorothy Strawn of the University of Washington said, "I'm seeing agreement from people of all ages and races, income groups and political viewpoint." The Rules Committee finally gave in, and the Senate passed the bill on January 30, 1970. The House followed a few days later.[3]

The bill allowed abortion only in the first seventeen weeks of pregnancy and included three other limitations. It required the husband's consent if living with his wife, or consent of a legal guardian for a girl under eighteen. It required ninety-day residency, and that abortion be performed in a medical facility approved by the State Board of Health.

The last requirement was particularly ironic since a Renton, Washington, physician had already challenged the old law with his own clinic. Dr. A. Frans Koome, a forty-year-old, Dutch-born father of two girls, announced the opening of his "Reproductive Crisis Clinic" for the practice of abortion in December 1969 and wrote Governor Daniel J. Evans that he had performed 140 abortions. The local police chief, Koome's next-door neighbor, raided the clinic, seized patient records, but soon found none of the women was willing to testify against their doctor. While the Washington State Medical Disciplinary Board called hearings with the intention of removing Koome's license, Koome kept on performing abortions even before the new law had passed.[4]

The referendum campaign was unique—not only the first time the abortion issue had been put to the voters, but the first time a state had been galvanized for nine months by frenzied debate. The huge sums raised by the Church's political fronts went into billboards and leaflets that accused such dignified proponents of abortion as medical societies and the clergy of fostering "murder." The lines between church and state were virtually eliminated—the minority leader of the House of Representatives, for example, addressing the May 13–14 forum which had been called by the Archbishop to train priests against the bill.

The feminist coalition struck back. "I deplore the arrogance and presumption of the Catholic Church in this matter," one feminist told a Seattle meeting. "You believe the fetus is a human being. Some people still believe witches ride around on broomsticks and a lot of other medieval, mystic hangovers." The Seattle Radical Women insisted, "We won't be glorified chattels any more."

On election day, November 3, 1970, the electorate approved the abortion bill by a vote of 56 to 44 percent. It was "a grand defeat for sexists and reactionaries," a University of Washington *Daily* columnist observed, and it climaxed a string of breakthroughs in 1970. With Washington added to California, the West Coast had been secured. New York was the anchor for the East—the District of Columbia, Maryland, and a few other states handling a limited share of the abortion demand. Now the critical problem for the movement remained the Midwest.[5]

In September 1969, Dr. Sidney Babbitz of Milwaukee, Wisconsin, was arrested on a charge of illegal abortion. Instead of defending the case on criminal grounds, his attorneys called in Joseph Nellis of Washington, D.C., who had represented Dr. Vuitch before the U.S. Supreme Court. Nellis shrewdly decided to go to the U.S. District Court to ask that the Wisconsin abortion law be declared unconstitutional.

On March 5, 1970, a panel of three Federal judges unanimously ruled in Babbitz's favor and supported the right of abortion before "quickening" (about four and a half months of fetal growth). Concluding that "the mother's right transcends that of such an embryo," the court announced "Upon a balance of relevant interests, we hold that a woman's right to refuse to carry an embryo during the early months of pregnancy may not be invaded by the state without a more compelling public necessity than is reflected in the statute in question."[6]

It was the first affirmative decision before a Federal panel, and cleared the way for early abortion in a clinic or doctor's office. With 38 percent of Wisconsin's population Roman Catholic, the reaction was violent. "Citizens Concerned for the Unborn" labeled the ruling "a disaster." A conservative legislator called it "typical of the sickness that is contagious in our Federal courts."

Although a few doctors and hospitals complied with the decision, the State Attorney General insisted that the ruling "legally affected only the right of Dr. Babbitz," and that other physicians relying on the judgment "run the risk of prosecution in the event the decision is reversed." Irritated that state officials "refuse to respect our judgment of unconstitutionality," the same three-judge Federal court announced on November 18 that "the only effective way to protect or effectuate our judgment is to issue an injunction permanently enjoining the defendants [the district attorney of Milwaukee, in particular] from henceforth prosecuting others." [7]

This injunction, a precedent in abortion litigation, which protected Babbitz and other doctors in their fight to perform abortion, went to the U.S. Supreme Court. Unfortunately, with recent rulings that Federal panels should generally abstain from state criminal proceedings, the Supreme Court vacated the injunction on April 19, 1971. Nellis then requested the U.S. Court of Appeals, 7th Circuit, to reinstate the injunction and finally to agree to a stay. Both requests were refused in August and October 1971.[8]

With Babbitz scheduled to go on trial for the original abortion charge, Nellis asked the Wisconsin Supreme Court for declaratory relief on the grounds the state law was unconstitutional, and that the doctor had been deprived of his constitutional rights. In January 1972, the court granted this petition, and then suddenly in April, reversed itself without a hearing. The first judicial breakthrough in the Midwest was wiped away. After two years of litigation, Dr. Babbitz now had to stand trial in criminal court.

To plan for an offensive in Midwest legislatures, NARAL had already called a conference in Chicago on January 9, 1971, "a high-level strategy meeting of key legislators and activists," as I wrote in the invitation. State senators and assemblymen, as well as leaders of our affiliates in Iowa, Illinois, Michigan, and Minnesota met with NARAL officers and veteran strategists like Assemblywoman Cook of New York to analyze the campaigns we would launch in the next months.

Almost before these campaigns got underway, the U.S. District Court for the Northern District of Illinois handed down another portentous decision on January 29. In a suit brought by women and physicians claiming that their constitutional rights had been infringed, the Federal panel by 2 to 1 declared the Illinois abortion law unconstitutional and sanctioned abortions in the first trimester of pregnancy. The Federal panel cited the U.S. Supreme Court's 1965 *Griswold* decision on contraception as a basis for the right of abortion—a line of reasoning I had urged in my writings since 1965. "A woman's interest in privacy and in control over her body is just as seriously interfered with by a law which prohibits abortions as it is by a law which prohibits the use of contraceptives," the court announced.

The first legal abortion under the decision was performed on February 1 at Grant Hospital in Chicago. With Cook County Hospital planning 125 a week, and all hospitals flooded with applicants, the Cook County State's Attorney asked Justice Thurgood Marshall of the U.S. Supreme Court for a temporary stay barring abortion until the high court had ruled on other cases before it. The Justice ordered the stay. The full Court refused to intervene. Within two weeks, the prospect of another Midwest state open to abortion had evaporated. At Chicago's Mt. Sinai Hospital, Dr. Miriam Wilson "reacted to Justice Marshall's decision with despair," reported the Chicago *Sun-Times*. "She said she did not know how she was going to explain the decision to her thirty-five patients 'who desperately don't want to be pregnant.' "[9]

Once again, the Midwest pendulum swung back to the offensive. On February 1, 1971, Dr. Alfred Kennan of the University of Wisconsin Medical School, a soft-voiced, sandy-haired professor of obstetrics and gynecology, opened the state's first freestanding abortion clinic, the Midwest Medical Center at Madison. His clinic at the time was protected by the original Federal court declaration of unconstitutionality in the Babbitz case. And although Catholic groups marched in protest, and the State Assembly (48 of whose 100 members were Catholics) passed a resolution urging the state to close the Center, Dr. Kennan continued to take a hundred cases a week, mainly referred by the Clergy Consultation Service, for over two months.[10]

On the afternoon of April 10, by order of the Dane County District Attorney, a raiding party of police closed the clinic, arrested Kennan and four of his staff, seized all records, and forcibly took a 17-year-old patient to the hospital for examination.

In a series of rallies and petitions, thousands of clergymen, physicians, professors, and students focused their anger on District Attorney Gerald Nichol, a Catholic. "Let him practice his religion on Sundays, and let us have the right to do what we want with our own lives," a Zero Population Growth spokesman announced.

The threat to Dr. Kennan mounted when the State Medical Examining Board called him for hearings on possible suspension of his license. His lawyer went to court to quash this subpoena, and brought suit before U.S. District Judge James E. Doyle to halt the District Attorney's prosecution of the clinic and its staff. On April 21, the D.A.

charged Kennan with criminal abortion. Since the Federal court's declaration of unconstitutionality in Babbitz still protected Wisconsin physicians at the time of Kennan's arrest, Judge Doyle issued a temporary restraining order, halting prosecution. The case then went to the U.S. Supreme Court, which affirmed the temporary restraining order. On May 24, 1971, the clinic reopened, the only bastion for abortion in the Midwest.

The next day, Ms. Anne Gaylor of the Wisconsin Committee to Legalize Abortion and NARAL testified before a State Assembly Committee. She reported the case of a young woman whose appointment had been canceled at the Kennan clinic after the raid. Unable to afford the trip to New York for abortion, she had jabbed a coat hanger into her uterus and punctured it. In panic, she called Clergy Consultation a hundred miles away. A counselor rushed her to the hospital, but she died within a few hours. "Tell the legislators," the counselor said, "that it is a terrible thing to watch a young girl die, and to know that her death was unnecessary, a total waste . . . because everyone who could help her was too intimidated by our unjust law to give her the help she needed."[11]

At a moment when the abortion campaign was at its peak, the President of the United States suddenly intervened. Since abortion laws were state laws, he had no excuse except in the case of military bases and government territory. President Richard Nixon used this slim wedge and expanded it into a national assault.

The Department of Defense had already liberalized its abortion policy in 1970, requiring U.S. military hospitals around the world to perform abortion with the approval of two doctors for all armed forces personnel and dependents regardless of local law. This policy was broadened even further in January 1971 by including nonmilitary hospitals, where abortion was legal, at government expense—even without approval from military physicians.[12]

On April 3, 1971, President Nixon countermanded his own Defense Department and prohibited abortion for military personnel and dependents except in states where it was already legalized. Using this order to inject "my own personal views," the President, a member of the Quaker faith, one of the first denominations to support abortion repeal, went on to attack abortion in general. "Unrestricted abortion policies, or abortion on demand," he announced, "I cannot square with my personal belief in the sanctity of human life—including the life of the yet unborn."

By seemingly including fetal life at the earliest stage, Nixon aligned himself solidly with the Catholic position. No exceptions were made for modest ALI-type laws to protect a woman's health. Neither women, their suffering, or their rights were mentioned in the President's 350-word statement. Obviously, Nixon had launched a "Catholic strategy" as blatant as his "Southern strategy."

Criticizing the President's moral stance, the United Church of Christ, Baptists, Methodists, and other Protestant denominations pointed out that, "The sanctity of life is grossly violated when the abortion laws, rulings and practices, supported by the President's actions, force a woman to endure an undesired pregnancy, and to bring forth an unwanted infant into an unloving environment."

But the danger of Nixon's attack went further. The Association of Planned Parenthood Physicians opposed his highly political manipulations "when this matter is being considered in legislatures and courts." Dr. Alan Guttmacher warned, Nixon's "remarks will be held by many as interfering in the due process of the law." The President had timed his message carefully. He had spoken at a moment when Midwest legislatures were grappling with repeal bills and his intervention was bound to reinforce Catholic and rural conservative blocs.[13]

In Iowa, the Iowa Association for Medical Control of Abortion, a NARAL affiliate, had built strong units in 120 cities and towns. Both major political parties, the Governor, and scores of influential organizations like the Iowa Medical Society supported repeal. All polls showed a majority of voters for a repeal law. Still, the money and manpower of Catholic Right to Life groups proved insurmountable. The opposition spent an estimated $50,000 to $70,000, the repealers only $2,200. Catholic priests preached against abortion constantly. Parishioners wrote letters and signed petitions at tables set up at church. Parochial school children were assigned letters to their legislators, and busloads of parishioners shuttled back and forth to the state capital.

By contrast, repeal groups like the PTAs and YWCAs sent few delegations to the capital. "We underestimated the fury of the opposition," Ms. Barbara Madden of the Iowa Association noted. "We ladies were just too 'nice.' "

The critical issue became the report from New York of twenty-six "live births" after saline abortions in late pregnancy. The newspapers played it in blazing headlines—"SEE 'LIVE BIRTHS' IN NEW YORK FIGURING IN 1971 IOWA DEBATE," announced the Des Moines *Tribune*. Its reporter called it "a major weapon to try to convince the 1971 Legislature to reject efforts to legalize abortion in the state." A nun on the Right to Life Committee told the press, "If people find out about these live births, then it will sway a lot of them." Catholic editors made certain the story blanketed the state. "Here is a baby that gasped and cried and was killed, an unprotected little innocent," a local Right to Life chairman told the legislature.[14]

Although NARAL tried to counter the damage with its study that showed that live births resulted from medical "inexpertness," and offered to train Iowa doctors in saline procedure, the campaign had been crippled. "Emotionalism was so high that we couldn't get legislators to talk," Ms. Madden reported. "They were sick of the subject, and just wanted to get rid of it and cut off their mail."

In Minnesota, NARAL's affiliate, the Minnesota Organization for Repeal of Abortion Laws, headed by Robert McCoy, had built an equally solid grass roots campaign. Both major parties supported repeal and for the first time in any state both party chairmen appeared together to speak for the bill. Governor Wendell Anderson, who had backed it as a state senator, added his support.

But the Minnesota Citizens Concerned for Life, with a hundred chapters across the state, spent an estimated $250,000 against repeal. The Catholic Hospital Association not only purchased full-page ads in television program guides, but a half-hour of prime TV time featuring the Archbishop and other Catholic officials. The Church's involvement in the campaign was notorious, the St. Cloud Diocesan Council, for example, appealing for donations to Father Paul Folsom of the Family Life Bureau, the Hibbing chapter of "Citizen Concerned" taking "memorials" in the name of Monsignor Patrick Byrnes.

"As you talk to legislators, you can sense that they're sick and tired of the issue," a lobbyist admitted. "It frightens them, and they wish it would go away." In March repeal strategists softened the bill in a last attempt to get it out of the committee, but by April it was buried for good.[15]

After these defeats, NARAL needed a new strategy to regain the offensive. The Michigan repeal groups, headed by Dr. Jack Stack, a NARAL board member, decided to gamble on Initiative and Referendum. This meant the collection of 213,000 signatures by a referendum petition for an abortion bill, followed by a referendum of voters at the polls. The collection of signatures alone was an onerous task—California repealers having failed to reach their quota a few years before. The further problem was that we could not get on the ballot until November 1972, delaying the offensive at least six months.

It was my belief that we also needed an immediate technique to force a confrontation in Michigan. The tragedy of Midwest abortion laws was that they primarily penalized the poor. With 600,000 legal abortions performed annually in New York, California, and other states, almost any woman with the plane fare to the East or West Coast could book a hospital or clinic appointment. But the poor, unable to afford fare, medical fee, or even care for their children while away, had no conceivable choice.

How could we focus attention on the poor? Our legal committee, mainly Prof. Means and Ralph Brown in Chicago, president of the Illinois repeal organization, gave the first clue. They suggested that the U.S. Supreme Court decision on Dr. Vuitch could support a physician anywhere performing abortion on mental health grounds. Further support could come from a majority of Federal court judges, 15 out of 23 who had already ruled in favor of a woman's constitutional right to terminate an unwanted pregnancy and to the aid of a physician in doing so. If we could find a doctor courageous enough to act on these precedents and publicly announce he was performing abortion for the poor, we would have a meaningful confrontation.

After weeks of telephoning physicians around the country, I found the ideal choice among NARAL's own officers. Dr. Edgar Keemer, our Midwest vice-president, was a prominent black physician in Detroit whose father had been professor at both the Howard and Meharry medical colleges. Keemer himself received his medical degree from Meharry in 1939, served ghetto patients in Detroit for thirty years, and had been an officer of the Detroit Medical Society and Civil Liberties Union.

Since Dr. Keemer stood the risk of legal indictment and loss of his medical license, I sought the help of the Michigan Clergy Counseling Service, whose 300 members made up one of the country's most prestigious referral groups. Its vice-president, the Rev. Ross Nicholson, agreed to come to Washington, D.C., to support the confrontation which NARAL would announce at its annual meeting on October 4, 1971.

Before a crowded press conference, "part of a concerted campaign to secure the invalidation or repeal of the Michigan law," as the *New York Times* called it, I announced "the first step in bringing abortion to the poor . . . so that the time may soon come when no woman because of her economic status will ever be denied equal rights to abortion." Dr. Keemer described the case he had aborted in his office a few days before despite the restrictive Michigan law—a forty-year-old mother of seven, who had become pregnant after giving up the pill because of side effects, and could not retain an IUD. A welfare recipient with no medical coverage and only $50 available for abortion, she could neither afford the fare to New York nor care for her family. Without Keemer's help, she would have resorted again to a back-alley practitioner as she had done twice before with serious complications. "Is that not a basic violation of constitutional rights?" Keemer demanded, pledging that he would continue to perform abortions for the poor referred by the Clergy Service.

"We see 5,000 indigent women a year," the Rev. Nicholson announced. "We talk about ways to beg, borrow, and raise money to get them to New York even with the medical fee waived. When these ways are exhausted, we sit and cry together in despair. In a practical sense, abortion is no longer against the law in Michigan. When 60,000 Michigan women per year obtain legal abortions elsewhere, it is no longer an illegal act. The Michigan Clergy Counseling Service will continue to refer poor and indigent women to competent doctors in Michigan under a recent interpretation of the Vuitch case. We support Dr. Keemer in this act and in his concern for poor people seeking abortions."

Speaking for the National Welfare Rights Organization, Dr. George Wiley, its executive director, concluded, "To us in welfare rights, control and self-determination in one's private personal life is one of those central issues that face women on welfare."

The confrontation made headlines throughout the Midwest, the

Detroit *Free Press* announcing, "DETROIT DOCTOR DOES ABORTIONS, SAYS IT'S LEGAL." Keemer was neither indicted nor even subpoenaed. Instead he became a local celebrity, featured on radio and television, and invited to speak at the University of Michigan, the University of Chicago, and other colleges. "Abortion is *not* illegal for Michigan women: it is only illegal for *poor* Michigan women," he told a medical meeting. "The Detroit Medical Society must not sit on its professional posterior while dollar discrimination stalks the ghetto like Bull Connor's dogs." The confrontation became more than one symbolic act. Keemer continued performing abortions for indigent patients—a breakthrough that established a physician's rights in Michigan without the slightest change in the law. He even gained semiofficial status from Medicaid, billing and receiving $75 for each in-office case.[16]

Another confrontation, in the Kansas courts, guaranteed a third Midwest clinic for abortion. The Kansas legislature in 1969 had passed a moderate ALI-type law under which 8,500 abortions were performed in its first year. About 2,000 took place at the clinic of Dr. Lynn D. Weller, Jr., a white obstetrician-gynecologist at Kansas City's Douglass Hospital, which served a predominantly black community. On July 28, 1971, the County Attorney notified Douglass it had violated the 1969 law which allowed abortions only in state-licensed hospitals accredited by the Joint Commission on Accreditation of Hospitals. Douglass was no longer accredited; in fact, only 80 of 169 Kansas hospitals held JCAH approval at the time.

Although Dr. Weller closed his abortion clinic, he, the hospital, and a group of women brought suit in Federal court. With Roy Lucas, president of the James Madison Constitutional Law Institute, as attorney, the plaintiffs asked for a declaratory judgment that the requirement of hospital accreditation and approval of three physicians for abortion infringed their fundamental rights to individual and marital privacy guaranteed by the Constitution.

On March 13, 1972, a three-judge panel of the U.S. District Court unanimously agreed that the accreditation policy does not "contribute to the decision-making process" and "singles out and classifies the abortion procedure apart from all other medical procedures." Declaring both accreditation and three-doctor approval "an unwarranted limitation upon the exercise of a fundamental right," the court ruled both provisions of the 1969 law unconstitutional. Dr. Weller's clinic reopened to become, with Dr. Kennan in Wisconsin and Dr. Keemer in Michigan, the vanguard of abortion in the Midwest.[17]

In Michigan, meanwhile, the drive for an Initiative and Referendum proved a strategic milestone. While a referendum on abortion had been ordered by the Washington State legislature, the Michigan abortion groups chose to go to the voters. The plan had risks, but one special bonus. If voters approved the new abortion law by referendum, it could only be overturned by a 75 percent majority of both legislative houses, and was thus virtually irrevocable.

The first step in Michigan originated from a legislative study commission in 1968, which showed that 84 percent of the state's physicians wanted a new abortion law, about half being for a free choice between doctor and patient and half for an ALI-type law. An ALI bill got to the Senate floor the next year. But despite the support of Governor William Milliken and Senator Lorraine Beebe's fervent speech on the anguish of women seeking abortion, including her own experience, the bill failed by three votes.

All organizations behind a new law now coalesced into the Coordinating Committee for Abortion Law Reform under the chairmanship of Dr. Jack Stack. A pragmatic politician and vice-chairman of the Republican State Finance Committee, Stack had also shown rare courage by convincing his local hospital to accept every application for abortion within its area solely on the approval of two physicians. When Senator Beebe started public hearings on abortion throughout Michigan, Stack and his committee used the hearings to rally and build community support.

The Coordinating Committee also backed proabortion candidates in the 1970 primaries and won most races. With four swing seats at stake in the general elections, the Committee won three, and mobilized a thousand women to defeat one Senator who had recently switched his vote against abortion. Unfortunately, Senator Beebe, a Republican in an overwhelmingly Democratic and Catholic district which she had only taken by 1 percent in 1966, succumbed to a vitriolic, antiabortion campaign.

In 1971, the abortion bill finally passed the Senate, although crippled by amendments. It remained buried in the House, however, and after months of futile pressure, the Coordinating Committee decided the only way to crack this impasse was to go to the electorate directly through Initiative petitions. The bill to be proposed by petition allowed abortion by free choice of doctor and patient in the first twenty weeks of pregnancy. It also provided that abortion be performed in a licensed hospital or facility approved by the State Department of Public Health. Since the Department firmly supported the petition campaign, any qualified freestanding clinic was expected to be approved and become as essential in Michigan as in New York.

One factor that led the Coordinating Committee to a twenty-week time limit instead of New York's twenty-four was the exaggerated publicity in the Midwest over New York's "living fetus" issue. Another factor was the legal advantage—Michigan does not require a birth, death, or stillborn certificate for the premature delivery of a fetus prior to twenty weeks. The Coordinating Committee, after sampling opinion throughout the state, concluded that twenty weeks was the most radical proposal that could win at the polls.

On September 15, 1971, the petition drive began with a press conference, supported by Ms. Helen Milliken, the Governor's wife, and Secretary of State Richard Austin, a black and a Democrat. The Republican State Central Committee endorsed it by resolution, and the National Committeewoman sent petitions to every county chairman.

A broad spectrum of organizations, from medical societies to almost all Protestant and Jewish groups, the Sierra Club, and unions, joined the drive. In campus towns, students raised money with bucket drives, and passed petitions from door to door, collecting 29,000 signatures from the University of Michigan and Ann Arbor residents, 25,000 from Michigan State University and Lansing.

An efficient team of coordinators, including Ms. Marianne Davis, Nancy Cleary, Gladys McLean, and Mary Lou Tanten, concentrated on key locations like football games, where canvassers signed up pregame picnickers at parking lots. One woman, a bowling enthusiast, went from bowling alley to bowling alley, gathering over 5,000 signatures. A 64-year-old man collected a thousand. Winter-sports fans covered the ski areas up north.

The most fertile territory turned out to be shopping malls, particularly during the buying surge before Christmas. Many owners protested canvassers at their doors. "At first we got kicked out of every mall in Michigan," Gladys McLean recalled. The women went back, armed with letters from the American Civil Liberties Union, insisting that malls were quasi-public. They negotiated with store managers, applied pressure through supporters who had relatives and friends in store management. They finally fought their way into every mall, although harassed by "Right to Life" mothers who planted themselves at store entrances and pushed their baby carriages between canvassers and potential signers.

On election day, canvassers even collected 5,000 signatures at the polls after the Coordinating Committee discovered an old legal ruling allowing petitions when the issue didn't appear on the ballot. The legislature closed the loophole shortly afterwards.

In early April 1972, the Coordinating Committee submitted 218,000 petition signatures—5,000 over the requirement—to the State Board of Canvassers. The Michigan Catholic Conference's attorneys tried to void them by claiming the proposed law unconstitutional, but the State Supreme Court turned down the suit. Meanwhile, the Committee filed more petitions for a total of 305,000. When "Right to Life" lawyers attacked the petitions for excessive inaccuracies a sampling proved them 85 percent accurate. The Board of Canvassers approved the petitions by a 4 to 0 vote and on April 18 Secretary of State Austin submitted the abortion bill to the legislature. When the legislature refused to act on the bill within the required forty days, it was officially placed on the ballot for a referendum on November 7.

As "Right to Life" groups intensified their pressure to overthrow the New York law in the winter of 1972, a new Michigan law took on added significance. The Catholic opposition inundated the state with billboards, television spots, and money—"perhaps half a million dollars worth" Dr. Stack estimated. Even in a Presidential year, the abortion referendum dominated the conscience and passions of the electorate for six months. The referendum for a liberalized abortion law was defeated with about 60 percent of the votes against 40 percent supporting it.

NOTES

1. Spokane *Valley Herald*, May 20, 1970; Seattle Radical Women, press release, March 26, 1969.

2. This, and preceding paragraph: Seattle *Post-Intelligencer*, April 20, 1969, p. 1; Washington *Post*, February 6, 1970; Seattle *Times*, March 21, 1969; March 28, 1969, p. 7; March 29, 1969.

3. This, and preceding paragraph: Seattle *Post-Intelligencer*, July 5, 1969; Seattle *Times*, January 25, 1970, Sec. C, p. 5; February 1, 1970.

4. *New York Times*, December 12, 1969, p. 36; Renton (Wash.) *Record Chronicle*, April 17, 1970.

5. This, and preceding paragraph: Seattle *Post-Intelligencer*, March 21, 1969; University of Washington *Daily*, November 10, 1970.

6. *Babbitz v. McCann*, 310 F. Supp. 293 (E.D. Wis., March 5, 1970).

7. This, and preceding paragraph: *New York Times*, March 15, 1970, p. 69; *Babbitz v. McCann*, 320 F. Supp. 219 (E.D. Wis., November 18, 1970).

8. 402 U.S. 903 (1971) vacated the injunction in light of *Younger v. Harris*, 401 U.S. 37 (1971), and companion cases.

9. This, and preceding paragraph: *Doe v. Scott*, 321 F. Supp. 1385 (N.D. Ill., January 29, 1971); Chicago *Tribune*, February 2, 1971; February 11, 1971, p. 1; Chicago *Sun-Times*, February 4, 1971; February 11, 1971.

10. *Babbitz v. McCann*, 310 F. Supp. 293 (E.D. Wis., March 5, 1970); *The Madisonian*, April 1, 1971.

11. This, and two preceding paragraphs: Wisconsin *State Journal*, April 21, 1971, p. 1; April 23, 1971, p. 1; *New York Times*, May 2, 1971, p. 36; Anne Gaylor, "Abortion in Wisconsin?" *ZPG National Reporter*, Vol. 3, No. 7, July, 1971, p. 1; *Kennan v. Warren*, 328 F. Supp. 525 (1971).

12. Memos of July 16 and 31, 1970, from Louis Rousselot, M.D., Assistant Secretary of Defense; *New York Times*, January 17, 1971, p. 43; January 21, 1971, p. 37.

13. This, and three preceding paragraphs: *New York Times*, April 4, 1971, p. 1; April 7, 1971, p. 43; Planned Parenthood-World Population press releases, April 14, 1971.

14. Des Moines *Tribune*, December 30, 1970, p. 1.

15. This, and preceding paragraph: St. Cloud (Minn.) *Visitor*, March 27, 1972; Chisholm (Minn.) *Free Press*, April 3, 1972; Minneapolis *Tribune*, March 7, 1971, p. 9B; March 19, 1971, p. 1B.

16. Detroit *Free Press*, October 5, 1971.

17. *Poe v. Menghini*, 339 F. Supp. 986 (D. Kan. 1972).

CHAPTER THIRTEEN

OVERTURNING THE OLD ABORTION LAWS IN FEDERAL AND STATE SUPREME COURTS

At least half the country supported repeal of abortion laws by the start of 1972, and almost all favored considerable liberalization, according to the polls. In a national study by the Opinion Research Corporation for the Presidential Commission on Population Growth, established by Congress and headed by John D. Rockefeller III, 50 percent wanted the decision on abortion left to a woman and her physician (72 percent for those who had completed college; 60 percent for those with annual incomes over $10,000).

While a hard-core 6 percent opposed all abortion, 39 percent of Roman Catholics backed the right of choice for a woman and her physician. An additional 41 percent of the total favored abortion under certain circumstances, generally the American Law Institute limitations.

Another survey by the Gallup Organization showed even stronger support. Fifty-seven percent wanted the decision on abortion left to a woman and her physician—54 percent of Catholics backing this stand.[1]*

* A more recent Gallup survey, conducted in June 1972 and published on August 24, 1972, revealed that 64 percent of the U.S. public (including 56 percent of Catholics) agreed that an abortion decision should be made solely by a woman and her physician.

This drastic swing in public opinion toward abortion, particularly among Catholics, would have a profound effect on the size of American families. Another study for the Population Commission reported that "American couples have changed their reproductive behavior radically over the course of the past five years, adjusting their fertility goals sharply downwards and increasing substantially their ability to stop childbearing at the wanted level." While the decline in birth expectations and in the number of unwanted children affected all couples, it was especially steep among Catholics.

In 1970, non-Catholic married women aged 20 to 24 wanted an average of 9 percent fewer children than in 1965 (2.35 children as compared to 2.57). But Catholic women in the same age group in that period cut their family expectations by 20 percent from 3.45 to 2.75 children.

A second index, measuring unwanted births that have already occurred, showed a startling drop of 45 percent among Catholic women in that period (an even higher 57 percent for Catholic, college women), and a drop of 32 percent for non-Catholics.

Obviously, Catholics had now adopted the same attitudes toward childbearing as the rest of the population, reducing the size of their families through use of the pill and other contraceptives, but more significantly, avoiding unwanted children through abortion when contraception failed. Even before legalization, my studies of the first 1,000 cases requesting in-office abortion showed 28 percent identified themselves as Catholics.[2]

The most hidebound legal and medical associations had made equally radical shifts. The American Bar Association's House of Delegates, "a traditionally conservative body heavily weighted with elderly corporate attorneys," as the *New York Times* put it, approved "abortion on demand" in the first 20 weeks of pregnancy without debate and only a handful of dissenting votes. The American College of Obstetricians and Gynecologists not only abolished all medical requirements for abortion, but also their rule for a second, consulting physician if the woman herself had requested the abortion.[3]

It was the courts, however, that produced even more sweeping gains for abortion in this period. The California Supreme Court had set the precedent in 1969 by declaring the old state law unconstitutional in *Belous*. Then the attack concentrated on the new California

"Therapeutic Abortion Act" of 1967. Lower courts declared it unconstitutional in the cases of Dr. Robert C. Robb and Dr. John S. Gwynne. Two other cases went to the Court of Appeals in 1971. The first involved Dr. Robert W. Barksdale. The court held that the accredited-hospital requirement, and approval of abortion in advance by a hospital committee, were "an unnecessary and unreasonable restraint," and that a woman has "a constitutional right to terminate her pregnancy" subject only to reasonable safeguards. Strangely enough, in the case of Dr. Robert R. Pettegrew in a different district, the court supported the constitutionality of the 1967 law.[4]

More decisive were the 1970 cases of *Roe v. Wade* in Texas and *Doe v. Bolton* in Georgia. The Texas case attacked the old law which allowed abortion only to save the "life" of the mother, similar to the majority of old state laws throughout the country. "Not only are the Texas Abortion Laws unconstitutionally overbroad, they are also unconstitutionally vague," the U.S. District Court concluded.

In Georgia, *Bolton* attacked the new, ALI-type "therapeutic" law which had been passed in over a dozen states since 1967. While the Federal court upheld the state's right to limit abortion to accredited hospitals and establish hospital committee approval as well as Georgia residency, it declared unconstitutional the most restrictive features of the law setting the medical basis for abortion. "Any such limiting restrictions"—confining abortion to injury to the health of the mother, danger of grave physical or mental defect to the child, or abortion as a result of pregnancy from rape—"must fail," the court concluded.

When the U.S. Supreme Court put both cases on its docket, and heard arguments on December 13, 1971, everyone expected that Texas and Georgia would eventually provide the critical high-court decision.[5]

Meanwhile, two Federal courts in Connecticut and New Jersey and two state supreme courts in Florida and Vermont would overthrow the old abortion laws of those states in a momentous judicial breakthrough. First came the flamboyant, almost medieval trial of Ms. Shirley Ann Wheeler in Florida. A winsome, freckle-faced woman of twenty-three, the eighth child of an alcoholic father who had abandoned his family and a mother who died in Shirley's infancy, she was raised by North Carolina relatives.

Unable to get a divorce from her first husband, she had lived with a common-law husband for three years when she became pregnant, went to an abortionist, and had to enter a hospital after hemorrhaging. The doctors found a fetus, claimed at the trial to be at least eighteen weeks old. Wheeler was arrested and convicted of manslaughter in July 1971, the first woman in America known to be held criminally liable for an abortion, probably the first in the English-speaking world.

The county prosecutor obviously pursued this bizarre case out of pique. "We, of course, could have made some arrangements if she had turned state's evidence against the abortionist, but she told us it was none of our business," he admitted.[6]

"I'm really terrified at the thought of going to jail, and damn if anyone here seems to care," Wheeler told a lawyer sent by the Women's National Abortion Action Coalition. "We are appalled that in the twentieth century such a miscarriage of justice should occur in the United States," Planned Parenthood of Western Missouri and Kansas telegraphed her.[7]

In October the court upheld her conviction and put her on two years' probation as absurd as the original arrest. She either had to get a divorce and marry her common-law husband or return to her family in North Carolina—"The next time she went to bed with a man, she had better make sure she had a marriage license hanging over it," the probation officer told a WONAAC reporter.[8]

Wheeler immediately appealed for a new trial with a supporting motion by Prof. Means. "I don't want to [go to jail], but I think I have the right to control my body the way I want to," she insisted.[9]

The Walsingham case was the first to reach the Florida Supreme Court. Six justices unanimously attacked the "arbitrary and unreasonable legislative interference and infringement" of the abortion law on the rights of woman and physician. In September 1971 a criminal court judge ruled the abortion law unconstitutional in the *Barquet* case, which incorporated Walsingham. After *Barquet* was appealed to the Supreme Court, the Miami *Herald* announced in a front-page, banner headline: "STATE HIGH COURT OVERTURNS ABORTION LAW." The court, ironically, hedged its decision, giving the state legislature sixty days to pass a valid law.[10]

Obviously, NARAL wanted to prevent a new law from being passed. Florida would then revert to English common law with abortion permissible at least until "quickening." The inflexible conservatism of the state, unfortunately, had stalled the development of a strong repeal organization. We now tried to weld local, proabortion groups together. Lee Gidding rushed to Miami for a coalition meeting, including NOW, ZPG, YWCA, the clergy, and the Catholics for Abortion Law Repeal, whose lobbyist was viewed "like a creature from another world" by legislators at Tallahassee. "We've just had it with keeping quiet," Ms. Nancy Bandez explained. "It's repulsive to me what the Catholic Church is doing."

Under pressure of the Supreme Court deadline, the legislature pushed through a bill even weaker than the ALI blueprint—"more of a temporary truce than a triumph for either side," the Miami *Herald* observed. With the Governor's signing on April 13, the gains of the court decision were diluted.[11]

The next crucial decision, in Vermont, produced more lasting advantages. The case was brought by a pregnant welfare recipient, "Jacqueline R.," unable to go outside the state for an abortion, and her physician, who claimed the restrictive 1846 law prevented him performing a medically indicated procedure. The judicial process may move faster in small states, for when the Vermont Supreme Court handed down its unanimous decision on January 14, 1972, "Jacqueline" still needed an abortion.

In a unique approach, the Supreme Court declared the old law "invalid" rather than unconstitutional. Vermont, among a handful of states, punishes only the physician, and specifically exempts the woman from criminal charges. Her only recourse, the court pointed out, became "self-induced abortion, uncounseled and unassisted by a doctor, in a situation where medical attention is imperative." Since the legislature "affirmed the right of a woman to abort," the court ruled, it "cannot simultaneously, by denying medical aid in all but cases where it is necessary to preserve her life, prohibit its safe exercise."[12]

This time, Vermont repeal groups, bolstered by NARAL and ZPG organizers, managed to block the legislature from passing a compromise bill diminishing the court's impact. Without a new law on the books, most, if not all, abortions were legal under common law. NARAL's policy had always been to exploit such an opening and organize an abortion clinic as quickly as possible. The problem was that the majority of gynecologists practiced in Burlington, and the city's predominantly Catholic population pressured hospitals against any relaxation of old restrictions. A magnificent court decision had produced an absurdity—the right to perform abortion, but no hospital with the backbone to act. After four months of hospital negotiations, a group of NARAL-affiliated physicians decided to break the impasse, and open a clinic of its own.

Almost on the heels of Florida and Vermont came a sweeping U.S. District Court decision in New Jersey. The case had been brought as a "class action" by members of the Princeton YWCA, nine doctors, and 1,200 women on behalf of all New Jersey women. On March 1, 1972, the Federal court ruled 2 to 1 that the state law was unconstitutional. It not only "chills and deters" the physician's rights under the First and Fourteenth Amendments, said the court; but violates a woman's "constitutional right of privacy cognizable under the Ninth and Fourteenth Amendments to determine for herself whether to bear a child or to terminate a pregnancy in its early stages, free from unreasonable interference by the state." [13]

No court had defined the grounds of unconstitutionality more decisively. Undeterred, the State Attorney General announced he would appeal, and with monstrous logic, said the decision meant nothing anyway. New Jersey would continue under the old law until the appeal reached the U.S. Supreme Court.

While NARAL was canvassing sympathetic gynecologists in an effort to establish a New Jersey clinic, the ideal candidate, cut from the mold of Michigan's Dr. Keemer, stepped forward on his own. Dr. Robert M. Livingston, a 37-year-old, Harvard-educated obstetrician-gynecologist with impressive credentials, appeared before the press at the office of the New Jersey Civil Liberties Union on March 30 to announce he had performed two abortions at his Englewood Cliffs office that morning.

"It's time that we stopped the nonsense and the charade and the debasing practice of making women who do not want to continue their pregnancies drive way out of state for something they should have legal access to here," Livingston stated. "I feel I am standing up to the problem, and I hope other doctors will too."

Ruffled by this defiance, the Deputy State Attorney General

claimed Livingston was "susceptible to arrest and indictment just like anyone else that commits a crime." Then he applied to the Federal court for a stay of its declaratory judgment, which was promptly denied. The county D.A., insisting he wouldn't be baited by Livingston or any doctor, told the press he would take the case to a grand jury when the facts warranted.[14]

Ignoring these verbal games, Livingston continued performing at least a dozen abortions a week. To heighten the confrontation, NARAL invited him as its principal luncheon speaker at its May 12 forum where he announced that if a second gynecologist could join his office, he would double his abortion case load immediately. Meanwhile, another team of veteran gynecologists prepared to open an abortion clinic in the southern part of the state.

The climax in this series of four momentous cases came in Connecticut. On April 18, 1972, the Federal District Court declared the state's 1860 law unconstitutional by a 2 to 1 vote. The opinion in this "class action," brought by a coalition of feminists called "Women vs. Connecticut," employed sharper language than any previous ruling. Based mainly on the Ninth Amendment right of privacy, it stated that ". . . Determining whether or not to bear a child is of fundamental importance to a woman." In examining a broad range of social and economic obstacles to childbearing, the court agreed that a woman with an unwanted child might find it "overtaxes her and her family's financial or emotional resources"; an unmarried mother will "suffer the stigma of having an illegitimate child." In ruling that the state could no longer interfere with a woman's rights, the court concluded "the state's interests are insufficient to take from the woman the decision after conception whether she will bear a child, and that she, as the appropriate decision maker, must be free to choose."

After this ringing decision in *Abele v. Markle*, and an injunction by the court, not merely a declaratory judgment, against Connecticut's abortion law, the State Attorney General sought a stay from the U.S. Supreme Court. In a similar 1971 case in Illinois, Justice Thurgood Marshall had immediately granted the stay. Now, on May 12, 1972, without even waiting for Ms. Catherine Roraback, counsel for the plaintiffs, to file opposition papers, Justice Marshall denied the stay after only two hours' consideration.[15]

Governor Thomas J. Meskill, a Republican and Catholic who had once trained for the priesthood, immediately reverted to an act of desperation that would turn the legislature into a circus. Calling it back into session, he and his leadership proposed a new bill—not the mild, ALI formula, as Florida had done, which might have stood up in the courts, but a bill even more restrictive than the 1860 law. The Governor sought to enact church dogma into law. The preamble to the bill declared, "The public policy of the state and the intent of the Legislature is to protect and preserve human life from the moment of conception. . . ."

"It is an atrocity, an atrocious bill," observed Ms. Jean Thornton, a Glastonbury Republican, and veteran opponent of abortion laws. "Are we once again going to hold our state up to ridicule above all others?"

With a strong patronage hold on his legislature, and an electorate about 43 percent Catholic, Meskill seemed unconcerned. One legislator, like many others, believed "the impetus for the bill as it was drafted came directly from the Hartford Archdiocese," the *New York Times* reported. "They didn't want any loopholes, and there weren't any." Another legislator, who switched from a liberal position to support of the bill, conceded, "The governor hands out all the goodies, and when he really wants to put the pressure on, it works." With most residents living in small communities dominated by the Catholic Church, the state had an exemplary record for toeing the clerical line, allowing the sale and use of contraceptives just seven years ago as a result of a U.S. Supreme Court decision.

The only real debate was a Senate attempt to soften the bill slightly by approving abortion for rape and incest. "It amounts to abortion on demand," snapped the Governor, quickly overriding the opposition. "A woman can merely claim she was raped, or it was an incestuous relationship. Everyone who wants an abortion will be reporting rape."

Senator Wilbur Smith, a black Democrat from Hartford, who supported the right of abortion in the first 24 weeks of pregnancy, insisted sarcastically that the Governor's bill should make abortion punishable by death since the fetus had been transformed into a person, and that the fetus be granted all rights of a citizen.

With six senators abandoning their position on rape and incest, the Governor's extremist bill passed both Senate and House easily, and Meskill signed it into law on May 23. Four high court decisions, invalidating four state laws in recent months, had been capped by this unique travesty of Federal court authority. Perhaps the Governor was simply putting on an exhibition for the archdiocese or his Catholic electorate. Perhaps he considered himself the pioneer in a new legislative drive to incorporate Catholic dogma wholesale into law. What really mattered now was not Meskill's showmanship but crucial cases from Texas and Georgia that would be decided by the U.S. Supreme Court.[16]*

A Federal court in Texas had already overturned the old "life only" law. A Federal court in Georgia had invalidated the restrictive causes for abortion approval in its ALI-type law. Both cases had been heard by the U.S. Supreme Court in 1971 with seven justices on the bench. On June 26, 1972, instead of handing down a decision, the Court ordered a rehearing for the fall when President Nixon's two latest appointments would be present. The long-awaited decision that could modify or repeal most of the nation's abortion statutes would unfortunately be postponed until 1973.[17]

NOTES

1. This, and two preceding paragraphs: *New York Times*, October 28, 1971, p. 1; *ASA Newsletter*, Vol. VI, No. 4–Vol. VII, No. 1, Winter 1971–Spring 1972.

2. This, and three preceding paragraphs: *New York Times*, May 30, 1972, p. 1; Lawrence Lader, "No In-Hospital Abortions," *Look*, January 21, 1969; Lader, "Why Birth Control Fails," *McCall's*, October, 1969.

3. *New York Times*, February 8, 1972, p. 37.

4. *People v. Belous*, 71 Cal. 2d 954, 458 P. 2d 194, 80 Cal. Reptr. 354 (1969); *People v. Robb*, Nos. 149005, 159061 (Mun. Ct., Orange Cty., Calif., January 7, 1970); *People v. Gwynne*, No. 173309 (Mun Ct., Orange Cty., Calif., June 16, 1970); *People v.*

* On September 20, 1972, a Federal District Court overthrew Governor Meskill's new law as an abridgment of the rights of a woman "to privacy and personal choice in matters of sex and family life."

Barksdale, 96 Cal. Rptr. 265 (1st Dist., 1971); *People v. Pettegrew*, 96 Cal. Rptr. 189 (1971).

5. *Roe v. Wade*, 314 F. Supp. 1217 (N.D. Tex., June 17, 1970), jurisdiction postponed, 402 U.S. 941 (1971); *Doe v. Bolton*, 319 F. Supp. 1048 (N.D. Ga., 1970) jurisdiction postponed, 402 U.S. 941 (1971).

6. *State of Florida v. Shirley Ann Wheeler*, Felony Court of Record, Volusia Cty., Fla., No. 1400.

7. *The Militant*, October 15, 1971, p. 4; Daytona Beach *Morning Journal*, October 15, 1971, p. 1.

8. *WONAAC Newsletter*, October 21, 1971, p. 1.

9. Daytona Beach *Morning Journal*, October 16, 1971, p. 1.

10. *Walsingham v. Florida*, 250 So. 2d 857 (Fla. 1971); *State of Florida v. Barquet*, 262 So. 2d 431 (Fla. 1972); Miami *Herald*, February 15, 1972, p. 1.

11. Miami *Herald*, April 8, 1972, p. 22A.

12. *Jacqueline R. and Beecham v. Leahy,* — Vt. —. 287A 2d 836 (1972).

13. *YWCA et al., v. Kugler* 342 F. Supp. 1048 (D. N.J., 1972).

14. This, and two preceding paragraphs: *New York Times*, March 31, 1972, p. 36.

15. *Abele v. Markle I*, 342 F. Supp. 800 (D. Conn., 1972); *Doe v. Scott*, 321 F. Supp. 1385 (N.D. Ill. 1970), appeals filed sub. nom., 39 U.S. L.W. 3438 (U.S. Mar. 29, 1971), (Nos. 70–105, 70–106).

16. This, and five preceding paragraphs: *New York Times*, May 17, 1972, p. 53; May 23, 1972, pp. 1, 23; May 25, 1972, p. 38; May 24, 1972, p. 51; May 20, 1972, p. 13; May 25, 1972, p. 38; *Griswold v. Connecticut*, 381 U.S. 479 (1965).

17. *Roe v. Wade*, No. 70–18; *Doe v. Bolton*, No. 70–40; *New York Times*, June 27, 1972, p. 25.

CHAPTER FOURTEEN

ORDEAL AND SURVIVAL: NEW YORK (1972)

We had seen the avalanche coming —NARAL had been raising money and working in legislative districts since late fall. But no one else seemed to believe it until Sunday, April 16, 1972, proclaimed "Right to Life Sunday" by Cardinal Cooke of New York. That morning at masses throughout New York State, every priest excoriated the abortion law, and the buses began to roll from as far away as Schenectady, carrying the faithful to Fifth Avenue for the largest and most boisterous antiabortion parade in history.

The fury of the attack had been set a few days before by an ad in the *Greenbush Area News of New Jersey*: a photograph of Adolph Hitler, a box score of deaths in recent wars and holocausts. The Korean war held fourth place with 34,000 dead Americans; the Vietnam war, third place with 45,000. Hitler was "still the record holder" with 6,000,000 dead Jews, but New York State came second—"only No. 2 but still trying until we repeal the abortion law." [1]

A few of us, mainly from the Women's National Abortion Action Coalition (WONAAC), gathered on the corner of 86th Street and Fifth Avenue, and watched the buses unload. They were almost all parochial school buses, crammed with marching bands and units from the Knights of Columbus and Right to Life chapters whose flags and banners inveighed in flashing colors against "murder" and the destruction of fetal "life." The cool, gray morning had suddenly turned bright and hot, and the boys and girls from the marching bands in their gaudy red and yellow and purple tunics stood laughing on the corner with their trumpets and drums, as if awaiting the opening of the big game and the charge of helmeted warriors from the locker room. We asked one young horn player about the abortion law and he said he hadn't read up on it. Why had he come? "Oh, we get paid for playing," he laughed.

We had not planned a counterdemonstration—only a few small groups stationed at 86th and 59th Streets with makeshift signs, a dozen Catholic women in our group with "Catholics for Abortion" scribbled hastily on cardboards clutched in front of them. The police had penned our group behind barricades on the east side of Fifth Avenue while the marchers assembled on the park side. The busloads unloading on nearby streets streamed past us. They were mainly middle-aged people, prim and determined in blue serge suits and flowered Sunday dresses. When they saw our signs, their faces flushed and hardened. Most of them screamed, only one word, like a small explosion, "Murderer! Murderer!" The sound rolled up the street. In that half-hour, there must have been a hundred faces thrust in front of mine with the same lacerating accusation, "Murderer!" I had debated abortion hundreds of times since 1965, but never had seen so much venom concentrated at one time.

The marching bands had started up across the street. When the WONAAC staff called the police a few days before, they had said a small group could walk down the opposite side of Fifth Avenue as long as there were no bullhorns or amplifying equipment. We sifted out of the barricades now, and started to move down the east side of the avenue. There was a burst of police whistles, a red-faced captain dashing over, ordering ten or fifteen subordinates to throw a cordon around us. We were shoved against the buildings, new barricades placed around us. When could we march? "When the parade is over," the captain announced. I asked him whether there was any law that prohibited a small group from following a parade down the other side of the street. "One more word out of you, and I put you in the wagon," he snapped.

We stood and watched the bands, the Knights of Columbus, the Right to Life and parochial school contingents pour down the avenue —10,000, the newspapers reported. It seemed macabre, all this money, organization, and fanaticism unleashed against a law that simply gave women (about a third of them Catholic women) the right to decide whether to bear a child. The law had worked well, halved maternal death rates and the rate of mangled underworld abortions that had always infested our hospitals. Statistics and health care, however, were meaningless in this frenzy. We were faced with a religious crusade based on the assumption of the Church hierarchy that its survival depended on forcing everyone else to accept its dogma. The bands and marchers seemed surprisingly like the crusaders of eight hundred years before—the knights and ragged children who had left Germany and France to pour across Europe to the Holy Land to convert the infidels by force or death. One crusade seemed as pointless as the other, and just as unlikely to change the course of history.

It had started in earnest on January 5, 1972—the buses left for Albany three days a week from every Nassau and Suffolk County parish, the *Long Island Catholic* announced. They came from Westchester, the Bronx, Queens, and other points of Catholic strength on the same inflexible schedule. It was a superbly organized and financed attack, concentrating on Catholic legislators and on Republicans with considerable Conservative and Right to Life blocs where the swing of a thousand votes could mean defeat for a senator or assemblyman. They came in groups of fifty and a hundred, mainly housewives and schoolchildren of fifteen and sixteen, shepherded by their teachers and priests, always armed with their brochures and grotesque, colored, fetus pictures.[2]

The pictures, drumming in the incessant message of murder, the letters and telegrams, spurred by parish sermons each Sunday, began to pile up on Capitol desks. Assemblywoman Constance Cook analyzed the vulnerable districts in late January—three shaky assemblymen in Westchester, four or five in the Bronx, a Long Island senator whose area had been redistricted to include new blocs of Catholic voters. The danger was becoming critical. We had only won the new law in 1970 by one vote in the Assembly and a handful in the Senate.

NARAL had assigned small campaign funds for organizing in Westchester and Suffolk Counties. We wanted to rouse the old coalition from two years back. But no one listened. Almost all organizations were confident of Governor Rockefeller's veto of the Donovan-Crawford bill, aimed at overthrowing the new law and reinstating the medieval restrictions existing before 1970. They thought the mere threat of a veto would keep the Catholic bill bottled up in committee. Our delegations to Albany and telegrams failed to materialize. "The great, new silent majority," the *Village Voice* described the old abortion coalition.[3]

By contrast, six hundred Right to Life members gathered on the Capitol steps at Albany on April 17, their chants reverberating through the offices above. The next day, a dozen women burst onto the floor of the Assembly while it was in session, screaming "Stop Abortion" at the startled legislators. When some refused to leave, guards had to carry them out of the chamber. A week later, during the dedication of the new Justice building on Albany's south mall, protesters in the audience stood up to shout against "this horrible [abortion] law," and had to be dragged out before Governor Rockefeller and other speakers could continue.[4]

The nightmare month started on April 17 when Assemblyman Leichter called to tell me the Donovan-Crawford bill would soon be forced out of committee. Lee Gidding, NARAL's executive director, and I worked around the clock, sitting on the phones, cajoling, pleading, hammering, until our voices were hoarse. Our objective was to try to keep Donovan-Crawford bottled in committee. Working through our most dependable allies like Planned Parenthood, Zero Population Growth, National Organization for Women, and WONAAC, we concentrated a flood of telegrams and phone calls on the Codes Committees of both houses.

To reach the public, I started with WBAI radio on April 21, then WMCA radio, Channel 5 TV, and other "talk shows" and interviews, begging listeners to bombard their legislators with telegrams. To reach the press, which had almost ignored the danger, I asked Borough President Sutton to hold a press conference on April 25 with distinguished speakers including the Mayor's wife, Ms. Mary Lindsay; Gordon Chase, the Health Services Administrator; Ms. Evelyn Cunningham, director of Governor Rockefeller's women's unit; Dr. Guttmacher of Planned Parenthood; and leaders of almost every Protestant and Jewish denomination. WONAAC held another press conference with Congresswoman Bella Abzug on April 28.

Meanwhile, we suffered two setbacks. The Rabbinical Council of America, an Orthodox Jewish group which had never supported abortion, but so far refrained from political opposition, now came out against the 1970 abortion law. For the first time in New York, the Catholic hierarchy had another denomination, small but significant, at its side. This loss was softened a few days later when the much larger Conservative movement in American Judaism announced its unequivocal support of the abortion law.

Even more disturbing, Governor Rockefeller on April 25 proposed a compromise amendment to the present law, limiting abortion to 16 rather than 24 weeks. The threat of the Governor's veto had been our main defense. Now it seemed obvious that the Republican leadership had retreated, either because they couldn't keep Donovan-Crawford bottled up, or were sure we didn't have the votes to defeat it once it got to the floor. The Governor's message inferred, "Let's hold something. At least a 16-week bill, which might draw votes from both camps, is better than nothing." The Governor also seemed to be saying his veto of Donovan-Crawford was no longer assured, and above all, that he didn't want to be forced into a veto.[5]

The worst part was that a 16-week bill really meant 12 weeks, and would produce a medical disaster. Since vacuum aspiration became risky after twelve weeks, most physicians put off abortion between twelve and sixteen weeks, after which saline induction could be used. Rockefeller's own assistant commissioner of preventive health services had previously testified that a 16-week limit "would deprive women of safe abortional procedures by forcing many more abortions into the 13- to 16-week interval—a period of great risk."[6]

Such a limit would force at least 40,000 women each year in New York back to underworld abortion, particularly the poor and uneducated who often failed to verify their pregnancies until the tenth or twelfth week. And it would deny abortion to the carrier of a mongoloid or other deformed fetus since tests for deformity cannot be completed until the nineteenth or twentieth week.

The danger had become so acute that NARAL now had to reach the public through a half-page ad in the *New York Times*. I raised $3,500 with a phone call to one of our dedicated contributors the morning of April 26, appeared on a radio show to plead for telegrams to Albany, and rushed to the NARAL office to write the ad in an hour, while Lee Gidding drew up a list of organizations, supporting the right of abortion, which would be boxed at the bottom.

In provocative type, the ad appealed to the reader: SAVE YOUR

RIGHT TO ABORTION. It warned that this right was "being destroyed this moment in Albany," and hit bluntly at the Catholic Church, "the most powerful tax-deductible lobby in history" which "wants to dictate your beliefs . . . wants to force women to have children against their will."

The first organized delegations, at least two months behind schedule, left for Albany by chartered bus that Friday morning, Drs. Guttmacher, Nathanson, and Tietze forming a special task force to convince legislators of the danger of a 16-week bill. When Senator Ohrenstein called a press conference for the delegations, Right to Life protestors infiltrated the crowd, trying to drown out speakers with shouting and clapping.

On April 29, the *New York Times* ran the first in a series of editorials, attacking the opposition's "emotion bordering on hysteria," and exhorting legislators to "have spine enough to resist the pressure groups." Another editorial warned that a New York defeat would "tend to condemn women of other states as well as New York's citizens to further prolongation of the deadly harms and heartbreaks of a medieval form of coercion."

On May 2, the last illusion of bottling up Donovan-Crawford was wiped away. Assembly Codes sent the bill to the floor.[7]

Crisis followed on crisis. While the May 6 rally for abortion in Union Square, planned by WONAAC weeks before, had been a low priority at the time, we now had to build a strong coalition in a few days, and I was tied to the phone till late at night lining up support. Still, Albany lobbying was an equal priority. The Assembly looked dubious, the Senate marginal.

On May 3, I tramped all day through the catacombs and rabbit-warrens of the old Capitol building, and the marble sterility of the new, office adjunct, cornering legislators when they were off the floor, or their legal counsels or secretaries. In a few wavering districts, I had to make specific commitments of canvassing and financial help in upcoming primaries and elections. In every district, I hammered at the votes our affiliate organizations could turn out—Puerto Rican, black, and Jewish groups in the Bronx, for example, and similar ethnic and religious blocs we could rally in other areas. Each office reported that our telegrams and phone calls had finally begun to make a dent.

The next day we sent over 500 people to Albany by bus; a delegation of physicians to hammer again at the medical dangers of a 16-week law; Ms. Mary Lindsay, who told a press conference that the abortion law was "probably the most important piece of legislation in the country so far as women's rights are concerned." Facing the crowd on the Capitol steps, she remarked pointedly, "We had 300,000 abortions in New York. I wish those 300,000 women would be standing outside the Capitol to show what they think about legal abortions." [8]

The climax of our demonstrations was the march down First Avenue to Union Square on Saturday, May 6—1,500 people with their signs and banners, led by folk-singers and their guitars. But where were the massive crowds, the 20,000 marchers that the Women's Rights demonstration had turned out two summers before? The speakers represented a broad coalition, Mary Lindsay again, Congresswomen Bella Abzug and Shirley Chisholm, Assemblyman Leichter. Speaking for NARAL, I branded the Catholic attack on the law "nothing but religious tyranny to impose one religious dogma on all women." I quoted Rev. Jesse Lyons of the Riverside Church, who demanded: "Is this abortion struggle part of a continuing battle in a religious war that is destined to divide or even destroy our country?"

Even as we were meeting, the White House delivered the crowning blow. A day before, President Nixon attacked the report by John D. Rockefeller III and the Commission on Population Growth, which vigorously supported the right of abortion and the New York law as a model for the rest of the country. This had some justification; it was the President's own commission. Now he took an unprecedented step by writing to Cardinal Cooke directly and aligning himself with the fury of the Catholic attack on the New York law. "I would personally like to associate myself with the convictions you deeply feel and eloquently express," the President stated.

It was a crude and shocking strategy to win Catholic and Conservative Democratic votes both in New York and the rest of the country. Nixon had not only taken the initiative in this alliance with the Church, but flaunted his Federal power in a state legislative struggle that was being decided in the next few days. "A blatant misuse of his high position," the *New York Times* criticized editorially. "Historians should find it hard to locate a parallel instance of a President openly working through a particular church to influence the action of a state government." Calling Nixon's intervention "as unwarranted as it was inflammatory," the New York *Post* warned, "The impact of the result will be felt throughout the country."

Whether or not the President reaped any political profit, he completely misjudged the reactions of Governor Rockefeller, his campaign manager in the state. "GOVERNOR REPORTED IRKED BY NIXON'S ABORTION VIEWS," the *Times* headlined its front-page story on May 9. As evidence of the Governor's "pique" that "his Legislature and his own office" could be "openly pressured by a President in this way," Rockefeller's office immediately referred all calls on the Nixon statement to the White House.

The repercussions of Nixon's gaffe produced an almost comic retreat two days later. John D. Ehrlichman, the President's leading adviser on domestic affairs, announced that Nixon had not intended "intentionally or accidentally" to embarrass the Governor. Ehrlichman said he had approved the letter to Cardinal Cooke on the condition it remain private, but someone else in the White House—"sloppy staff work," it was called—authorized the Cardinal to release it. "Suspicions persisted in some quarter here," the *Times* concluded, "that the President fully intended that the letter, or at least its substance, be made public knowledge, and simply underestimated, or dismissed the embarrassment this would cause the Governor."

In their investigation of this "feckless intrusion," the political columnists Rowland Evans and Robert Novak insisted that the release of the letter had been fully authorized by President Nixon. Without consulting his campaign manager, John Mitchell, who was as angered as Rockefeller by the blunder, the President had not given his letter of endorsement "a second thought." [9]

Rockefeller, too, indulged in some backtracking. On May 6, obviously swayed by medical arguments against a 16-week bill, he announced he would now favor an 18-week bill. We had scored a point, but as word leaked down from Albany that many influential legislators would go for the Governor's compromise, it seemed to me that the 1970 law was being sacrificed for political expediency. It was a gamble either way. But I preferred to gamble on holding the Senate, or on a veto if we lost it, rather than yielding to Catholic pressure. Even if the 18-week bill passed, it solved nothing and only stalled the Catholic confrontation for a year.

By Monday afternoon, however, despite the compromise drive,

the opposition seemed strong enough to get the Crawford bill on the floor. Yet there were a few glimmers of hope. The Governor's mail, overwhelmingly against the abortion law the previous week, had now turned about 3,000 to 2,600 in our favor. Assembly Minority Leader Steingut's mail, previously almost completely against the law, turned 80 percent in our favor. Assemblyman Manuel Ramos, a Bronx Democrat who had voted against the 1970 law, committed himself to its support. Assemblyman Anthony Stella, a Bronx Democrat and an anti-vote last time, conveniently developed a sudden illness which would keep him from Albany and eliminate an opposing vote.

Frantically, that afternoon and evening we concentrated on a half-dozen swing votes—some of us making an appeal for telegrams on WBAI and WRVR, Prof. Means and I talking from 8 p.m. to midnight on NBC. On May 9, the Assembly chamber was cleared of visitors at 1:40 p.m. The debate, a series of forty-one speeches, essentially repeated the pattern of 1970. Dominick Di Carlo of Brooklyn demanded for the opposition, "Can we tear a child apart limb from limb because of an accident of fate that he has not yet been born?" Constance Cook, speaking as the only mother in the legislature of "two very wanted, very beloved children" insisted that the only issue was whether abortion would be done "in a hospital or in a motel room." Mary Ann Krupsak, a Catholic whose courage was amplified by the fact she would be running in a new and conservative district, stated, "Gentlemen, you cannot become pregnant. You cannot understand that. You don't respect women or you would never introduce a bill of this sort." [10]

As expected, the vote to overthrow the abortion law was carried 79 to 68 with two absent (Alfred Lama of Brooklyn, who had supported the 1970 bill, as well as Stella). In 1970, we had won with 75 votes, Speaker Duryea, who had no need to vote at this time, being the decisive 76th. Thus, we had dropped seven votes—five affirmatives in 1970 who had switched this time.

The worst erosion came with three Westchester Republicans—Peter Biondo, Gordon Burrows, and Edward Myer III, a new legislator. They had all been considered committed to abortion. Months before, when Right to Life groups threatened them with primaries, NARAL had rallied our affiliates in their districts and pledged to help in a primary fight. But they had stalled off an alliance. Lieutenant

Governor Malcolm Wilson, a Catholic with immense influence and patronage in Westchester, had undoubtedly exerted superior pressure. To make matters worse, Myer at the last minute accepted Conservative Party endorsement.

Two unfortunate switches came from Armando Montana in the Bronx and Chester Straub in Brooklyn, Catholics who had stood up under bitter personal harassment last time but now collapsed. We had probably failed to give them adequate support.

All Tuesday evening and Wednesday morning, we made a desperate concentration on Senate votes. With the decision hanging on Senators Norman Levy of Nassau and Paul Bookson of Manhattan, both Jewish, we were on the phone hour after hour with every Jewish organization and rabbi in the area in a last plea to persuade the two legislators.

The Senate debate began shortly before noon on May 10, the galleries soon being emptied by police after a telephone caller warned that a bomb had been placed nearby. With the words "murder" and "barbaric slaughter of innocents" pounded incessantly into the legislators, Senator James H. Donovan of Chadwicks even had packets of photographs of fetuses placed on every desk. "This is lobbying during the debate," shouted Senator Joseph Galiber of the Bronx.

"You have no right to come to the floor of this body and ask us to enact into law church doctrine," insisted Senator Fred Ohrenstein of Manhattan. Observing that his Catholic faith made him opposed to abortion personally, Senator Thomas Laverne of Rochester concluded, "I cannot impose my view on everyone as a point of law." [11]

The Senate then voted to overthrow the abortion law by 30 to 27 compared with 31 to 26 in our favor in 1970. The four votes that defeated us included George Murphy in Nassau, who had replaced Senator Speno after his death, and Richard Schermerhorn of Orange—the first an unshakable Catholic in a district that his predecessor, also a Catholic, had found strongly for abortion in 1970 and so supported it; the second, a fervent conservative and antiabortionist who had defeated Senator Dominick in 1970.

The two votes that should have gone our way, and given us the Senate, remain inexplicable. Levy had been elected in place of Norman Lent, a Catholic who had voted for the abortion law in a proabortion district and then won a seat in Congress. The only explanation is that Levy's whole record—his vote for a one-year residence requirement for welfare cases, for example—locked him into a totally conservative position. Bookson, who had voted for the law the last time, had now been partially redistricted. But neither the small bloc of Catholic and Orthodox Jewish votes in his old Manhattan area or in the appended area in Brooklyn could account for this sudden reversal.

Everything now depended on Rockefeller's veto. Despite his pledge to stick by it, his compromise offer of a 16- and then an 18-week law, and the pressure of the Church and Cardinal Cooke, who personally appealed to the Governor against a veto, put his ultimate decision in doubt. NARAL was frantically involved in our national conference, planned months before and starting Thursday night, but we worked through the weekend to deluge the Governor with telegrams. The public at last seemed convinced that the right to abortion hung by a fragile thread. Western Union lines were so swamped it generally took a half-hour to reach an operator (although some calls admittedly came from the opposition). For the first time, our phone "trees" worked effectively, and every contact seemed to produce another ten telegrams.

After squeezing in a last, WNEW radio taping to appeal for telegrams on Saturday, May 13, I came home to hear on a news flash that the Governor had vetoed the Donovan-Crawford bill. It was a vigorously worded message. Rockefeller struck at "the extremes of personal vilification and political coercion brought to bear on members of the Legislature" and at "an emotional climate in which the truth about abortions and about the present state abortion law have become distorted almost beyond recognition."

Criticizing the vehemence of Catholic pressure groups, the Governor added, "I do not believe it is right for one group to impose its vision of morality on an entire society. Nor is it just or practical for the state to attempt to dictate the innermost personal beliefs and conduct of its citizens." Abortions would not have ended through the overthrow of the 1970 law, he noted. They would simply have been diverted, particularly among the poor, to back-room abortion mills.

"I can see no justifications now," he concluded, "for repealing this reform and thus condemning hundreds of thousands of women to the dark ages again."

We had squeaked through almost miraculously, saved by the

Governor's resolute stand. The right of abortion, and concomitant gains in maternal health standards, would be preserved for another year. But politically the abortion law remained in peril. The Governor, supposedly in line for a Cabinet appointment or Federal post if Nixon was reelected, might not be in Albany to save the law again by the spring of 1973. His automatic successor, Lieutenant Governor Wilson, was a bitter enemy of abortion.

We had learned the fury of the Catholic lobby: the use of untaxed funds such as the Right to Life committee's rent-free office at the New York Archdiocese, the total involvement of churches and priests in political races despite the illegality of tax-free money for campaigning. At best, Right to Life groups represented 15 or 20 percent of the dectorate. Yet this hard core behind the Donovan-Crawford bill had produced startling results through an intense concentration of money and manpower on a score of wavering and frightened legislators.[12]

The abortion movement, by contrast, had ignored all danger signals, and never harnessed a majority of the electorate, as it had done in 1970. Except for NARAL's early start, and organizations like Planned Parenthood, WONAAC, ZPG, and the clergy, which had entered the campaign by April, neither the public nor our original coalition became even partially mobilized until the Donovan-Crawford bill passed the Assembly.

No explanation of this apathy seems adequate. Perhaps the public was content to sit back and count on the Governor's veto. Perhaps it was so convinced of the worth of the law, and the remarkable health record achieved, that its destruction appeared inconceivable.

The peril was intensified by the number of antiabortion candidates that Right to Life groups entered in the June, 1972, primaries. The Coalition for Free Choice in Abortion put together a sizable campaign fund to support friendly legislators in tight races, and defeat a selected list of opponents. The shock of the last few months had finally awakened the abortion movement. Unless it could change the tone of the legislature in the primaries and general elections that fall, the chances of stopping another Catholic attack in 1973 were disturbingly slim.

NOTES

1. *Greenbush Area News of New Jersey*, April 13, 1972.

2. *Long Island Catholic*, December 16, 1971.

3. *Village Voice*, April 27, 1972, p. 27.

4. *New York Times*, April 18, 1972, p. 43; April 19, 1972, p. 94; April 25, 1972, p. 40.

5. This, and preceding paragraph: *New York Times*, April 24, 1972, p. 72; April 26, 1972, p. 31; United Synagogue of America, press release, May 5, 1972.

6. Dale E. Harrow, M.D., New York State Department of Health, before State Senate Committee on Health, February 10, 1971.

7. This, and preceding paragraph: *New York Times*, April 28, 1972, p. 20; April 29, 1972, p. 30; May 3, 1972, pp. 18, 46.

8. New York *Daily News*, May 5, 1972, p. 5.

9. This, and five preceding paragraphs: *New York Times*, May 7, 1972, p. 1; May 8, 1972, pp. 32, 36; May 9, 1972, p. 1; May 11, 1972, p. 1; New York *Post*, May 22, 1972, p. 31.

10. This, and preceding paragraph: New York *Post*, May 9, 1972, pp. 3, 70; *New York Times*, News of the Week, May 14, 1972, p. 4.

11. *New York Times*, May 11, 1972, p. 1.

12. This, and preceding paragraph: *New York Times*, May 14, 1972, pp. 1, 62; May 8, 1972, pp. 1, 43; October 28, 1971, p. 1; Association for the Study of Abortion *Newsletter*, Vol. VI, No. 4–Vol. VII, No. 1, p. 1.

CHAPTER FIFTEEN

CLIMAX TO REVOLT

No other social revolution in our country has achieved such immediate and sweeping results as the campaign for legalized abortion. While only about 8,000 legal abortions were performed in 1966, the number soared to over 600,000 in 1972. In six years, the abortion campaign became one of the most explosive issues of our time.

Eighteen new laws were passed to legalize abortion—radical laws in Alaska, Hawaii, New York, and Washington; moderate ALI laws in thirteen other states, with California law broadened so that it fell somewhere between the two groups. As a result of court decisions, the District of Columbia, and to a lesser extent, Wisconsin and New Jersey, were opened to legalized abortion. High courts declared the medieval statutes of six states invalid, two of these cases receiving a final hearing before the U.S. Supreme Court in the fall of 1972.

What distinguishes abortion from most other social campaigns is that it became a people's revolt, developed at the precinct level of politics. Striking deep into the national conscience, enveloping our most fundamental instincts on sex and procreation, it galvanized the democratic political process as no other issue but the Vietnam war. But in contrast to Vietnam where the individual's will, and often that of his representatives in Congress, were thwarted by the power of the White

House and Pentagon, abortion provided a rare chance for decision-making by the people.

By the very nature of its base in the individual's right of free choice in childbearing and the individual's opposition to dictation by church or state, the abortion movement soon took in a broad range of support from every economic, social, and political stratum. This coalition—conservative Republicans, reform Democrats, millionaires, welfare rights organizations, militant Socialists, Catholic legislators and laymen (despite the hierarchy's bitter enmity), even black power delegations when they got over their fear of genocide—gave the movement its unique strength.

For Women's Liberation, abortion became the great catalyst. Whether they aimed at moderate goals like job equality, or the complete dissolution of the nuclear family, the feminists quickly realized that all their programs depended on a woman's control of her own body and fertility. "The ultimate freedom remains the right of every woman to legalized abortion," I had predicted in 1966. The disparate elements of feminism could not only coalesce around abortion; it also gave them a universal issue with boundless emotional impact. Even the Equal Rights Amendment, passed by Congress in 1972 after a campaign of 49 years, never roused mass participation. A sit-in at an all-male bar produced only a day's titillation in the headlines. Abortion proved the only issue that could draw all segments of women to the barricades. And radical politicians, like the Young Socialist Alliance, eventually sought to build a mass base around abortion through WONAAC, on the premise that once women have mobilized for a highly personal right, they could expand their demands to other areas.[1]

The most critical effect of legalized abortion was on the number of unwanted and unplanned births. When 600,000 legal abortions annually are correlated with 2.65 million unwanted and unplanned births to married couples alone between 1966 and 1970, according to the National Fertility Study, abortion obviously could fill a desperate void in fertility control.[2]

The new abortion laws showed their impact by the end of 1971. The number of births dropped 159,000 in 1971 over 1970, a decrease of 4 percent. In March 1972, after a declining birth rate for 13 of the previous 14 months, there were 31,000 fewer births than the same month the year before—a reduction that could cut the 1972 total by hundreds of thousands if the trend continued. (Even with 800,000 more women of childbearing age than the year before!)

While other birth control techniques and motivations contributed to this startling pattern, the impact of abortion is particularly evident from geographic analysis. In New York City, with the most extensive abortion facilities in the country, the number of births dropped 12 percent, three times that of the nation as a whole. In the mid-Atlantic states, in New England, on the West Coast, including Alaska and Hawaii—all with immediate or close access to legalized abortion—the number of births dropped 8.3 percent, 6 percent, and 7.2 percent respectively, again far more sharply than the rest of the country.[3]

By guaranteeing that no child comes into this world unwanted, unloved, and uncared for, legalized abortion produced immeasurable gains in psychiatric and social health. "There can be nothing more destructive to a child's spirit than being unwanted, and there are few things more disruptive to a woman's spirit than being forced without love or need into motherhood," concludes the Group for the Advancement of Psychiatry.[4]

The gains in maternal health have been proved by New York City statistics—a decrease of over 50 percent in "incomplete" or butchered abortions by back-alley practitioners; a similar decrease in maternal mortality rates; a 10 percent decline in illegitimacy rates. The health of two groups was particularly benefited. Legalized abortion cut the number of unwanted births both for teenage girls and older women at a time when childbearing, and the survival potential of the infant, take on accelerated risks.[5]

Above all, the abortion movement destroyed to a large extent the system of exploitation in which generations of women had been trapped. The savage ordeal of underworld abortions, its generally substandard medical care at exaggerated prices, its debasing secrecy and harassment by police, even the hypocrisy of so-called "therapeutic" abortion where women crawled and begged before hospital committees—these had been largely replaced by the dignity and safety of legalized abortion.

Commercialization, unfortunately, has still not been eliminated.

While the cost of first-trimester abortion runs about $150 in New York and about $200 in most legalized states, the owners and medical staffs of commercial clinics continue to make excessive profits by handling heavy case loads in brief periods. Commercial referral services, although banned in New York, continue to operate elsewhere, squeezing unnecessary fees from women, on top of clinic costs.

It is unlikely this problem will be solved until abortion care becomes part of public health medicine. Health services of essential importance, such as cancer tests, immunization, and venereal disease detection, have long been provided to rich as well as poor by Federal and local government funding. Abortion certainly ranks among these priorities. The benefits to society from increased maternal and child health, from the lowering of illegitimacy rates, and certainly from the achievement of a stable population recommended by the Presidential Commission on Population Growth, all demand that abortion care be rated as a national priority, free and available to all under government support.

The severest test of a social revolution is the inclusion of seemingly unattainable demands into the daily practices of a people. In 1966, when I wrote that "abortion as well as marital privacy deserves the protection of the Constitution," only a handful of radicals had the effrontery to classify abortion as an "inalienable right," and insist on a platform of free choice in childbearing by abortion as well as contraception. Yet by 1969, the California Supreme Court had incorporated similar language into its Belous opinion. And by 1972, almost a dozen high court decisions had affirmed and reaffirmed these rights.[6]

The rapid advance of legalized abortion in turn gave the feminist movement an explosive boost. Abortion provided the prime weapon against sexism and the "biological imperative"—the prison of unwanted childbearing that had chained most women to the role of housekeepers, nurses, and cooks under male dominance. Once sex had been detached from pregnancy, Women's Liberation could construct its own ethics on the ash-heap of puritan morality. The single woman could no longer be terrorized by social ostracism; the married woman no longer forced into deeper subservience by an unwanted child. "Protecting the mother's morals . . . turns out to mean deterring her from having sexual relations," Federal District Judge Jon O. Newman pointed out in the decision overthrowing Connecticut's abortion law, and "the Supreme Court has decided that such a purpose cannot validate invasion of a woman's right to privacy in matters of family and sex." [7]

The dependence of women on men (which Ms. Germaine Greer built into her castration thesis in *The Female Eunuch*)[8] and other targets of Women's Liberation—the menial housewife, programmed into a cheap, controllable source of breeding, child care, and domestic labor through theological, economic, and social systems—had now been deprived of their essential prop.

The immediate evidence showed that women grasped this opportunity for independence. In December 1971 there were 3,000 fewer marriages than the same month the year before despite the sharp increase of women of marriageable age. In a survey of students on fifty campuses by the John D. Rockefeller III Fund, almost one-third of those polled considered marriage "obsolete" (seven out of ten still aiming eventually for legal marriage). While about a third of all women remained unmarried by age 21 in 1960, the number of single women at this age soared to almost 50 percent by 1970.[9]

If women were marrying later, or sometimes not at all, the impact of abortion became particularly evident among teenagers, a group that had previously borne a high proportion of illegitimate births, or suffered the traditional shotgun marriage. With the Joint Program for the Study of Abortion study of 73,000 abortions at sixty-six institutions across the country showing almost 25 percent performed on teenagers, the pattern of enforced marriage seemed to be headed for oblivion.[10]

In addition to the decline of births to married women, the feminists have also promoted a trend toward childless marriage. "The best thing I can do for mankind is never to have children," a young valedictorian told her graduating class at Mills College, California, a few years ago. "Given the complexities of the task and the urgent need to further curb our birth rate, it would be far wiser to regard parenthood as a specialized occupation—and childlessness as our cultural norm," insists Ms. Ellen Peck, author of *The Baby Trap* and an officer of the National Organization for Non-Parents, which spearheads the movement.

The impact of legalized abortion has given Women's Liberation a base for the complete reorganization of the institution of marriage itself. The feminist can now turn her marriage into an equal partnership with her husband. Child-care centers, equal division of income and property no matter who produces the larger share, a contract before marriage which fairly divides domestic responsibilities—all these are techniques to enlarge her freedom. In addition, the feminist demands a complete restructuring of sexual morality. "End the double standard of sexual morality in all facets of life," Seattle Radical Women announces in its manifesto. Guarantee the right to "extramarital sexual relations free from criminal sanctions of 'adultery.' " [11] Or as Victoria Claflin Woodhull, one of the earliest feminists, put it, "I have an inalienable constitutional and natural right to love whom I may, to love as long or as short a period as I can, to change that love every day if I please."

The most radical feminists want an even more sweeping revolt—the end of the nuclear family itself. "If women are to effect a significant amelioration in their condition, it seems obvious that they must refuse to marry," Germaine Greer insists. Once we abolish the "patriarchal family," she concludes, we have abolished "a necessary substructure of the authoritarian state." [12]

But whether the radical feminist chooses a commune or solitary living, whether she prefers homosexuality or a male partner, for a month or years, her challenge has already eroded the nuclear family. Security, once the cornerstone of the marriage contract, has lost its appeal, particularly in middle-class circles. Critics, like Ann Richardson Roiphe, complain that the radicals "would have us abandon ugly security for free flight." [13] Actually they have replaced one security with another—the security of a husband's salary and homestead for the biological security of abortion, and the deeper, psychological security of their own personal development.

Other critics claim that the revolt virtually means the death of sex, returning "the human species to the condition of neuter-sexed amoebae," as Dr. Fiona Graham of the William Allenson White Institute has written. "They are not feminists but psychological nihilists. They deny evolution, sexual differentiation and reproduction." [14]

The real issue in the feminist revolt, however, is not the death of sex but the rebirth of sex. The extremists, whom Dr. Graham attacks, may never become more than an isolated phenomenon, at best a tenth of all women over the next decade. But serious erosion of the nuclear family will come from a much larger mass of feminist converts who will shape family and husband to their own ideal of equality, and remake the laws and traditions of puritan morality in their own image. What we will have is a new birth of sex, not just among youth, but married and single women of all ages—an explosion of sexuality that threatens and terrifies the guardians of ancestral virtues whether in the churches or the White House. It is this threat that makes the Catholic Church as well as President Nixon lash out at legalized abortion. And when the President opposes sex education and contraception for teenagers as doing "nothing to preserve and strengthen close family relations," he is really defending traditional marriage against the new sexuality.

With contraception, and now abortion, eradicating the old puritan bludgeon of fear, the barriers against cohabitation on most college campuses have been wiped out. Parietal rules have become a tidbit of gossip for aging alumni. Even at home, parents are being forced to accept, albeit grudgingly, the joint occupance of a son's or daughter's room by a companion of the opposite sex. "My whole attitude towards sex has changed enormously in recent years," one father admitted to a *New York Times* reporter. "I feel generally that the sexual ethics of young people now are better than those I had as a boy. It wasn't ethics then; it was hypocrisy." [15]

A recent study for the Presidential Commission on Population Growth shows that nearly half of all unmarried women have had sexual intercourse by the age of nineteen. While more blacks than whites had intercourse in each age group, 16 percent of the whites admitted to four or more partners, less than 11 percent of the blacks did so.[16]

This attack on traditional standards of morality and marriage, spurred by contraception, but particularly by abortion, undoubtedly represents for President Nixon and his "middle America" a plot against the American way of life itself. It must seem to them the eruption of a nihilistic hedonism which could destroy the puritan work ethic on which the nation was built—the Calvinistic concentration on work, profit, and success as the consuming objective of man's energies, depending to a large extent on the suppression of sexuality. (As a minor example, consider the prohibitions against sex as a deterrent to athletic prowess that school and college coaches have always tried to impose on their teams.) The new sexuality, therefore, becomes an indictment of The Establishment and three hundred years of moral discipline. The President's abhorrence of legalized abortion partly stems from a political strategy of wooing Catholic votes. But more fundamentally it represents the conviction that laws and customs controlling sex through fear are still the patriotic way to keep the structure of society in its ancient mold.

Similarly, the impact of legalized abortion raises a startling challenge to what Prof. Mary Daly of Boston College calls "patriarchal authoritarianism," notably in the Catholic hierarchy. In its most vivid form, it symbolizes the struggle between the individual and the institution which has regimented and controlled much of society's ethical choices for two thousand years. "What the women's movement is saying is that decisions will be made affecting the processes of 'nature,' and that women as individuals will make the decisions in matters most intimately concerning themselves," Prof. Daly, herself a Catholic theologian, points out. "I think that this, on the deepest level, is what authoritarian religion fears."

This struggle between individual choice and authoritarianism has already been accelerated "into a situation in which open war is declared between feminism in this country and official Roman Catholicism," Prof. Daly concludes. "As this issue surfaces more and more, women are seeing the church as their enemy. For its part, the institutional church is focusing its tremendous lobbying power on the issue." [17]

Abortion has thus become the most volcanic ethical struggle of our time—incorporating an alliance far beyond feminism—simply because it threatens Catholicism more seriously than any other issue. It has reached the stage of open church-state conflict because most of the public considers abortion, as well as contraception, a private judgment, and the Church's furious lobbying, an invasion of the individual's bedroom.

The authoritarian control of the Church over family and procreation has been threatened on many levels. The termination of the fetus—or murder, as the Church sees it—is only a starting point. What the Church fears equally is the rejection of its dogma by a large proportion of its communicants and the increasing use of abortion by Catholics as a backup to contraception. Concomitantly, it fears a sharp decline in the size of Catholic families and the acceptance by Catholic women, as the Population Commission study proves, of the same small-family goals as the rest of the country. The whole structure of authority is further threatened when the single Catholic woman need no longer be forced into marriage against her will, or bear an illegitimate child for a Catholic foundling home—children that often become priests and nuns, who, when adopted, become the source of considerable financial contributions to the Church from adopting parents.

The heightening of this conflict may have already crippled the ecumenical tradition—a thesis enunciated at a NARAL national meeting by a leading Protestant spokesman. The Catholic hierarchy has not only moved its debate in 1972 to the level of frenzy and vituperation; authoritarianism precludes any role for individual choice. Thus, Dean Thomas L. Shaffer of Notre Dame Law School protests that ". . . every defender of abortion reform I have met refuse[s] to go into the evidence of life—biological, behavioral, ethical or affective." [18] This is an absurdity of fact, considering the hundreds of books, articles, conferences, and public discussions devoted to such debate by proponents of abortion. It is also an absurdity of logic. What Dean Shaffer and other Catholic officials seem to want is an evaluation of the evidence by authorities, by committees of biologists, behavioralists, or ethical experts who will make the decisions for all women on when life begins.

The Church cannot seem to accept that its committee of experts may come out with different answers than another committee. Or that no matter what a committee rules, many of us will simply reject it. Legalized abortion, in sum, is the culmination of the struggle of individualism versus authoritarianism. In the most personal terms possible, I can only conclude that my wife's life, health, and desire to terminate a pregnancy rate far above the claims of the fetus no matter what a committee of biologists or moralists rule as to its living characteristics. Neither church nor state nor any committee will ever force my wife to have a child against her will despite the penalities or hardships we might suffer to preserve that right of choice.

The Church seems to be going to any lengths to enforce its authority. The insistence on a Connecticut law, establishing life from the moment of conception, by a Catholic governor and Catholic-controlled legislature, immediately after a Federal court declared the old statute unconstitutional, was a frightening precedent both of law and power politics. The same desperate approach has since been initiated in the Massachusetts legislature, and may be followed in other legislatures with strong Catholic influence. We can dread the possibility that the Church may continue to ride roughshod over further high courts, and even the U.S. Supreme Court, by going to Congress with a bill defining when life begins. Such tactics would make legalized abortion a permanent and bloody battleground in church-state relations.

Not only the Catholic Church, but even some adherents of the abortion movement reject abortion as a population control measure. This amounts to semantics. While the obvious technique of population control is voluntary sterilization—a man or woman by his or her act proclaiming that no further children are wanted—every contraceptive use, and every abortion, not only prevents a potential or actual pregnancy at that moment, but increases the chances of fewer births and greater population control that month or year. While proponents of abortion call it a backup measure to contraception, in practical fact, an increasing number of women are including it in the contraceptive package by *choice*. A woman who gives up the pill because of side effects or other reasons may choose the IUD despite its failure rate on the theory she can always compensate for a failure through legalized abortion.

It seems absurd to keep denying the function of abortion in population control—denial stemming from the fear that population control implies compulsion. Yet we had better face the fact that some form of compulsion—even the psychological compulsion of overcrowding, environmental chaos, and other factors that have brought the family goals of non-Catholic women down to 2.35 children and Catholic women to 2.75 children—is not only healthy, but imperative.

The facts on population growth have been analyzed so exhaustively that it is only necessary to outline the mathematical threat. While world population in 1650 numbered a half-billion with a doubling time of 250 years, by 1970 the total had soared to 3.6 billions, which will be doubled, at the present growth rate, in 33 years. Even if population stability, or zero population growth, were achieved in 60 years, we would still have 15 billion people crowding the earth.[19]

The collateral menace, as projected by Club of Rome scientists in their study, *The Limits of Growth*, is that reckless industrialization will consume resources, exploding population will outstrip food and industrial supplies, and runaway pollution will overwhelm the biosphere by the year 2020. In their *Blueprint for Survival*, Sir Julian Huxley and dozens of Britain's most noted scholars warn that population and industrial expansion are rushing us to "the breakdown of society, and the irreversible disruption of the life support systems within the lifetime of our children." [20]

The projection for the United States has improved slightly. In March 1972 the average family size dropped to 2.136 children, just a fraction above the replacement level of 2.110. If we miraculously were able to reach ZPG, and maintain it for 70 years with immigration held at the present level, we would then level off at about 270 or 280 millions. But if we could only hold to 2.3 children per family—a distinct threat with the rapid increase of women entering the fertile period—our population would double in 80 years. Perhaps the worst danger from pollution and environmental chaos is the increasing concentration of population in a few metropolitan regions on the East and West Coasts—75 percent of Americans living on less than 2 percent of our land area—where a population is shooting up at a rate faster than in India.[21]

The critical obstacle to the small family has always been the high rate of unwanted pregnancies. A few years ago, Profs. Ryder and Westoff of Princeton University found that about one-half of all couples, intending to limit their families after the second, third, and fourth pregnancies, were unsuccessful. Their more recent study, as we have seen, shows about 550,000 unwanted births annually among married couples.[22]

While legalized abortion has started to diminish unwanted births, it is primarily the unwanted pregnancy that must be eliminated—a target that depends on the development of an ideal contraceptive, perhaps an injection that requires only one decision by the woman, and protects her permanently without failure rate or side effects unless she should want to terminate its protection. All present techniques fall short of these standards. The problems of motivation and application, even with the pill, and the constant chance of forgetting a daily dosage, are too complex. Failure rates add to the obstacles. The highly touted IUD still has a failure rate of 3 percent, which means that about 30 of every 1,000 women each year will become pregnant against their will. While the rate improves after a year or more, many women have to give it up because of bleeding or expulsion.[23]

In addition, a recent Planned Parenthood study shows that a fourth of all women who want to limit their families fail both through ignorance and dependence on ineffective, "drugstore" methods—mainly the poor without access to competent medical advice and care.[24]

The most effective techniques at this time are abortion and voluntary sterilization. Abortion has prevented 600,000 unwanted births in the last year, perhaps a few hundred thousand more since the number of secret abortions is unknown. Sterilization's impact increases at a steep rate of mathematical progression—each procedure permanently removing the man or woman as a future parent. The latest medical statistics, uncorroborated and possibly high, show 750,000 male and 250,000 female sterilizations annually. Another barometer of demand is that the first vasectomy clinic was started in New York in 1969. Three years later, almost 200 had sprung up across the country. If close to 1,000,000 sterilizations continue to be performed annually, an increasingly larger segment of the fertile population, particularly with the trend toward sterilization for the young wife or husband after one or two children, will be removed from potential parenthood.

In addition to permanence, the great advantage of voluntary sterilization is the simplicity of technique—the male requiring fifteen minutes or so in a doctor's office, the new female techniques of laparoscopy and culdoscopy replacing the traditional hospital stay with a four-hour clinic visit. There are subtler advantages. Most couples worry about the tragic possibility that a spouse and children could be killed in an accident, and the survivor could remarry and want another family. Under old methods, the chances of restoring fertility reached 40 percent at best. But new research—the implantation of a tiny valve in the male vas, for example—may make it possible by 1975 for the doctor to leave the valve in the "off" position until the male decides to restore his fertility and have the valve switched "on." Another backup, already in use, are sperm "banks." The male can deposit his sperm at banks around the country where it will be kept permanently frozen. If he decides on a child, and surgery fails to restore his fertility, the sperm can be unfrozen and often successfully used to produce a pregnancy through artificial insemination.[25]

Since abortion and sterilization have been such important factors in bringing down the birth rate, it would seem logical that the government would do everything possible to extend their impact. The Presidential Commission on Population strongly supported both techniques as well as calling for immediate stabilization of our population. Logic, however, has never concerned President Nixon's political aims. He rejected the major recommendations of his own commission, particularly on abortion. His Secretary of Health, Education, and Welfare, who had established an advisory board on abortion policy, promptly urged that legalized abortion be opposed. Although no state law prohibits sterilization, and Association for Voluntary Sterilization records show almost one-third of all applicants listing themselves as Catholics, even approved and existing sterilization programs were blocked.[26]

In June 1971 the Office of Economic Opportunity approved a sterilization program around the country with a sizable budget. In January 1972 guidelines were finally cleared, but then suddenly impounded. The funding for one project had started, but the $682,000 that was supposed to be invested elsewhere disappeared. O.E.O.'s director of health affairs suddenly developed reservations about costs and priorities of sterilization, but denied this reversal in policy had anything to do with White House orders.[27]

The federal government thus refuses to develop either a population policy or support two of its essential ingredients, abortion and voluntary sterilization (although copious government funds for sterilization have gone to India, which might raise some questions about why Nixon wants small families abroad but not in the U.S.). We need a concrete population policy here immediately, and the vague blueprints of a few population groups for a two-child-family target are not enough. Sir Julian Huxley's scientific team urged, among other essentials, that Britain must cut its population in half. Prof. Paul Ehrlich of Stanford University, former president of ZPG, Inc., calls for a United States cutback from the present 210 million to 150 million.[28]

This cutback, requiring a determined drive for a one-child family, must be achieved quickly, in my opinion. Despite the problems of economic and social dislocation—a sharp drop in the number of school pupils, for example—during the transition period, only the one-child family can produce stabilization within a reasonable time, and eventually bring us to 150 million and a reasonable balance between our population, resources, and environmental demands.

The voluntary approach just cannot work fast enough, and we

have delayed even mild forms of population control too long. We are dealing now with sanity and survival. We must accept the principle that "having a child is no longer a matter of private will, but of public welfare," as Dr. Ashley Montagu, the anthropologist, has put it. "Whatever endangers the public welfare should, therefore, be carefully regulated."

We accept death controls without question—the extension of life through public health programs, and prolongation of terminal illness often against the patient's will, which have reduced deaths to about one for every two births in the world and are partly responsible for our runaway population. Why do we draw back from the slightest controls over birth?

As a start, we should set the minimum age of marriage at twenty-three, which will postpone childbearing and eliminate some pregnancies of hasty, young marriages. The states have long set minimum ages of marriage, and raising the minimum should not be a serious inconvenience. Premarital pregnancies could be terminated at a woman's choice by legalized abortion.

A more effective step would be economic penalties against couples who bear three or more children; perhaps for a second child, in the transition period. Since penalties must not discriminate against any economic, social, or racial group, particularly the poor, they would have to be based on graduated income. A family with $6,000 income, for example, might be taxed $600 for a second child, $800 for a third; while a family with $50,000 would pay $15,000 and $17,500.

Technology, which has not been too successful in producing the ideal contraceptive, may do better with abortion in helping to achieve the one-child family. The overwhelming obstacle to abortion from the standpoint of the Catholic Church is the presence of a fetus, even an inch of tissue in early gestation. But what if abortion, or "potential abortion," could be carried out before the presence of a fetus was even known? What if the procedure could be kept completely under the woman's control? These are the possibilities offered by a new drug—already mentioned as a "miracle drug"—the prostaglandins.

Chemically, the prostaglandins are a group of fourteen fatty acids found in almost all body tissues. Used in minute amounts, injected into the cervix, into the amniotic sac through the abdomen or in other ways, different members of the prostaglandin family have proved remarkably effective in aborting both first trimester and second trimester pregnancies.

Far more portentous in its religious and political implications, however, is the use of the prostaglandins as a monthly contraceptive, actually a "periconceptional contraceptive," administered by vaginal tampon, suppository, or perhaps orally. The woman need never know if she is pregnant or not. The prostaglandins will start menstruation whether she is pregnant, or simply has had an unexpected delay in the onset of her regular menses. In fact, she may only have to use it three or four times a year, whenever her period seems late.

Particularly for some Catholic women, who may still feel guilt over vacuum abortion, the prostaglandin approach removes any knowledge of the existence of a fetus. More importantly, it should undercut in large part the Church's objections to potential "murder," when even the most determined theologian could not prove that conception had taken place. For all women, it becomes the final gift by eliminating medical bureaucracy and costs—the tampons or oral dosages hopefully available through drugstores or clinic outlets.

Although successful tests have been conducted on hundreds of women in Britain, Uganda, Sweden, and more recently the United States, moving "at rocket speed," as Dr. Charles H. Hendricks of the University of North Carolina Medical School puts it, the previous disappointments in fertility control should temper current enthusiasm. Yet scores of prestigious researchers around the world have produced increasingly optimistic results—more studies on prostaglandins appearing in the last year than on any other drug. Dr. Hendricks insists it "represents a landmark in mankind's struggle to protect himself from his own fertility." [29]

What the abortion movement accomplished in six years was to shake up the country as it has only been shaken by the abolitionists and Alabama bus boycotts and early peace marchers. This raucous, overangry, and scrambled collection of 75 national and state organizations emerged from a few pioneers and stayed glued together simply because we knew it had to be done. We knew that abortion wasn't just central to a woman's right of choice. It was central to everything in life and how we wanted to live it.

If it started as an expression of Jean-Paul Sartre's dictum that the responsibility of the intellectual today is action, many of us also seized on the movement as an outlet for our frustrations with a system and government that increasingly rendered the voter impotent to control his own destiny. Abortion not only involved us in an essential moral issue, but offered the possibility of achievement and radical change. It offered adventure in a democratic process grown flaccid from lack of commitment. The referral networks brought many of us to the knife-edge of danger that gave the movement its aura of passion and joy.

The greatest strength of the early abortion radicals was that we grasped the nature of the problem long before it had surfaced, and clung to our demands despite ridicule, public vilification, and danger from existing laws. In our stubborn way we knew we were right, no matter how many opposed us.

A final tribute to our rightness came from the highest court of New York State, the Court of Appeals, which on July 7, 1972, by a 5 to 2 vote ruled against Prof. Robert Byrn's attempt to have the fetus declared a human person with all rights under the Fourteenth Amendment. Noting that "unborn children have never been recognized as persons in the law in the whole sense," the court concluded, "the Constitution does not confer or require legal personality for the unborn."

Another, final affirmation of our platform came from U.S. District Judge Joseph H. Young in a second case involving Dr. Milan Vuitch in Maryland. Vuitch had been arrested in 1968 for performing abortion in his Maryland clinic in conflict with Maryland law, which allowed abortion only in accredited hospitals. It had been my contention from the start that physicians like Vuitch, along with other early referral services, had produced records of safety and skill in clinic and in-office abortion equal to any hospital.

In overthrowing the hospital requirement of the Maryland law on June 22, 1972, and affirming that "a woman does have a constitutionally protected 'fundamental personal right' to seek an abortion," Judge Young declared ". . . it is not alleged that clinical abortions actually *were* unsafe in 1968—only that the medical profession had not at that time recognized their safety. It would be manifestly unfair to require Dr. Vuitch to serve a prison term solely because he may have recognized a fact which many of his colleagues had not." [30]

Dr. Vuitch and a few of us who demanded the right of clinic

abortion as early as 1965 not only recognized the facts, but had the persistence to make the medical profession, the courts, and most of the public finally recognize them with us.

We were determined to prove that radicalism hadn't been washed out of the American dream. It was a test of individualism against church and bureaucracy. Explosions like the abortion fight are needed to bring the system back to fundamentals. The abortion movement reminded people that social revolution is a continuing process, and the meaning of America disappears when the revolution stops. Perhaps more important than producing 600,000 legal abortions in 1972, the abortion movement affirmed that an act of faith can become revolution.

NOTES

1. Lawrence Lader, *Abortion* (New York: Bobbs-Merrill Co. Inc.; 1966; Boston: Beacon Press, 1967), p. 167; *New York Times*, March 23, 1972, p. 1.

2. "The 1970 National Fertility Study," *Family Planning Perspectives*, Vol. 4, No. 2, April 1972, p. 12. Final analysis of statistics is expected to show unplanned and unwanted births at over 550,000 annually.

3. *Ibid.*, p. 7; and *New York Times*, May 24, 1972, p. 7.

4. "The Right to Abortion: A Psychiatric View," Group for the Advancement of Psychiatry, Committee on Psychiatry and the Law, Report No. 75, New York, 1969.

5. *Family Planning Perspectives, op. cit.*, pp. 12–13.

6. Lader, *op. cit.*, p. 173.

7. *Abele v. Markle I*, 342 F. Supp. 800 (D. Conn., 1972).

8. Germaine Greer, *The Female Eunuch* (New York: Bantam Books, Inc., 1972).

9. Center for Optimum Environments *Newsletter* (Hartford, Conn.), Volume 2, No. 2, January–February, 1972, p. 5; "Marital Status and Living Arrangements: March 1971," No. 225, Government Printing Office, Washington, D.C., p. 20.

10. Christopher Tietze and Sarah Sewit, "Joint Program for the Study of Abortion (JPSA)," *Studies in Family Planning,* The Population Council, New York, Vol. 3, No. 6, June, 1972, p. 100.

11. "Program and Structures," Seattle Radical Women, October, 1969.

12. Greer, *op. cit.,* pp. 340, 350.

13. Ann Richardson Roiphe, "The Family Is Out of Fashion," *New York Times Sunday Magazine*, August 15, 1971, p. 10.

14. William Allenson White Institute *Newsletter*, Vol. VI, No. 2, Winter 1971–1972, p. 9.

15. *New York Times*, May 15, 1972, p. 1.

16. *New York Times*, May 10, 1972, p. 9.

17. This, and preceding paragraph: Mary Daly, "Abortion and Sexual Caste," *Commonweal*, Vol. 95, February 4, 1972, p. 415.

18. *New York Times*, June 19, 1972, p. 32.

19. *The Ecologist* (London), Vol. 2, No. 1, January 1972.

20. Dennis L. Meadows *et al., Limits of Growth* (New York: Universe Books, 1972), pp. 34, 37, 38.

21. *New York Times*, May 24, 1972, p. 7; "Population and the American Future: Excerpts," *Studies in Family Planning*, The Population Council, New York, Vol. 3, No. 5, May 1972, pp. 77–95; *Life*, May 19, 1972, p. 47.

22. Norman B. Ryder and Charles F. Westoff, *Reproduction in the United States; 1965* (Princeton, N.J.: Princeton University Press, 1971), p. 322.

23. Christopher Tietze, "Ranking of Contraceptive Methods by Levels of Effectiveness," Excerpta Medica International Congress Series No. 224, Proceedings of VIII Annual Meeting, American Association of Planned Parenthood Physicians, Boston, Massachusetts, April 1970, *Advances in Planned Parenthood*, Vol. 5.

24. *New York Times*, June 6, 1972, p. 16.

25. Lawrence Lader, *Foolproof Birth Control: Male and Female Sterilization* (Boston: Beacon Press, 1972).

26. *New York Times*, June 21, 1972, p. 48.

27. *New York Times*, May 28, 1972; Washington *Star*, June 1, 1972.

28. *New York Times*, January 14, 1972, p. 1.

29. Charles H. Hendricks, "Prostaglandins and Therapeutic Abortion: Summary of Present Status" (unpublished), from Brook Lodge Symposium, Augusta, Mich., June 12–14, 1972. This and other prostaglandins abstracts are available from The Upjohn Co. through Manning, Selvage, & Lee, Inc. New York.

30. This, and two preceding paragraphs: *New York Times*, July 8, 1972, p. 1; *State of Maryland v. Vuitch*, Civil No. 71-1129 Y (U.S. Dist. Ct., Dist. of Maryland, June 22, 1972).

BIBLIOGRAPHY

This is not a definitive bibliography on abortion, but rather a list of sources that were most valuable to the author. It rarely includes sources already cited by the author in *Abortion* (1966, 1967); and only occasionally repeats citations from the chapter footnotes.

The most comprehensive and up-to-date bibliography on abortion has been compiled by Dr. Christopher Tietze of The Population Council, New York, to whom the author is deeply indebted for many of his references. Another authoritative bibliography covering the early period of abortion, *An Annotated Bibliography of Induced Abortion*, was edited by Dr. Gunnar K. af Geijerstam of the University of Michigan's Center for Population Planning in 1969. Ms. Mildred B. Beck of the National Center for Family Planning Services, U.S. Department of Health, Education, and Welfare, has also drawn up a valuable list of references. A number of important articles and court decisions are available in reprint from the Association for the Study of Abortion, New York.

Abortion Rights Association of New York, *Listing of Selected New York State Abortion Clinics*, issued by the Medical Responsibilities Committee, Abortion Rights Association of New York, June 1972.

Aimakhu, V. E., "Vacuum aspiration in the management of abortions," *International Surgery*, 57:13–16, January 1972.

American Friends Service Committee, *Who Shall Live? Man's Control Over Birth and Death* (New York: Hill and Wang, 1970).

American Journal of Obstetrics and Gynecology, "A statement on abortion by one hundred professors of obstetrics," *American Journal of Obstetrics and Gynecology*, 112:992–998, 1 April 1972.

American Journal of Public Health, Vol. 61, No. 3: 487–542, March 1971.

American Medical Association, "Special issue: medicolegal aspects of abortion," *The Citation*, 24:65–80, 15 December 1971.

American Public Health Association, "Recommended standards for abortion services: adopted by the Executive Board of the APHA at the 98th annual meeting in Houston, Texas, October 29, 1970," *American Journal of Public Health*, 61:396–398, February 1971.

Anderson, G. G., "Clinical reports on induction of abortion: efficiency and side effects: intravenous administration, report IV," *Prostaglandins in Fertility Control* (World Health Organization), (Stockholm: Karolinska Institutet, 1971), pp. 85–88.

Anderson, G. G., and L. Speroff, "Prostaglandins and abortion," *Clinical Obstetrics and Gynecology*, 14:245–257, March 1971.

Anwyl, J. H., "The role of private counseling for problem pregnancies," *Clinical Obstetrics and Gynecology*, 14:1225–1229, December 1971.

Arnold, C. B., R. C. Lerner, and S. Wassertheil, "New York state obstetricians and the new abortion law: attitudes toward the law and willingness to perform abortions," presented at the Annual Meeting of the Population Association of America, Washington, D.C., 24 April 1971.

Ballard, W. M., "California abortion statistics for 1971," *California Medicine*, 116:55, April 1972.

Bardis, P. D., "Abortion and public opinion: a research note," *Journal of Marriage and the Family*, 34:111, February 1972.

Beasley, J. D., P. M. Sarrel, L. Lader, K. R. Niswander, P. E. Sutton, and K. R. Whittemore, "Abortion and poverty: the social discrimination involved in the practice of abortion," *Abortion in a Changing World*, edited by R. E. Hall, 2:21–38 (New York: Columbia University Press, 1970).

Beck, M. B., "Abortion: the mental health consequences of unwantedness," *Seminars in Psychiatry*, 2:263–274, August 1970.

Beck, M. B., "The destiny of the unwanted child: the issue of compulsory pregnancy," *Abortion and the Unwanted Child* (California Committee on Therapeutic Abortion), (New York: Springer, 1971), pp. 59–71.

Beck, M. B., S. H. Newman, and S. Lewit, "Abortion: a national public and mental health problem: past, present, and proposed research," *American Journal of Public Health*, 59:2131–2143, December 1969.

Beric, B. M., and M. Kupresanin, "Vacuum aspiration, using paracervical block, for legal abortion as an outpatient procedure up to the 12th week of pregnancy," *Lancet*, 2:619–620, 18 September 1971.

Berk, H., J. Ullman, and J. Berger, "Experience and complications with the use of hypertonic intra-amniotic saline solution," *Surgery, Gynecology, and Obstetrics*, 133:955–958, December 1971.

Blake, J., "Abortion and public opinion: the 1960–1970 decade," *Science*, 171:540–549, 12 February 1971.

Branch, B. N., "Counseling in abortion services," *Abortion Techniques and Services*, edited by S. Lewit (Amsterdam: Excerpta Medica, 1972), pp. 122–124.

Buckle, A. E., M. M. Anderson, and K. C. Loung, "Vacuum aspiration of the uterus in therapeutic abortion," *British Medical Journal*, 1:456–457, 23 May 1970.

Bumpass, L., and C. F. Westoff, "Unwanted births and U.S. population growth," *Family Planning Perspectives*, Vol. 2, No. 4: 9–11, October 1970.

Bygdeman, M., and N. Wiqvist, "Prostaglandins: a new group of abortifacient substances," *Advances in Planned Parenthood*, 7:139–145 (Amsterdam: Excerpta Medica, 1972).

California Committee on Therapeutic Abortion, *Abortion and the Unwanted Child* (New York: Springer, 1971).

Callahan, D., *Abortion: Law, Choice and Morality* (London: Collier-Macmillan, 1970).

Callahan, D., "Contraception and abortion: American Catholic responses," *Annals of the American Academy of Political and Social Science*, 387:109–117, January 1970.

Canada: Minister of Industry, Trade, and Commerce, "Therapeutic abortions in Canada, 1971," *Statistics Canada*, 3 May 1972.

Cisler, L., "Abortion law repeal (sort of)," *Notes (From the Second Year): Radical Feminism*, 1970.

Cobb, J. C., "Abortion in Colorado 1967–1969: changing attitudes and practices since the new law," *Advances in Planned Parenthood*, edited by A. J. Sobrero and C. McKee, 5:186–189 (Amsterdam: Excerpta Medica International Congress Series No. 207, 1970).

Commission on Population Growth and the American Future, *Population and the American Future* (Washington, D.C.: U.S. Government Printing Office, 1972).

Cooke, R. E., A. E. Hellegers, R. G. Hoyt, and H. W. Richardson, eds., *The Terrible Choice: the Abortion Dilemma, Based on the Proceedings of the International Conference on Abortion Sponsored by the Harvard Divinity School and the Joseph P. Kennedy Jr. Foundation* (New York: Bantam Books, 1968).

Cushner, I. M., "The aftermath of abortion legislation in Maryland: problems and projections," *Advances in Planned Parenthood*, edited by A. J. Sobrero and R. M. Harvey, 6:158–163 (Amsterdam: Excerpta Medica International Congress Series No. 224, 1971).

Cushner, I. M., "Induced abortion by saline injection," *Abortion Techniques and Services*, edited by S. Lewit (Amsterdam: Excerpta Medica, 1972), pp. 23–26.

Diggory, P., "The unwanted pregnancy," *Journal of Biosocial Science* (Suppl.), 3:127–132, June 1971.

Embrey, M. P., "Induction of abortion by prostaglandins E (PGE_1 and PGE_2)," *Journal of Reproductive Medicine*, 6:15–18, June 1971.

Fairchild, E., and A. J. Penfield, "Should family planning clinics perform abortions?" *Family Planning Perspectives*, 3:15–17, April 1971.

Furstenburg, F. F., "Attitudes toward abortion among young blacks," *Studies in Family Planning*, 3:66–69, April 1972.

Gabrielson, I. W., S. Goldsmith, and L. Potts, "Adolescent attitudes toward abortion: effects on contraceptive practice," *American Journal of Public Health*, 61:730–738, April 1971.

Goldsmith, S., "Teenagers and abortion: some special considerations," *Abortion Techniques and Services*, edited by S. Lewit (Amsterdam: Excerpta Medica, 1972), pp. 147–150.

Goldsmith, S., and A. J. Margolis, "Aspiration abortion without cervical dilation," *American Journal of Obstetrics and Gynecology*, 110:580–582, 15 June 1971.

Goldsmith, S., L. Potts, L. Green, and R. Miller, "Counseling and referral for legal abortion in California's Bay Area," *Family Planning Perspectives*, 2:14–19, June 1970.

Granfield, D., *The Abortion Decision* (New York: Doubleday & Co. Inc., 1969), p. 240.

Group for the Advancement of Psychiatry, *The Right to Abortion: A Psychiatric View*, Volume VII, No. 75, October 1969, pp. 175–290.

Guttmacher, A. F., ed., *The Case for Legalized Abortion Now* (Berkeley, Calif: Diablo Press, 1967).

Guttmacher, A. F., and H. F. Pilpel, "Abortion and the unwanted child," *Family Planning Perspectives*, 2:16–24, March 1970.

Hall, R. E., ed., *Abortion in a Changing World: Proceedings of an International Conference Convened in Hot Springs, Virginia, November 17–20, 1968, by the Association for the Study of Abortion* (New York: Columbia University Press, 1970), 2 vols.

Hall, R. E., *A Doctor's Guide to Having an Abortion* (New York: New American Library, 1971).

Hall, R. E., "Induced abortion in New York City: a report of six separate studies," *American Journal of Obstetrics and Gynecology*, 110:601–611, 1 July 1971.

Hardin, G., "Abortion—or compulsory pregnancy?," *Journal of Marriage and the Family*, 30:246–251, May 1968.

Hardin, G., "Blueprints, DNA, and abortion: a scientific and ethical analysis," *Medical Opinion & Review*, 3:74–85, February 1967.

Hardin, G., "Semantic aspects of abortion," *ETC: A Review of General Semantics*, 24:263–281, September 1967.

Harting, D., and H. J. Hunter, "Abortion techniques and services: a review and critique," *American Journal of Public Health*, Vol. 61, No. 10: 2085–2105, October 1971.

Hern, W. M., "Is pregnancy really normal?" *Family Planning Perspectives*, 3:5–10, January 1971.

Holzman, ed., "Implementation of legal abortion: a national problem," *Clinical Obstetrics and Gynecology*, 14:1109–1344, December 1971.

Horden, H., *Legal Abortion, The English Experience* (Oxford: Pergamon Press, 1971).

International Planned Parenthood Federation, "Abortion—a world survey," *International Planned Parenthood News* (Suppl.), 216:1–4, March 1972.

Karim, S. M. M., "Prostaglandins as abortifacients," *New England Journal of Medicine*, 285:1534–1535, 30 December 1971.

Karim, S. M. M., "The use of prostaglandins in abortion," *Abortion Techniques and Services*, edited by S. Lewit (Amsterdam: Excerpta Medica, 1972), pp. 68–77.

Karim, S. M. M., and G. M. Filshie, "The use of prostaglandin E_2 for therapeutic abortion," *Journal of Obstetrics and Gynaecology of the British Commonwealth*, 79:1–13, January 1972.

Keemer, E. B., "Looking back at Luenbach: 296 non-hospital abortions," *Journal of the National Medical Association*, 62:291–293, July 1970.

Keller, C., and P. Copeland, "Counseling the abortion patient is more than talk," *American Journal of Nursing*, 72:102–106, January 1972.

Kerenyi, T. D., "Outpatient intra-amniotic injection of hypertonic saline," *Clinical Obstetrics and Gynecology*, 14:124–140, March 1971.

Lader, L., *Abortion* (Indianapolis: Bobbs-Merrill, 1966; Boston: Beacon Press, 1967).

Lader, L., "First exclusive survey of non-hospital abortions," *Look* Magazine, 21 January 1969.

Lader, L., *Foolproof Birth Control: Male and Female Sterilization* (Boston: Beacon Press, 1972).

Lader, L., "The mother who chose abortion," *Redbook*, February 1968.

Lader, L., "The new abortion laws; a discussion of the ethical and medical considerations that underlie," *Parent's Magazine*, April 1968.

Lamm, R. D., "The reproductive revolution," *American Bar Association Journal*, 56:41–44, January 1970.

Lamm, R. D., "Therapeutic abortion: the role of state government," *Clinical Obstetrics and Gynecology*, 14:1204–1207, December 1971.

Long, W. N., B. R. Bradshaw, and M. Burge, "Black attitudes regarding contraception, abortion, and sterilization," *Abortion Techniques and Services*, edited by S. Lewit (Amsterdam: Excerpta Medica, 1972), pp. 151–160.

McLaughlin, M. C., "Abortion standards, New York City Board of Health," *Clinical Obstetrics and Gynecology*, 14:25–35, March 1971.

Meadows, D. H., D. L. Meadows, and J. Randers, *The Limits to Growth* (New York: Universe Books, 1972).

Means, C. C., "Does a foetus possess constitutional or other legal rights?" *Abortion Techniques and Services*, edited by S. Lewit (Amsterdam: Excerpta Medica, 1972), pp. 92–95.

Means, C. C., "The law of New York concerning abortion and the status of the foetus, 1664–1968: a case of cessation of constitutionality," *New York Law Forum*, 14:411–515, Fall 1968.

Means, C. C., "The phoenix of abortional freedom: is a penumbral or ninth-amendment right about to arise from the nineteenth-century legislative ashes of a fourteenth-century common-law liberty?" *New York Law Forum*, 17:335–410, 1971.

Metters, J. S., and P. J. D. Milton, "How safe is abortion?" *Lancet*, 1:197–198, 22 January 1972.

Moore, E. C., "Abortion and public policy: what are the issues?" *New York Law Forum*, 17:411–436, 1971.

Muller, C. "Abortion: financial impact on the patient," *Clinical Obstetrics and Gynecology*, 14:1302–1312, December 1971.

Muller, C., "Health insurance for abortion costs: a survey," *Family Planning Perspectives*, 2:12–20, October 1970.

Muller, C., "Socioeconomic outcomes of restricted access to abortion," *American Journal of Public Health*, 61:1110–1118, June 1971.

Nathanson, B. N., "Ambulatory abortion: experience with 26,000 cases (July 1, 1970–August 1, 1971)," *New England Journal of Medicine*, 286:403–407, 24 February 1972.

Nathanson, B. N., "Suction curettage for early abortion: experience with 645 cases," *Clinical Obstetrics and Gynecology*, 14:99–106, March 1971.

Newman, S. H., M. B. Beck, and S. Lewit, eds., *Abortion, Obtained and Denied* (New York: The Population Council, 1971).

New York: Laws and Statutes, "Brief in support of defendants-respondents by two amici curiae: National Association for Repeal of Abortion Laws and Prof. Cyril C. Means, Jr.," State of New York, Court of Appeals, 1972.

New York City Department of Health: Health Services Administration, "Abortion report," *Health Services Administration News*, 20 February 1972.

Overstreet, E. W., "The role of the university hospital in solving the logistic problems of legal abortion," *Clinical Obstetrics and Gynecology*, 14:1243–1247, December 1971.

Pakter, J., and F. Nelson, "Abortion in New York City: the first nine months," *Family Planning Perspectives*, 3:5–12, July 1971.

Penfield, A. J., "Abortion services, facilities, equipment, transport time," *Abortion Techniques and Services*, edited by S. Lewit (Amsterdam: Excerpta Medica, 1972), pp. 173–175.

Penfield, A. J., "A Planned Parenthood abortion service," *Advances in Planned Parenthood*, 7:185–186, Amsterdam: Excerpta Medica, 1972.

Pennsylvania Abortion Law Commission, *Report of the Pennsylvania Abortion Law Commission*, June 1972.

Pharriss, B. B., "Prostaglandin therapy: potential for untoward effects," *Advances in Planned Parenthood*, 7:146–150 (Amsterdam: Excerpta Medica, 1972).

Phelan, L. C., and P. T. Maginnis, *The Abortion Handbook for Responsible Women* (North Hollywood, Calif.: Contact Books, 1969).

Pilpel, H., "The right of abortion," *The Atlantic Monthly*, June 1969.

Reiterman, C., ed., *Abortion and the Unwanted Child* (New York: Springer Publishing Co., 1971).

Roemer, R., "Abortion laws: present and future," *Abortion Techniques and Services*, edited by S. Lewit (Amsterdam: Excerpta Medica, 1972), pp. 100–103.

Rosen, H., "Abortion in America," *American Journal of Psychiatry*, 126:1299–1301, March 1970.

Rovinsky, J. J., "Abortion in New York City," *Advances in Planned Parenthood*, 7:169–174 (Amsterdam: Excerpta Medica, 1972).

Rozovsky, L. E., "Legal abortions in Canada," *Canadian Hospital*, 48:39–41, February 1971.

Sanders, M. K., "The right not to be born," *Harper's Magazine*, April 1970.

Schaefer, G., "Technique of dilatation and curettage for abortion," *Clinical Obstetrics and Gynecology*, 14:85–98, March 1971.

Schulder, D., and F. Kennedy, *Abortion Rap* (New York: McGraw-Hill, 1971).

Schulman, H., I. H. Kaiser, and G. Randolph, "Outpatient saline abortion," *Obstetrics and Gynecology,* 37:521–526, March 1971.

Schwartz, R. A., "The abortion laws: a severe case of resistance to change," *Ohio State Medical Journal*, 67:33–38, January 1971.

Shainess, N., "Abortion: inalienable right," *New York State Journal of Medicine*, 1772–1775, 1 July 1972.

Simpson, W., "The doctor, abortion, and the law," *Journal of the Canadian Medical Association*, 87:821, 13 October 1962.

Smith, E. M., "Counseling for women who seek abortion," *Social Work*, 17:62–69, March 1972.

Stone, M. L., M. Gordon, and J. Rovinsky, "The impact of a liberalized abortion law on the medical schools," *American Journal of Obstetrics and Gynecology*, 111:728–735, 1 November 1971.

Taymor, M. L., "Abortion law in Massachusetts," *New England Journal of Medicine*, 283:602, 10 September 1970.

Thompston, J. R., "A defense of abortion," *Philosophy & Public Affairs*, 1:47–66, Fall 1971.

Tietze, C., "Abortion on request: its consequences for population trends and public health," *Seminars in Psychiatry*, 2:375–381, August 1970.

Tietze, C., "Demographic aspects of abortion in the United States," *International Population Conference, Congrès International de la Population* (International Union for the Scientific Study of Population), 2:1208–1217 (Liege, 1971).

Tietze, C., "The potential impact of legal abortions on population growth in the United States," Report prepared for the Commission on Population Growth and the American Future, Revised December 1971, p. 13.

Tietze, C., and S. Lewit, "Abortion," *Scientific American*, 220:21–27, January 1969.

Tietze, C., and S. Lewit, "Early complications of abortions under medical auspices: a preliminary report," *Studies in Family Planning*, 2:137–143, July 1971.

Tietze, C., and S. Lewit, "Joint Program for the Study of Abortion (JPSA): Early medical complications of legal abortion," *Studies in Family Planning*, 3:97–122, June 1972.

United Kingdom: Office of Population Censuses and Surveys, *The Registrar General's Quarterly Return for England and Wales. Quarter Ended 31 December 1971*. No. 492, 4th Quarter 1971 (London: Her Majesty's Stationery Office, 1972).

Wassertheil, S., C. B. Arnold, R. C. Lerner, and S. L. Heimrath, "Women obstetricians in New York and state abortion law," *Health Services Reports*, 87:328–335, April 1972.

Westoff, C. F., E. C. Moore, and N. B. Ryder, "The structure of attitudes towards abortion," *Milbank Memorial Fund Quarterly*, XLVII (1), Pt. 1: 11–34, January 1969.

Wertheimer, R., "Understanding the Abortion Agreement," *Philosophy & Public Affairs*, 1:67–95, Fall 1971.

World Health Organization, *Abortion Laws: a Survey of Current World Legislation* (Geneva, 1971). Also *International Digest of Health Legislation*, 21:437–512, 1970.

Whittington, H. G., "Role of the counselor in abortion," *Abortion Techniques and Services*, edited by S. Lewit (Amsterdam: Excerpta Medica, 1972), pp. 120–121.

Zarky, N. G., "Legal problems of counseling and referral," *Abortion Techniques and Services*, edited by S. Lewit (Amsterdam: Excerpta Medica, 1972), pp. 104–107.

INDEX

Abele v. Markle: 192
Abortion: ambulatory, 150, 156; determining need, 3, 14, 47; in hospitals, 21–22, 46, 50, 68, 85, 86, 110–111, 113, 117, 152–153, 154, 155, 157, 211; late pregnancy, 164–166, 177, 200; non-hospital, 4, 92–93, 151, 153, 154, 155–157; Sanger and, 20; self-induced, 13, 23, 27, 32
Abortion, illegal: 85, 86; underworld, 2, 13, 20, 22–23, 73, 81, 166, 198, 200, 206
Abortion, legal: and abortion committees, 21–22, 111, 188; and guidelines, 149–150, 153, 154; implementing, 149–167; grounds for, family health, 47; woman's health, 2, 14–15, 113; woman's life, 2, 14, 110, 157, 188
Abortion (Lader): 60
Abortion Action Now: 171
Abortion committees: 13, 21–22, 111, 188, 211
Abortion counseling: 43, 46, 48, 76, 151, 154
Abortion guidelines: 149–150, 153, 154
Abortion Information Agency, commercial referrals: 164
Abortionists, underworld: 22–23, 81
Abortion laws: 21; Alaska, 109, 117–120, 209; California, 50, 66–70; Colorado, 35, 49, 62–65, 84–85; District of Columbia, 1–2, 14; Florida, 188–190; Georgia, 188; Great Britain, 47–48; Hawaii, 109, 115–117, 209; local ordinances, 159–161; New Jersey, 191–192, 209; New York, 114, 122–144, 209; North Carolina, 62, 65–66, 85–86; Texas, 188; Vermont, 190–191; Washington, 170–172, 209
Abortion referral services: 1, 2, 16, 25, 42–43, 50, 51, 53, 72, 80, 84, 92, 94, 97, 98, 102, 107, 108, 109, 164; clergy and, 43–46, 48–51, 56, 75, 76, 100, 103–104, 111, 125, 154, 180; commercial, 163–164, 212
Abortion reform: Alaska, 109, 117–120, 209; California, 50, 66–70, 86, 106, 109–111, 167*n.*; Colorado, 35, 49, 62–65, 84–85, 106; Connecticut, 192–194, 217; counterreform efforts, 159–161, 198–207; District of Columbia, 14, 111–115, 209; Hawaii, 109, 114, 115–117, 209; Illinois, 174–175; Iowa, 177–178; Kansas, 84, 181; legislative, 56–57, 59–60, 63–67, 69–70, 122–144, 170–172, 182; Maryland, 84; Massachusetts, 218; Michigan, 178–184; Minnesota, 178; New York, 56–57, 59–60, 122–144, 209; North Carolina, 62, 65–66, 85–86; Vermont, 190–191; Washington, 170–172, 209; Wisconsin, 173–174, 175–176, 209. *See also* Courts
Abortion Reform Association: 131
Abzug, Bella: 199, 202
Alaska, abortion laws in: 109, 114, 117–120
Aldrich, Bailey: 80
ALI plan: 57–58, 61, 62, 63, 65, 70, 84, 118, 181, 182, 186, 188
Alliance for Humane Abortion: 117–118, 120
Alvares, Walter C.: 90
Amatniek, Kathy: 82
Ambulatory abortion: 150, 156
American Baptist Convention: 90
American Bar Association, position on abortion: 187
American Civil Liberties Union: 77, 90, 113, 127, 131; California, 33, 74; New Jersey, 191; New Mexico, 34; New York, 26, 58, 125
American College of Obstetricians and Gynecologists: 187
American Ethical Society: 147
American Jewish Congress: 125, 134, 137
American Law Institute: 57
American Medical Association: 151
Americans for Democratic Action: 58, 125
Anderson, Wendell: 178
Anthony, Susan B.: 35
Anwyl, the Rev. J. Hugh: 50, 111
Arkansas, abortion laws in: 84*n.*
Arrests: 1, 2, 11, 54, 74–76, 78–80, 98–100, 173, 175, 224; injunction against, 173
Association for the Study of Abortion: 26, 58, 61
Association for Voluntary Sterilization: 221
Austin, Richard: 183, 184
Authoritarianism: 215–217

Babbitz, Dr. Sidney: 173–174
Babcock, Primula: 118
Baird, Evie: 53, 80
Baird, William: 16, 50, 51–55, 78–80, 116, 125, 160, 161
Balletta, Vincent, Jr.: 127
Bandez, Nancy: 190
Barbee, Lloyd: 60
Barksdale, Dr. Robert W.: 188
Barquet case: 189
Bartlett, Kenneth: 131
"Battered child" syndrome: 24
Beebe, Lorraine: 182
Beilenson, Anthony: 56, 67, 69, 70
Belous, Dr. Leon: 72–74, 104, 106, 109, 111
Bermingham, John: 63
Biddle, Craig: 69
Bielby, the Rev. Carl: 49
Billé, Constance: 81, 95, 120
Biondo, Peter: 204
Birth control: 20, 30, 59, 84, 187, 211, 215, 219–223; contraceptives, 39, 40, 193, 218, 219; dispensing contraceptives, 12, 52, 54, 78, 161; and right to privacy, 12, 161; Sanger and, 18–19, 56; voluntary sterilization, 218, 220–221
Birth rate: 210–211, 213, 219, 220
"Blaine amendment": 128
Blue Cross–Blue Shield, abortion coverage: 151
Blumenthal, Albert H.: 59, 122, 123, 129, 130, 138, 144
Boal, R. Bradley: 162
Bogage, Rabbi Lewis: 49
Bookson, Paul: 134, 135, 205, 206
Booth, William: 51
Bourne, Dr. Aleck: 56

Brennan, Justice William J.: 161
Breslow, Dr. Lester: 90, 94
Brown, Arlene Emery: 130
Brown, Helen Gurley: 159
Brown, Louis: 26, 96, 98–104, 107
Brown, Margaret: 98, 99, 102, 107
Brown, Ralph: 179
Brunelle, Dr. Pierre: 75
Brush, Ellen: 91
Brydges, Earl: 59, 122, 128, 132, 135, 144, 149, 159
Burdick, Dr. Lalor: 97
Burke, Patrick: 2
Burns, John A.: 117
Burrows, Gordon: 204
Byrn, Robert: 163, 224
Byrnes, Msgr. Patrick: 178

California: 31; abortion laws in, 50, 66–70, 86; Clergy Service, 50, 111; reform, 66–70, 86, 109–111
California Committee on Therapeutic Abortion (CCTA): 67, 68
Canada, abortion in: 51
Canfield, Elizabeth: 110
Cardell, the Rev. Nicholas: 131
Carmen, Arlene: 45, 46, 47, 105, 152
Catheter technique: 51
Catholic Church: political role, 21, 32, 43, 59, 63–64, 66, 69, 72, 103, 116–117, 123, 124, 128, 135, 138, 139, 161–163, 170–171, 178, 193, 196–198, 201, 206, 207; position on abortion, 114, 161–162, 215–218, 222
Catholics: attitude toward abortion, 67, 186–187, 217; attitude toward birth control, 187; and NOW, 37
Catholics for Abortion Law Repeal: 190
CCTA. *See* California Committee on Therapeutic Abortion
Censorship: 33–34
Center for Reproductive and Sexual Health: 156
Chase, Gordon: 155, 158, 167, 199
Childcare centers: 40, 214
Chisholm, Shirley: 90, 97, 202
Cisler, Lucinda: 50, 129, 130
Citizens Committee for Abortion Law Repeal: 131
Clapp, James: 129, 130
Clark, Justice Tom C.: 13, 112
Cleary, Nancy: 183
Clergy and Lay Advocates for Hospital Abortion Performance: 152
Clergy Consultation Service on Abortion: 42, 43, 44, 48, 56, 58, 152, 154, 164, 175, 176; California, 50, 111; Chicago, 76; Cleveland, 74; Colorado, 49; Michigan, 49
Cleveland *Plain Dealer*: 75
Clinics: birth control, 12; Canada, 51; freestanding, 150–151, 153, 154, 155, 156–157, 166, 175–176; Mexico, 28, 30, 51, 73; NARAL, 113–114, 115, 191; Parents Aid Society, 53, 160; Puerto Rico, 45–46; sterilization, 220
Cohen, Dr. Harvey: 85
Colorado, abortion laws in: 35, 49, 62–65, 84–85; Clergy Service, 49
Commercial abortion services: 163–164, 211–212
Committee for the Cook-Leichter Bill: 130–131, 133
Common law, legality of abortion: 190, 191
Comstock, Anthony: 35
Confrontation tactics: 33–34, 51–52, 54, 79–80, 104–108, 129–130, 150–152, 179–180
Connecticut: abortion reform in, 192–194, 217; birth control law, 12
Connolly, Abp. Thomas A.: 161
Constitution, New York: 128
Constitution, U.S.: First Amendment, 12, 104, 128, 191; Fifth Amendment, 15, 104, 105, 106; Ninth Amendment, 191, 192; Fourteenth Amendment, 158, 191
Cook, Constance: 92, 123, 124, 125, 129, 130, 135–145 *passim*, 174, 198, 204
Cooke, Terence Cardinal: 144, 196, 202, 206
Coordinating Committee for Abortion Law Reform: 182, 184
Cost: abortions, 23, 26, 45–46, 47, 51, 85, 86, 101, 115, 149, 151, 153, 154, 155, 156, 211–212; referrals, 107, 163–164, 212
Council of Churches: 116, 131, 170
Counterreform efforts, abortion: 159–161, 198–207
Courts and abortion reform: 15, 74, 106, 108, 109, 111, 114–115, 158, 161, 163, 173, 188–194, 209
Cunningham, Evelyn: 199
Cusack, Ruth: 126, 128, 129
Cushner, Dr. Irvin: 152

Daly, Mary: 216
Davis, Marianne: 183
Day, Theodore: 134
Deaths from abortion: 23, 48, 65, 154, 156, 166, 198, 211
Delaware, abortion laws in: 84*n.*
DeLorenzo, Alan: 123
DeLorenzo, Anita: 123
Demonstrations: 39, 52, 82–83, 95–96, 114, 120, 137, 171, 196–197, 199, 201–202
DeSapio, Carmine: 44
DeSelincourt, Hugh: 19
DeSelincourt, Janet: 20
Detroit *Free Press*: 78
Diamond, Dr. Milton: 117
DiCarlo, Domenick: 60, 204
Dingle, Kay: 131
District of Columbia: abortion laws in, 1–2, 14; reform in, 111–115
Doctors. *See* Medical profession
Dodder, the Rev. Clyde: 49
Doe v. Bolton: 188
Domenick, Clinton: 127, 133, 134, 144, 159, 205
Donovan, James H.: 157, 158, 159, 161, 205
Dorsen, Norman: 115
Dowd, Joseph: 136
Doyle, James F.: 175
Draper, William H.: 90
Drinan, Robert F.: 79
Duryea, Perry: 122, 128, 136, 138, 139, 140, 141, 142, 146, 204

Eastern Europe, abortion in: 30

Eddy, the Rev. Robert: 131
Edey, Dr. Helen: 91
Ehrlich, Paul: 221
Ehrlichman, John D.: 203
Elkind, Elizabeth: 131, 143
Ellenhorn, David: 99, 100, 104
Ellis, Havelock: 19
Episcopal Church, attitude toward abortion: 58
Erickson, Jan: 118
Erikson, Erik H.: 24
Evans, Daniel J.: 172
Evans, Rowland: 203
Eve, Arthur: 131, 137, 141, 142, 147

Family, feminists and the: 214–215
Faust, Jean: 36, 37
Feminine Mystique (Friedan): 35, 37, 40
Ferebee, Dr. Dorothy: 112
Fetus: defective, 68, 69; as a person, 163, 224; rights of, 23, 222; saline abortion and, 164–165
Fields, Sylvia: 123
Finch, Robert H.: 69
Fink, Stanley, 136
Finkbine, Sherri: 43
Fletcher, the Rev. Joseph: 90
Folsom, Father Paul: 178
Frey, Ruth: 130
Friedan, Betty: 18, 34, 36–40, 90, 94, 95, 97
Friedman, Leo: 28

Galiber, Joseph: 205
Gaylor, Anne: 175
Gelobter, Barbara: 129, 137, 141
Georgia, abortion laws in: 84*n.*
German measles: 44, 68
Gesell, Arnold: 15, 111
Gidding, Lee: 95, 190, 199, 200
Ginsberg, Martin: 122, 123–124
Gold, Edwin M.: 90
Goldenberg, Dr. Samuel: 170
Graham, Dr. Fiona: 214
Graham, Ross: 133, 134, 135
Grand jury proceedings: 104–108
Great Britain, abortion in: 42, 47–48, 76
Greer, Germaine: 213, 214
Greitzer, Carol: 97, 132, 150
Griswold v. Connecticut: 12, 20, 174
Gurner, Rowena: 32–33
Gusberg, Dr. S. B.: 152
Gustafson, Carl: 63
Guttmacher, Dr. Alan: 84, 90, 177, 199, 201
Gwynne, Dr. John S.: 188

Hall, Dr. Robert: 58
Hansen, Stephen: 146
Hardin, Garrett: 20, 32, 58, 89
Hare, the Rev. Robert W.: 74–76
Harvey, Dr. Hale: 154, 156
Hawaii, abortion laws in: 109, 114, 115–117
Hayes, Joan: 116
Health, and abortion: mental, 2, 14–15, 57, 113, 115; physical, 2, 57, 110, 115, 157, 166, 188
Health Services Administration (HSA), New York City: 153, 155, 158
Hellman, Dr. Louis M.: 58
Hendricks, Dr. Charles H.: 223
Henrie, Dr. W. J. Bryan: 4, 5–7, 22, 72
Hinand, the Rev. Allen: 49
Hogan, Mark: 62, 64
Holloman, Dr. John: 153
Hospitals: 13, 46, 50, 68, 85, 86, 110–111, 113, 117, 152–153, 154, 155, 157; abortion committees, 13, 21–22, 111, 188, 211; accreditation and abortion, 181, 188; Catholic, 140; military, 176
Huntington, Prescott: 132, 135–136
Huxley, Sir Julian: 219, 221

Illegitimacy rates: 211
Illinois, abortion reform in: 174–175
Illinois Committee for Medical Control of Abortion (ICMCA): 61
Incest, abortion laws and: 44, 193
Industrialization: 218–219
Ingraham, Dr. Hollis S.: 150
Iowa, abortion reform in: 177–178

Jack, Hulan: 138, 139, 140, 141, 142, 147
Jain, Dr. Sagar C.: 70
Japan, abortion in: 30, 54
Jews. *See* Judaism
Johnson, Lyndon B.: 81
Jonas, Milton: 136
Jones, Arthur H.: 65–66, 86
Judaism, position on abortion: 59, 134, 162, 199–200

Kansas, abortion reform in: 84, 181
Keemer, Dr. Edgar: 179, 180, 181, 191
Kennan, Dr. Alfred: 175, 181
Kerenyi, Dr. Thomas: 165–166
Ketchum, Dr. Jesse: 76, 77
Kim, Dr. Young W.: 159
Kinsolving, the Rev. Lester: 44
Knights of Columbus: 116, 196–197
Knox, John: 31
Koch, Ed: 153
Koome, Dr. A. Frans: 172
Krassner, Paul: 26, 45, 105, 106, 107
Krumm, the Rev. John: 44
Krupsak, Mary Anne: 127, 137, 141, 142, 147, 159, 204
Kummer, Dr. Jerome: 110

Lader, Lawrence: referrals, 25–26, 45, 50, 56, 72, 89, 107, 125; and Sanger, 18–20
Lairtus, Dr. Karl: 73–74
Lama, Alfred: 204
Lamm, Richard: 62–65, 85
Lassoe, John V. P., Jr.: 58
Laverne, Thomas: 127, 133, 144, 159, 205
Leasure, Kenneth: 136
Leavy, Zad: 109
Leichter, Franz: 92, 124, 126–127, 130, 135, 136, 151, 199, 202
Lent, Norman: 82–83, 124, 205
Levy, Norman: 205–206
Lindsay, John V.: 132
Lindsay, Mary: 199, 202
Linsky, Martin: 80

Lippes, Dr. Jack: 153
Lisa, Joseph: 139, 141, 142, 147
Livingston, Dr. Robert M.: 191–192
Local ordinances: 159–161
London, Ephraim: 12, 45, 105
Love, John A.: 65
Lucas, Roy: 105, 181
Lutheran Church, attitude toward abortion: 58
Lyons, the Rev. Jesse: 44, 45, 47, 103, 104, 105, 107, 202

Macaulay, Donald: 54
McClintock, Beatrice: 91, 95
McCoy, Robert: 50–51, 178
McIntyre, James F. Cardinal: 69
McLaughlin, Dr. Mary: 150
McLean, Gladys: 183
McNulty, Dr. James V.: 68–69
Madden, Barbara: 177, 178
Madeiros, Abp. Humberto S.: 161
Maginnis, Patricia: 7, 16, 20, 27, 30–31, 32–34, 43, 50, 58, 61, 70, 72
Mandel, Marvin: 84
Mannes, Marya: 90
Margolies, Rabbi Israel: 43
Marino, Ralph: 133
Marriage: 213–214, 222
Marshall, the Rev. Robert F.: 77
Marshall, Justice Thurgood: 174, 192
Maryland, abortion laws in: 84
Massachusetts: 217–218; Baird in, 54, 78–80; Hare and, 74–76
Means, Cyril: 12, 45, 104, 105, 109, 163, 179, 189, 204
Medicaid, and abortion: 152, 157–158, 159, 160, 181
Medical insurance, abortion coverage: 151–152
Medical procedures, advances: 13, 20, 165–166
Medical profession: 112, 114, 118; and referrals, 26; support within for abortion reform, 14, 73, 101, 112
Mercorella, Anthony: 140
Meskill, Thomas J.: 193–194
Mexico, abortion clinics in: 28, 30, 51, 73
Michaels, George: 142–143, 144–147
Michigan: abortion reform in, 178–184; Clergy Service, 49, 76–78, 179, 180
Midwest Medical Center: 175
Milam, Lorenzo: 171
Miller, Herbert: 138, 139
Miller, Keith: 120
Milliken, Helen: 183
Milliken, William: 182
Mills, Louise: 91
Minnesota, abortion reform in: 178
Minority groups, and abortion: 22, 46, 86, 137, 210
Mitchell, John: 203
Montagu, Dr. Ashley: 222
Montana, Armando: 205
Moody, the Rev. Howard: 42–43, 44, 47, 48, 93, 96, 103, 105, 152, 153, 154, 162
Moore, Emily: 130
Moore, Hugh: 91
Morris, Norval: 61
Morrow, Dr. Laura: 112
Mott, Stewart: 91
Munger, Charles T.: 110
Murphy, George: 205
Myer, Edward, III: 204, 205
Myers, Dr. Lonny: 61–62, 82, 88–89, 90–91, 96, 97

NARAL. *See* National Association for Repeal of Abortion Laws
Nassau Medical Center: 160
Nathanson, Dr. Bernard: 46, 95, 114, 132, 150, 151, 152, 156, 157, 165, 201
National Association for Repeal of Abortion Laws (NARAL): 86, 104, 113, 124, 131, 136, 147, 150, 151, 153, 164, 165, 190, 200, 207; formation, 88–97
National Organization for Women (NOW): 35, 36–37, 38, 82, 125, 126, 137, 190, 199
Neier, Aryeh: 12, 26
Nellis, Joseph L.: 12, 13, 14, 114, 173–174
Neuberger, Maurine: 81, 90
New Jersey, abortion laws in: 191–192
Newman, Jon O.: 212
New Mexico, abortion laws in: 84*n.*
New Orleans, abortion in: 46
New York: abortion reform, 56–57, 59–60, 114, 122–144; abortion reform implemented, 149–167; counterreform efforts, 198–207
New Yorkers for Abortion Law Repeal: 92, 129, 130, 139
New York Times: 151, 201
Nichol, Gerald: 175
Nicholson, the Rev. Ross: 179, 180
Nickerson, Eugene: 132
Nienhueser, Helen: 117, 118, 119
Niles, Dalwin: 134
Nixon, Richard M.: 176, 202–203, 215, 221
North Carolina, abortion laws in: 62, 65–66, 85–86
Novak, Robert: 203

Ober, Dr. William: 12
O'Boyle, Patrick Cardinal: 114
Ohrenstein, Manfred: 57, 58, 124, 127, 134, 136, 201, 205
Oregon, abortion laws in: 84*n.*

Parents Aid Society: 51, 52, 53, 160
Parietal rules: 40, 215
Parker, the Rev. Theodore: 43
Parsons, the Rev. E. Spenser: 61, 77
Passanante, William: 127, 134
Paterson, Basil: 60, 127, 133, 134, 137
Peck, Ellen: 213
Pettegrew, Dr. Robert R.: 188
Phelan, Lana: 30–31, 32, 33–34, 81, 97
Physician's right of medical decision: 3, 14, 47, 115
Pilpel, Harriet: 12
Planned Parenthood Federation: 30, 51, 84, 147, 155, 160, 164, 199, 207
Plunkett, Thomas F.: 77, 78
Poland, Kay: 119
Police: 2, 27, 28, 73–74, 99

Pollution: 218–219
Poor, abortion and: 13, 15, 20, 22, 26, 46, 85, 86, 101, 102, 112, 113, 160, 179, 206
Population control: 218, 221–223
Population growth: 14, 218–219, 221–222
Post-abortion recovery: 93, 101, 156–157, 166, 211
Powers, James E.: 135
Presbytery of Cleveland: 75–76
Presidential Advisory Council on the Status of Women: 81
Presidential Commission on Population Growth: 186, 187, 202, 212, 215, 221
Privacy, right to: 12, 15, 109, 161, 174, 191, 192, 194*n.*, 213
Prostaglandins: 222–223
Protestant Council of Churches: 58
Protestantism, position on abortion: 59, 75–76, 162, 177
Public education: abortion, 51–52, 92, 125; contraception, 46, 51–52; self-abortion, 32, 33
Publicity: 32, 57, 61, 67, 93, 129, 183, 200–201, 204. *See also* Sensationalism
Public opinion: 67, 83, 108, 109, 114, 115, 116, 117, 122, 137, 183–184, 186–187, 209–210
Puerto Rico, abortion in: 42, 45–46, 76

Rabbinical Council of America: 199–200
Rader, John: 117, 118, 119, 120
Ramos, Manuel: 142, 204
Rangel, Charles: 127, 140
Rape, abortion laws and: 44, 69, 188, 193
Reagan, Ronald: 66, 69
Referendum, abortion reform by: 172, 181, 183
Rein, Edith: 60–61
Religion. *See under* various denominations, *i.e.*, Catholic Church; Judaism
Repeal position, abortion reform: 70, 78, 81, 83, 92, 94, 109, 116–117, 125, 132, 135
Residency requirements: 70, 117, 142, 167, 172, 188
"Right to Life" groups: 33, 69, 159, 160, 161, 177, 184, 196–198, 199, 204, 207
Robb, Dr. Robert C.: 188
Roberts, Burton: 100–101, 102–103, 107, 108
Robinson, Florence. *See* Vuitch, Florence
Rockefeller, John D., III: 186, 202
Rockefeller, Nelson: 126, 127, 128, 144, 157, 198, 199, 200, 203, 206–207
Roe v. Wade: 188
Roiphe, Ann Richardson: 214
Roman Catholic Church. *See* Catholic Church; Catholics; Right to Life groups
Roraback, Catherine: 192
Rubella. *See* German Measles
Rubenfeld, Leonard: 160
Ruskin, Evey: 118
Russell, Dr. Keith: 67, 86, 110
Ryder, Norman B.: 219

Saline technique: 164–166, 177–178, 200
Sandler, Leonard: 104
"San Francisco nine": 67–69, 72
Sanger, Margaret: 11, 16, 18–20, 31, 35, 36, 39, 56
Sargent, Francis: 80
Scanlan, Bishop John: 117
Schaef, the Rev. Finley: 44, 45, 103, 104, 105, 107
Schermerhorn, Richard: 205
Schwartz, Dr. Richard A.: 75
Self-abortion: 13, 23, 27, 32, 166
Sensationalism: 100–101, 159, 162, 196, 198
Sexual morality: changes in, 40, 212–215
Shaffer, the Rev. John: 119
Shaffer, Thomas L.: 217
Shaw, the Rev. Canon Don: 90
Sherman, Gordon: 90
Shively, Dr. J. Paul: 67
Sitnick, Joseph: 12, 13, 14
Smith, Francis Xavier: 163
Smith, Ruth P.: 62, 88–89, 91, 95, 130
Smith, Wilbur: 193
Society for Humane Abortion: 27, 28, 34
Soll, Pat: 118
Soviet Union, abortion in: 30
Speech, right to free: 33–34, 78
Spencer-Roberts Associates: 69
Speno, Edward: 124, 128, 132, 205
Stack, Dr. Jack: 178, 182, 184
Steel, Ruth: 62, 65
Steingut, Stanley: 124, 204
Steinhoff, Dr. Patricia: 117
Stella, Anthony: 139, 141, 142, 147, 204
Sterilization, voluntary: 218, 220–221
Straub, Chester: 205
Straut, the Rev. Charles: 49
Strawn, Dorothy: 171
Sunnen, Joseph: 110, 162
Sutton, Percy: 56, 57, 58, 59, 90, 94, 95, 96, 125, 132, 137, 141, 150, 151, 152, 153, 199

Tanten, Mary Lou: 183
Teenagers, and abortion: 47, 213
Thaler, Seymour: 83, 133
Thornton, Jean: 193
Ticktin, Rabbi Max: 76–78
Tietze, Dr. Christopher: 109, 153, 157, 201
Travia, Anthony J.: 59
Truppin, Dr. Michael: 155

Unitarian-Universalists, attitude toward abortion: 43, 58, 90, 125, 131
Unwanted births: 20, 167, 187, 192, 210–211, 219–220
U.S. Equal Employment Opportunity Commission: 36
U.S. Office of Economic Opportunity: 221
U.S. Supreme Court: 12, 114–115, 161, 173, 188, 194

Vermont, abortion reform in: 190–191
Vuitch, Florence Robinson: 10, 11
Vuitch, Dr. Milan: 1–4, 8–12, 15, 22, 26, 72, 96, 104, 110, 111, 112, 114, 173, 224

Wager, Eli: 146
Wallace, the Rev. Robert: 78*n.*
Washington, abortion reform in: 170–172
Weller, Dr. Lynn D., Jr.: 181
Wells, H. G.: 19, 20
Westoff, Charles F.: 219

Wheeler, Shirley Ann: 188–189
Wheelwright, the Rev. Farley: 49, 75
Wiley, Dr. George: 180
Williams, Dr. Ben C.: 85
Williams, Bill: 20
Wilson, Malcolm: 135, 205, 207
Wilson, Dr. Miriam: 174–175
Wilson, Dr. Rodman: 118
Wirin, A. L.: 74
Wisconsin: abortion reform in, 173–174, 175–176; Baird in, 79
Women's Abortion Project: 153, 164
Women's Liberation groups: 38, 39, 81, 82, 113, 131, 152, 153, 172. *See also* National Organization for Women
Women's liberation movement: 35–36, 39–40, 80–82, 144, 210, 212–215
Women's Medical Center: 151–152
Women's Medical Services: 154, 155, 156
Women's National Abortion Action Coalition (WONAAC): 189, 196, 197, 199, 207, 210
Women's rights: 15, 20–21, 134, 213; abortion, 36, 106, 108, 190, 194*n.*, 202; contraception, 106; sovereignty of her body, 13, 18, 21, 109, 174; suffrage, 35
Woodhull, Victoria Claflin: 214

Yano; Vincent: 116, 117
Young, Coleman: 78
Young, Joseph H.: 224

Zero Population Growth (ZPG): 116, 164, 190, 199, 207

SUMMATION OF THE MAJORITY OPINION OF THE UNITED STATES SUPREME COURT IN THE CASE OF *ROE v. WADE* BY JUSTICE HARRY A. BLACKMUN JANUARY 22, 1973 (No. 70-18)

To summarize and to repeat:

1. A state criminal abortion statute of the current Texas type that excepts from criminality only a *life saving* procedure on behalf of the mother, without regard to pregnancy stage and without recognition of the other interests involved, is violative of the Due Process Clause of the Fourteenth Amendment.

(a) For the stage prior to approximately the end of the first trimester, the abortion decision and its effectuation must be left to the medical judgment of the pregnant woman's attending physician.

(b) For the stage subsequent to approximately the end of the first trimester, the State in promoting its interest in the health of the mother, may, if it chooses, regulate the abortion procedure in ways that are reasonably related to maternal health.

(c) For the stage subsequent to viability the State, in promoting its interest in the potentiality of human life, may, if it chooses, regulate, and even proscribe, abortion except where it is necessary, in appropriate medical judgment, for